Mothering the Race

Mothering the Race

Women's Narratives of
Reproduction, 1890–1930

ALLISON BERG

University of Illinois Press

URBANA AND CHICAGO

Library of Congress Cataloging-in-Publication Data
Berg, Allison, 1963–
Mothering the race : women's narratives of reproduction, 1890–1930 /
Allison Berg.
p.   cm.
Includes bibliographical references and index.
ISBN 0-252-02690-X (cloth)
1. Motherhood—United States—History.
2. Racism—United States—History. 3. Motherhood in literature.
4. Fertility in literature. I. Title.
HQ759.B459   2002
306.874'3'0973—dc21   2001001490

For Michael

Contents

Acknowledgments

I HAVE MANY people to thank for the support and encouragement that made this book possible. First, I thank the friends, colleagues, and teachers who read and commented on my work in progress: Robin Bates, Pat Brantlinger, Don Cook, Kathryn Flannery, Susan Gubar, Jean Kowaleski, Björn Krondorfer, Michael Largey, Carolyn Mitchell, Mike Nelson, Laura Plummer, Celia Rabinowitz, Lori Robison, Jorge Rogachevsky, Sheila Sullivan, Karen Suyemoto, Katharina von Kellenbach, Ellen Weinauer, Lori Williams, and Eric Wolfe. You made the inevitably lonely process of writing much less so. The anonymous readers for the University of Illinois Press helped this become a better book, and my editor, Willis Regier, made the publication process as seamless as possible. Special thanks to my undergraduate research assistants, Haley Sinclair and Allison Youatt, for able assistance with last-minute fact checking.

My work on this project was punctuated by biweekly cross-country commutes, the fate of many an academic who is half of a dual career couple. I thank my colleagues and students at St. Mary's College of Maryland for providing a stimulating and nurturing environment during my five years there and former provost Mel Endy for making the two-career shuffle more manageable with generous pretenure leave time. Since coming to James Madison College at Michigan State University, I have benefited greatly from being part of such a rich and collegial interdisciplinary community. Thanks, especially, to Gene Burns, Leslie Butler, Ron Dorr, Richard Evans, Sherman Garnett, Julia Grant, Grant Littke, Michael Schechter, Curtis Stokes, Colleen Tremonte, and Dick Zinman for your friendship and support. A faculty development grant from James Madison College provided a reduced teaching load at a crucial stage of the project.

Finally, I thank my family, Sandra Sampson, Charles Sampson, Rondi Berg, Steven Berg, and Amy Blythe, as well as Arthur Largey, Marjorie Largey, and Maryanne Boltz, for their unflagging support. My husband, Michael Largey, never doubted that the innumerable drafts that he critiqued would one day be a book; at the same time, he never failed to provide diversions that kept my academic pursuits in proper perspective. My life outside books is infinitely richer because of him.

* * *

I am grateful for permission to reprint portions of chapter 2 and the epilogue, which appeared in the following publications:

"Reconstructing Motherhood: Pauline Hopkins's *Contending Forces*," *Studies in American Fiction* 24 (Autumn 1996): 131–50. © 1996 by Northeastern University.

"Other Mothers: Public Policy, Popular Culture, and Recent Hollywood Films," in *Race in 21st Century America,* ed. Curtis Stokes, Theresa Melendez, and Genice Rhodes-Reed (East Lansing: Michigan State University Press, 2001), 181–91. © 2001 by Michigan State University Press.

Mothering the Race

Introduction: The Politics of
Race and Reproduction

IN HIS ANNUAL MESSAGE to Congress in 1906, President Theodore Roosevelt chastised middle-class, white American women for their "willful sterility ... the one sin for which the penalty is national death, race death" (7428). In 1992 Vice President Dan Quayle rebuked the same group of women when he criticized the willful fertility of television's Murphy Brown, accusing her of glorifying unwed motherhood and "mocking the importance of fathers" (Wines A12). While Roosevelt and Quayle objected to different reproductive behaviors—to insufficient and inappropriate childbearing, respectively— both drew upon cultural discourses linking race and reproduction to lament women's deviation from a traditional ideal of motherhood. Quayle's comments could be dismissed as a belated appeal to the values of June Cleaver, the 1950s mass-culture icon of American motherhood, but they gain additional resonance if we hear them as echoing early twentieth-century invocations of True Motherhood, an elastic concept that could be invoked as readily to justify the New Woman's demand for suffrage as to uphold traditional maternal behaviors in the interests of "the race."[1]

In the decades after Reconstruction and throughout the Progressive Era, the racial value of reproduction was emphasized not only by white writers responding to the specter of race suicide but also by black writers stressing the imperative of racial uplift. Roosevelt's warning that the falling birthrate among native-born white women would lead to "race death" reflects both his own fear that college-educated, middle-class women might choose vocations other than marriage and motherhood and a more widespread cultural anxiety regarding what Lothrop Stoddard called the "rising tide of color against white world supremacy." Stoddard's racist diatribe, published in 1920, reflected the common white perception that immigrants and African Americans would soon overwhelm the white, native population through unchecked reproduction. But if white women were frequently criticized because their apparent abnegation of motherhood compromised white racial supremacy, black women were frequently praised, in racial uplift literature, for their maternal contributions to black racial advancement. The African American educator E. Azalia Hackley underscored both the power and the responsibility of black maternity when she wrote in her 1916 guidebook for girls that "the colored mother . . . may bless or curse each succeeding generation; she may change race history" (181). Although for very different reasons, "true" mothers, black or white, were responsible not only for literally bearing a child but also for symbolically bearing a race.

Dan Quayle's censure of Murphy Brown depended upon a similar, though less explicit, yoking of race and reproduction. Quayle's comments, delivered in response to the violence provoked by the acquittal of four white police officers in the beating of Rodney King, a black Los Angeles motorist, deflected attention from real race and class conflicts onto a fictional mother, who became both symptom and cause of a nationwide crisis of values. Specifically, Quayle saw in Murphy Brown's unwed maternity an example of the "breakdown of the family structure," which was, in his view, responsible for the "lawless social anarchy" represented by the April 1992 riots in Los Angeles (qtd. in Prasch 25). Ignoring both the immediate cause of the riots—the legal exoneration of the police officers' violence—and the obvious race and class differences between Murphy Brown and the inner-city teenagers whose reproductive choices he feared she might influence, Quayle equated single motherhood with social anarchy, much as Roosevelt equated reproductive "sterility" with white racial decline.

Given the general context of welfare-reform rhetoric in the 1990s, which frequently capitalized on the stereotypical image of the black "welfare queen," and given the specific context of Quayle's remarks, which were delivered as part of a larger critique of the "culture of poverty" that he saw typified in South Central Los Angeles, Quayle's characterization of the white Murphy Brown as a reckless reproducer drew upon a long-standing image of the "bad" black mother. As Rhonda M. Williams and Carla L. Peterson have argued, it is "the blackening of gender deviancy that marks 'welfare mothers' as threatening cultural aberrations and compels draconian shifts in social policy. The 'welfare queens' that haunt popular landscapes are African Americans. We are told that their unwillingness to marry leads to fatherless homes, criminally inclined sons and daughters" (13). If, as Dorothy Roberts suggests in *Killing the Black Body,* contemporary disparagements of black motherhood help to "persuade people that racial inequality is perpetuated by Black people themselves" (5), Quayle's use of Murphy Brown as a proxy for single mothers of color enabled him to trace the origins of the Los Angeles riots not to the disillusionment and rage produced by a miscarriage of justice but to "deviant" reproductive behaviors associated, in the popular imagination, with black women.

Of course, nothing is unique about either politician's recourse to mother blaming; as a recent collection of essays makes clear, "bad" mothers have been held responsible for an array of twentieth-century problems, from teenage delinquency to serial murders (Ladd-Taylor and Umanski 5). What bears noting is that while both Roosevelt and Quayle attributed national crises to deviant maternal behaviors, neither specified the norm from which these behaviors diverged, perhaps because they assumed the qualities of a good mother to be a matter of national consensus, transcending differences of race, class, or culture. Given the rapidly changing definitions of motherhood in each era, their assumption of a normative model of maternity testifies to the persistence of a maternal mystique—the belief that mothers share certain essential and timeless qualities—even as the material conditions and cultural meanings of motherhood undergo radical change.

The speed of such change at the beginning of the twentieth century can be measured by comparing Roosevelt's view of the nonreproductive woman with Margaret Sanger's claim, fifteen years later, that "they who today deny the right of a woman to control her own body speak with the hardihood of invincible ignorance or with the folly of those blind ones who in all ages have opposed the light of progress. Few there are to insist openly that woman remain a passive instrument of reproduction" (*Woman* 211). Where Roosevelt invoked the authority of biblical tradition, alluding to the wages of reproductive "sin," Sanger associated herself with the "light of progress," the very spirit of the modern. For Sanger, and for thousands of women who responded enthusiastically to her early speaking tours, access to birth control information was the most important prerequisite to female emancipation, which was itself a cardinal feature of the new century. As Mrs. Lulu MacClure Clarke of St. Louis wrote to Sanger after her 1916 speaking tour, "even if women can't help much, don't know how to speak in public or write for the press, etc., yet they are awakening up all over the nation and waiting for someone to lead the way" (qtd. in Gordon 231).

Clarke's letter invoked a metaphor prevalent in turn-of-the-century Anglo-American feminist literature—from Kate Chopin's 1899 novel, *The Awakening*, to the suffragist Florence Guertin Tuttle's nonfictional treatise *The Awakening of Woman* (1915)—yet it underestimated the role that women's writing and public speaking had already played in the very awakening that she lauded.[2] As Anne Ruggles Gere has demonstrated, the implicitly politicized literacy practices of two million American women active in the women's club movement provided a means of "produc[ing] and consum[ing] discourses that enabled them to explore and change social formations" (53). Since the influence of the women's club movement extended not only to its members but also to their innumerable sisters, mothers, daughters, and friends, allowing them to "imagine themselves as participants in a widespread activity that connected them with multiple but invisible others" (21), the deliberate program of reading and writing encouraged across a wide variety of women's clubs no doubt helped spur women's claim to a more prominent role in a self-consciously national culture.

Yet while it is true that "through writing and reading, [women] established new and intimate relationships that extended across the open spaces of the expanding nation" (Gere 21), this very expansion threatened the ideal of a unified national culture. Certainly, the redefinition of nation necessary to incorporate both massive influxes of immigrants and new imperialist ventures helped to fuel the popularity of evolutionary discourses, which at once proclaimed the unity of the human "family" and imposed hierarchies of mental, social, and sexual development within this family. Indeed, the Progressive Era's master narrative seemed to require that all forms of progress be measured in specifically racial terms. Daniel G. Brinton's *Races and Peoples* (1890), for example, asserted that "the adult who retains the more numerous fetal, infantile or simian traits, is unquestionably inferior to him whose development has progressed beyond them. . . . Measured by these criteria, the European or white race stands at the head of the list, the African or negro at its foot" (48).

The perception that each woman had a hereditary obligation to advance her own race's destiny, in a process understood to be inherently competitive, worked against the prospect of a unified women's movement, particularly because not only antifeminists but many feminists upheld the primacy of women's duty to reproduce race. Thus, even as the suffragist Rheta Childe Dorr argued for the expansion of women's traditional responsibilities to include municipal mothering, she bolstered her claim with an argument from nature, asserting that "woman's work is race preservation, race improvement, and who opposes her, or interferes with her, simply fights nature, and nature never loses her battles" (330). Annie Marion MacLean was more succinct in her 1910 study, *Wage-Earning Women,* where she argued that "the prime function of woman must ever be the perpetuation of the race" (178).[3] But was this "function" inevitably at odds with women's own emancipation? Or could the laws of nature embodied in what the novelist Pauline Hopkins called the "mighty working of evolution" provide an impetus for reconceiving motherhood as a site of female agency as well as racial advancement? Such questions elicited a range of answers in nonfiction from the turn of the century, from Lester Ward's optimistic claim that "woman *is* the race, and the race can be lifted up only as she is raised up" (275) to Charlotte Perkins Gilman's lament that "the female segregated to the uses of sex alone naturally deteriorates in racial development, and naturally transmits that deterioration to her offspring" (*Women* 183).

This study examines early twentieth-century fictional portrayals of motherhood as they reflect and contribute to larger public debates about the relationship between race, reproduction, and female agency. I focus exclusively on African American and native white women's participation in such debates for two reasons. First, although the "maternal function of the immigrant woman was especially productive of racial anxiety" (Irving 3), and social workers intent on Americanizing immigrants were accordingly enjoined to "go after the women" (Sanchez 250), the targeted immigrant mothers—like the Native American mothers whose children were removed to boarding schools—had relatively little public voice in debates about how, or whether, to raise children.[4] Second, the unprecedented flowering of black women's fiction at the turn of the century; black women's prolific contributions to the nonfictional literature of racial uplift, in which the black mother was a pivotal figure; and the predominance of white middle-class women in the feminist, birth control, and eugenics movements meant that the most explicit and extensive cross-racial dialogues about motherhood took place between African American and native white women.[5]

On the one hand, the specter of white race suicide and the imperative of black racial uplift made motherhood both a cultural ideal and a racial duty, for black and white women alike. On the other hand, feminist activists from Anna Julia Cooper to Emma Goldman sought to expand woman's role beyond what Kate Chopin termed the "mother-woman." Thus, while much social scientific, medical, and popular literature of this era emphasized motherhood's contributions to black or white race progress, insisting that women literally and figuratively "mother the race," an identifiable cross-racial tradition of women's fiction rejected a strictly instrumental definition of maternity, imagining mothers as subjects and agents in their own right. By focusing on critical fictions of maternity—novels and short stories whose depiction of pregnancy, childbirth, and child rearing work against dominant ideologies of motherhood—I reveal how women's fiction in this period questioned the apparently natural relationship between female biology and racial destiny, challenging traditional ideas about gender, sexuality, race, and motherhood. I argue that while motherhood was a primary site of racial hierarchy during the first third of the twentieth century, the belief that motherhood was a universal identity provided a means of engagement for women writers and activists across lines of color and class. That even the most "liberatory" narratives tended to reproduce dominant racial ideologies testifies to the persistence of racial hierarchy within first-wave feminist movements. At the same time, a cross-racial, cross-class analysis reveals a shared project of denaturalizing maternity by confronting the distortions of successive maternal ideals, from the nineteenth-century True Mother to the twentieth-century New Mother.[6]

My analysis builds on a vast body of feminist scholarship on motherhood, beginning with Adrienne Rich's *Of Woman Born: Motherhood as Experience and Institution,* whose subtitle reflects the inevitable tension between the experience of motherhood and its cultural meanings. While several recent studies have examined nineteenth- and twentieth-century literary representations of motherhood from psychoanalytic and trans-Atlantic perspectives, *Mothering the Race* takes a narrower historical and geographic focus.[7] By focusing on the four decades between 1890 and 1930—defined in retrospect as the Progressive Era but proudly dubbed the "Woman's Era" by the female activists who figured so prominently in its reform efforts—I offer a more detailed and historicized account of how racially specific notions of motherhood colored both literary and political discourses of female emancipation.

The ongoing interdependency of black and white constructions of maternity, as well as the level of explicit and implicit cross-racial dialogue apparent at the turn of the century, prompt me to undertake an intertextual study of black and white women writers, though such an undertaking is fraught with difficulties. As Hazel Carby pointed out in 1987, scholarship that purports to offer cross-racial and cross-class analysis has too often had predictable political consequences: "First, in order to establish the common grounds for a unified women's movement, material differences in the lives of working-class and middle-class women or white and black women have been dismissed. [Second], the search to establish that these bonds of sisterhood have always existed has led to a feminist historiography and criticism which denies the hierarchical structuring of the relations between black and white women and often takes the concerns of middle-class, articulate white women as a norm" (*Reconstructing* 17). More recently, Ann duCille has critiqued the current trend in literary studies, in which the figure of the black woman in literature has become a "kind of sacred text" ("Occult" 591). DuCille argues that while the "hyperstatic alterity" of the black woman has boosted the careers of any number of traditionally trained white academics who have abandoned a well-mined white literary tradition in order to capitalize on multiculturalism, it has not granted a commensurate measure of scholarly respect, academic prestige, or institutional power to the black feminist critics who first unearthed the riches of black women's writing.[8]

Unfortunately, a desire not to replicate such biases has perpetuated the de facto segregation of feminist literary studies. Carby's groundbreaking study made vivid the many ways that black women writers used literature to challenge dominant notions of femininity and sexuality from the antebellum period through the Harlem Renaissance, and it helped to generate a wave of black feminist scholarship attentive to the specificity as well as the variety of black female experience. While more recent efforts to examine whiteness as a racial identity have demonstrated the reciprocity of black and white racial formations, relatively few studies of American women writers have explored the intersections and contradictions of racial ideologies as they are manifested across black- and white-authored texts. Certainly, interracial studies of U.S. women's literary traditions are still less common than works that treat African American women's writing as a separate tradition.[9]

Yet recent historical scholarship on the origins of maternalist politics and the welfare state—including Seth Koven and Sonya Michel's *Mothers of a New World;* Molly Ladd-Taylor's *Mother-Work;* and Gwendolyn Mink's *The Wages of Motherhood*—suggests that the reconstruction of maternal ideals in the Progressive Era provides particularly fruitful ground for cross-racial literary analysis.[10] As Mink argues, "The socialization of motherhood found its logic in the prevailing gender ideology and found its force in the race anxieties of what, in practice, was white men's democracy" ("Lady," 1990, 93). Drawing on this scholarship, as well as on black feminist scholarship that defines the novel as a form of "cultural and political intervention" (Carby, *Reconstructing* 61), *Mothering the Race* offers an integrated analysis of motherhood as it appears in African American and white women's fictions, revealing the mutual dependency of black and white constructions of maternity, as well as the interanimations of race and class in fictions across the color line.

Women's fictional representations of motherhood both participated and intervened in what we might call a national project of rational reproduction, a project in which maternity figured as a precious natural resource.[11] If, as Anne McClintock has argued, "women are typically constructed as symbolic bearers of the nation, but are denied any direct relation to national agency" (261), why, in the period between 1890 and 1930, did African American and white women writers draw so insistently upon motherhood as a literary and political trope through which to *gain* national agency? As a number of scholars have demonstrated, the nineteenth century saw the boundary between public and private inextricably linked to the boundary between male and female, with gender differences understood to be inherent and immutable. Rita Felski argues that "the distinction between a striving, competitive masculinity, and a nurturant, domestic femininity, while a feasible ideal only for a minority of middle-class households, nevertheless became a guiding rubric within which various aspects of culture were subsumed" (*Gender* 18). Of course, the gendered boundaries between public and private were neither absolute nor impermeable in the nineteenth century; the ideologies of Republican Motherhood and True Womanhood relied as much on the assumed interdependence as the necessary division of the public and private spheres. Yet by the 1890s such boundaries threatened to disappear entirely. With the emergence of social Darwinist, nativist, and eugenics discourses, motherhood, once aligned with the domestic and private, became a primary site of racial competition and thus associated with the masculine public sphere. If the New Woman posed a threat because she challenged Victorian definitions of femininity, the New Mother provoked particular anxiety because her role in racial reproduction collapsed traditional divisions between public and private, imbuing the "private" experience of motherhood with metaphors of the marketplace.

Yet this same collapse, along with the increasing publicity given to discussions of birth control, opened up a new discursive space for articulating ideas about motherhood across lines of race, class, and genre. Sometimes the cross-racial "conversation" was explicitly competitive, if not hostile, as when the white author Olga Louise Cadija bemoaned that "by the time the average white woman marries, the average colored woman is the mother of several children" and issued a call to save America from becoming a "black-peopled country" (qtd. in Williams, "Some Perils" 6). Cadija's indictment of women's clubs as contributing to white race suicide, and her attendant jabs at the black women's club movement, prompted the African American club woman Fannie Barrier Williams to decry Cadija's "unwarrantable ignorance of our social status" and to reaffirm, somewhat defensively, that "home, and everything contained in that name, [is] the most important and precious of [black women's] thought and effort" ("Some Perils" 6). But the tensions surrounding motherhood could also occasion more productive interchanges: Margaret Sanger's *Birth Control Review* published a special issue devoted to the "Negro Woman" that featured Angelina Weld Grimké's antilynching, pro–birth control short story, "The Closing Door"; the African American playwright Mary Burrill's *They That Sit in Darkness* drew on Margaret Sanger's account of her own conversion to the cause of birth control to dramatize the plight of impoverished black women; and Sanger herself acknowledged the need for depictions of motherhood that would "give us something that we cannot obtain from any number of 'maternity surveys' or 'biometric computations' of vital statistics—the never-told factor of maternal anguish and sacrifice" (*Motherhood* 42). In the chapters that follow I demonstrate that only by considering together the fictions of black and white, working-class and elite women writers, and only by considering literary depictions of maternity in the context of the rise of interventionary reproductive science, can we appreciate the multiple valences of motherhood in this era. I am interested not only in the diverse strategies by which women writers and activists interrogated, rejected, and sometimes reclaimed nineteenth-century maternal ideals but also in the resilience of such ideals, and the racial order that they implicitly support, in the production and reception of maternal fictions.[12]

Chapter 1, "Maternal Metaphors: Articulating Gender, Race, and Nation at the Turn of the Century," traces the interpenetration of racial and sexual ideologies in the construction of the "race mother," a woman whose maternal labors were viewed as contributing positively to racial progress. Analyzing the rhetorical strategies of black and white women speakers at the World's Congress of Representative Women (1893) and at the annual National Congresses of Mothers (beginning in 1897), I argue that as motherhood emerged as an increasingly public, political, and racialized discourse, it both served as a point of connection and as a marker of difference between African American and white women. Indeed, the maternalist values undergirding black racial uplift and white feminist reform efforts at once depended on and reinforced hierarchies of race and class.

Chapter 2, "Reconstructing Motherhood: Pauline Hopkins's *Contending Forces* and the Rhetoric of Racial Uplift," examines Hopkins's portrayal of the black mother as a racially redemptive figure and as a counter to racial and sexual stereotypes fueled by social Darwinist discourses. I argue that Hopkins, to a greater extent than her black feminist contemporaries, historicized and problematized the white ideal of True Womanhood on which the black race mother was based, using multiple and contradictory images of mothers to undercut notions of racial or maternal essences. The contradictions of *Contending Forces* reflect the inherent tensions in racial uplift ideology, tensions that Hopkins negotiated in her role as literary editor of the *Colored American Magazine,* where she sought both to document race progress and to protest ongoing violence. By insisting on the relevance of slave mothers' experiences to those of twentieth-century black mothers, Hopkins demonstrated both the historical limitations and the potential power of black motherhood as a site of racial uplift.

While motherhood proves both personally fulfilling and racially redemptive in *Contending Forces,* it appears lethal to female subjectivity in novels of sexual awakening by Kate Chopin and Edith Wharton. Chapter 3, "The Romance 'Plot': Reproducing Silence, Reinscribing Race in *The Awakening* and *Summer,*" explores the contradictions in each novel's implicit argument that romantic love betrays women by securing "mothers for the race" at the expense of the female subject. In both novels female sexual agency proves illusory because sex leads inevitably to maternity, which is associated with linguistic paralysis, physical confinement, and death; yet both Chopin and Wharton ultimately uphold motherhood as an inescapable racial imperative. Like their contemporary, Charlotte Perkins Gilman, whose evolutionary feminism provides a useful framework for examining the competing goals of female emancipation and racial advancement, Chopin and Wharton critiqued the unnatural construction of womanhood under patriarchy, particularly as it is inscribed and reproduced through language. Yet unlike Gilman, who predicated racial advancement on the emancipation of women, Chopin and Wharton conceded the biological primacy of reproducing race.

The final two chapters focus on two novels of the 1920s—Edith Summers Kelley's *Weeds* and Nella Larsen's *Quicksand*—that offer sobering accounts of women's continued sexual subjugation during the supposedly liberated Jazz Age. In these remarkably similar texts an ambitious, artistic heroine becomes a prisoner of biology, defeated by the physical demands of excessive childbirth. Where Chopin and Wharton offer groundbreaking portrayals of women's sexual desire, Kelley and Larsen "write beyond the ending" to represent the material effects of childbirth and motherhood, though with significantly different emphases. *Weeds* (1923), which focuses on a white working-class woman, connects the unrewarded labors of child rearing to the capitalist exploitation of tenant farmers. *Quicksand* (1928), the story of a black middle-class woman, reveals the artistic and reproductive colonization of the black female body within an emerging black nationalism, explicitly gendered male.

Chapter 4, "Hard Labor: Edith Summers Kelley's *Weeds* and the Language of Eugenics," examines Kelley's novel within the context of the birth control and eugenics movements, with particular attention to the rhetorical strategies of Margaret Sanger. In a decade when the power of mother love was invoked in direct proportion to the threat of the nonmaternal New Woman, Kelley created a mother figure utterly devoid of maternal instinct, who comes to view her children as "greedy vampires." By attributing an apparently "natural" sexual order to the manmade structure of capitalism, Kelley contested the logic of determinism that structures the male naturalist novel, even as she rejected the lingering romanticism of *The Awakening,* whose ending she explicitly rewrote. Yet while Kelley's realism precludes an emancipatory ending, her detailed rendering of childbirth suggests that childbearing itself has the potential to transform female consciousness.

Chapter 5, "Fatal Contractions: Nella Larsen's *Quicksand* and the New Negro Mother," places Larsen's nightmarish representation of maternity in the dual context of antilynching polemics and Harlem Renaissance aesthetics. I argue that Larsen, unlike many of her contemporaries, rejected an instrumental definition of black womanhood, focusing on the creative rather than the procreative potential of her artist-heroine. Her biracial heroine's search for a stable racial identity generates a peripatetic plot that symbolically bridges white European modernism and black southern folk culture. Yet her heroine's only "artistic" production—of black children from whom she feels profoundly alienated—highlights not only her lack of reproductive agency but also the intractability of binary racial categories.

Exploring the economic and psychological consequences of maternity, Kelley and Larsen challenge the assumption that women find their deepest satisfaction—and the race its highest achievement—in and through motherhood. By 1929 a male critic reviewing women's new fiction for the *Bookman* was forced to conclude that "love, passion, matrimony and babies are not the preponderating interests of all women that men have thought them to be" and that "the maternal instinct so highly sentimentalized by the old novelists" was nothing more than an "imaginative illusion" (Herrick, "Feline" 4–5). Yet, as I suggest in a brief epilogue, "Representing Motherhood at Century's End," recent representations of motherhood in literature and film, including Toni Morrison's *Beloved* and Anna Quindlen's *One True Thing*, revive and revise notions of maternal instinct in ways that reflect our current preoccupations with motherhood and race.

The reemergence of the "problem" of maternity at the turn of the twenty-first century is in some ways predictable, for as Elaine Showalter's study of gender and culture at the last fin de siècle demonstrates, "in periods of cultural insecurity, when there are fears of regression and degeneration, the longing for strict border controls around the definition of gender, as well as race, class, and nationality, becomes especially intense" (*Sexual Anarchy* 4). Speaking primarily of the British context, Showalter argues that "racial boundaries were among the most important lines of demarcation . . . [because] fears not only of colonial rebellion but also of racial mingling, crossbreeding, and intermarriage, fueled scientific and political interest in establishing clear lines of demarcation between black and white" (5). While such fears necessarily inform the problematic nexus of race and maternity, *Sexual Anarchy,* like most scholarship on the New Woman in the United States and Britain, does not explore the question of motherhood in any detail, perhaps because the New

Woman is typically associated with a rejection of maternity.[13] Yet far from dismissing maternity out of hand, the writers I discuss are exceedingly ambivalent about, but never indifferent to, motherhood. Moreover, in the U.S. context the permeability of racial boundaries was precisely what marked the previous fin de siècle as modern, and the cross-fertilization of African American and white writing was what gave women's literature of this era its distinctive flavor, bearing out Fannie Barrier Williams's observation that "American literature needs for its greatest variety and its deeper soundings that which will be written into it out of the hearts of these self-emancipating [black] women" ("Intellectual Progress" 700).

By putting black and white, canonical and noncanonical writers in dialogue, I identify as part of an emerging tradition a group of writers who, while very much engaged in the modern project of redefining reproduction, typically have not been viewed as modernists. Indeed, to the extent that the novels considered here attempted to tell the "real" story of motherhood, by and large adhering to a realist aesthetic, they might be viewed as antimodernist. Yet the necessary association of the modern with formal experimentation has been challenged by recent re-readings of literary modernism—particularly Sandra M. Gilbert and Susan Gubar's three-volume *No Man's Land;* Marianne De Koven's *Rich and Strange;* and Suzanne Clark's *Sentimental Modernism*—which have identified both the crucial role that gender played in the development of a modernist aesthetic and the gendered values and assumptions that have excluded most women from the modernist canon, and in so doing downplayed their importance to twentieth-century literary history.

Clark's rhetorical approach is particularly useful in thinking about the de facto marginalization, within a modernist aesthetic, of women's writing about maternity. Clark argues that "in order to avoid admitting the rhetorical situation of literature, which engages it inevitably in culture, history, and desire, American modernist literary criticism endorsed a formalism which avoided ideology by calling women ideological, and rejected their sensible attachments to the everyday" (6). Inasmuch as motherhood epitomizes women's traditional (though no longer inevitable) attachment to the body—and beyond this to the "everyday" realities of child rearing—a maternal thematics would seem particularly irreconcilable with high modernism's valorization of disembodied textuality, much as motherhood itself has appeared incompatible with artistic creation. Certainly, male modernists' wholesale rejection of sentiment served to marginalize texts that purported to tell a mother's story, while the continued association of the maternal with the sentimental has obscured how insistently early twentieth-century women writers revised the perceived inadequacies of nineteenth-century women's fiction precisely through their representations of motherhood.[14]

My primary intent, however, is not to delineate the formal innovations of the novels under consideration but to examine how fictions of maternity served as forms of cultural intervention, even as they reproduced the racial and sexual ideologies that they sought to critique. While it is tempting to judge historical texts according to current feminist criteria, it is important to recall Rita Felski's observation in *Beyond Feminist Aesthetics* that "the political value of literary texts from the standpoint of feminism can be determined only by an investigation of their social functions and effects in relation to the interests of women in a particular historical context, and not by attempting to deduce an abstract literary theory of 'masculine' and 'feminine,' 'subversive' and 'reactionary' forms in isolation from the social conditions of their production and reception" (2). Rather than identifying "dominant" and "subversive" ideologies of motherhood in this era, I read women's fictional and nonfictional narratives of reproduction as part of a "historical conversation of multiple voices engaged in continuing conflict" (Mailloux 58).

We can begin to chart the conflict-laden terrain of motherhood by noting the virulence with which some critics objected to Kate Chopin's unmaternal heroine as "morbid," "vulgar," and likely to foster "unholy imaginations and unclean desires" (Culley 167–69); the censorship of the childbirth scene in Edith Summers Kelley's *Weeds;* or the perception that Angelina Weld Grimké's play *Rachel* advocated black "race suicide." At the same time, if the reading habits of women's clubs are at all representative, we can assume that even critical depictions of maternity would have been read with careful attention by civic-minded women convinced that novels could "[teach] and [improve] readers, connecting them with remote places and persons, and touching hearts and minds" (Gere 243). Perhaps, as was the case when Pauline Hopkins read part of her forthcoming novel *Contending Forces* to members of Boston's Woman's Era Club, revisionary depictions of motherhood were read collectively, as part of a larger consideration of the "Woman Problem." Certainly, critics did their part to link women's fiction to the much-debated politics of reproduction, as when a reviewer of Kelley's *Weeds* asserted that "it will be very profitable for legislators to consider whether scientific birth control or primitive methods of abortion furnish the better solution [to] the problem of a degenerating physical stock, due to excessive childbearing" (Sherman 363).

By placing women's fictions of maternity within the historical context of racial uplift, feminist, birth control, and eugenics discourses, I hope to demonstrate how fiction both participates in and challenges the construction of maternal and racial hierarchies. Indeed, if we consider women's critical fictions as part of what Felski calls a "counter-public sphere," we can examine the "mediations between literature, feminist ideology, and the broader social domain" (*Beyond* 9) as part of a revolution in reproduction that both inspired and gained force through literary revisions of maternity. Acknowledging that this revolution was at once sustained and constrained by notions of racial mothering not only complicates our understanding of first-wave feminist movements but also provides an impetus for reexamining the intersections of racial and reproductive discourses in contemporary literature, popular culture, and public policy debates.

1. Maternal Metaphors: Articulating Gender, Race, and Nation at the Turn of the Century

IN HER CONTRIBUTION to a volume of essays titled *A New Negro for a New Century: An Accurate and Up-to-Date Record of the Upward Struggles of the Negro Race* (1900), Fannie Barrier Williams lamented the lack of attention paid to the black mother's role in the "upward struggle," noting that "the negro as an 'alien' race, as a 'problem,' as an 'industrial factor' . . . [is] well known and instantly recognized; but colored women as mothers, as homemakers, as the center and source of the social life of the race have received little or no attention" ("Club Movement" 379). Seeking wider publicity for the black mother's role in shaping the new century's "New Negro," Williams laid claim to a social identity that Charlotte Perkins Gilman had recently repudiated when she argued in *Women and Economics* (1898) that "as a sex specialized to reproduction, [woman gives up] all personal activity, all honest independence, all useful and progressive economic service for her glorious consecration to the uses of maternity" (198–99).

Two decades later Margaret Sanger would stress the eugenic importance of selective motherhood, reminding her readers that the United States could only "gather perfect fruit from perfect trees" and that the "race is but the amplification of the mother body" (*Woman* 233). In the same year the African American playwright and poet Angelina Weld Grimké registered her ambivalence about the relationship between white and black women by chastising the former for their persistent racism. Yet she held out hope for cross-racial understanding based on a common maternal experience: "The white women of this country are about the worst enemies with which the colored race has to contend. . . . [But] if anything can make all women sisters underneath their skins, it is motherhood" ("'Rachel' the Play" 414).

Though Williams, Gilman, Sanger, and Grimké never met to discuss their views of motherhood, they were all participants in a national conversation about what Gilman termed the "uses of maternity." This conversation took on particular urgency during the Progressive Era, when nativists, maternalists, pacifists, and feminists began to discuss motherhood as part of a larger politics of population. Thus, when Emma Goldman denounced the "defenders of authority [who] dread the advent of a free motherhood," she linked the cultural imperative to bear children to a host of political interests, asking: "Who would fight wars? Who would create wealth? Who would make the policeman, the jailer, if woman were to refuse the indiscriminate breeding of children? The race, the race! shouts the king, the president, the capitalist, the priest. The race must be preserved, though woman be degraded to a mere machine" (13). Goldman's formulation assumed an inverse relationship between the needs of the race and the emancipation of women, yet the concept of the "race mother" that emerged at the turn of the century was used not only to reinforce woman's traditional reproductive role but also to articulate mothers' vital role in racial and national progress.

Taking up the much-debated relationship between race and reproduction, and between female agency and national destiny, Williams, Gilman, Sanger, and Grimké speak to questions of power and universality that continue to animate feminist scholarship on motherhood. On the question of maternal power Williams and Gilman are diametrically opposed. For Williams mothers are an unrecognized, but unquestionably vital, factor in national life; for Gilman mothers are peripheral to the life of the nation and have forfeited independent personhood through the offices of maternity. On the question of universality Sanger and Grimké are equally at odds. Where Sanger asserts a biologically determined, culturally impermeable system of reproduction in which "like begets like" (*Woman* 233), Grimké suggests that the cross-cultural experience of motherhood might get "underneath" racial difference to uncover a set of shared interests.

Even more striking is the contrast between Gilman's and Sanger's descriptions of mothers as passive reproductive vehicles and Williams's and Grimké's assumption that mothers are active social agents, a contrast that suggests a disjuncture between white and black conceptions of motherhood. While many white feminists were characterizing marriage and motherhood as a form of sex slavery, postbellum texts by black women used domesticity as the privileged sign of emancipation. As Claudia Tate argues, black women writers at the turn of the century "represented freedom not simply as a desired political condition but as domestic ambitions—marriage, motherhood, and home—in which women have authority as well as men" (*Domestic* 49).

Yet at cross-racial forums like the World's Congress of Representative Women (1893) and the National Congresses of Mothers (beginning in 1897),

African American and white women could agree with Frances E. W. Harper that "more than the increase of wealth, the power of armies, and the strength of fleets is the need of good homes . . . and good mothers" ("Woman's" 436). Despite the implicit racial hierarchy that governed such forums, these national meetings testified to motherhood's powerful role in public as well as private life while selectively and strategically promoting the idea that, as mothers or potential mothers, all women were, to paraphrase Grimké, sisters under the skin.

This notion has little credibility for a generation of feminist scholars trained to suspect any assertion of gender essentialism. The literary critic Barbara Omolade's observation that "black women are not white women with color" (248) embodies the current emphasis on the particularity and irreducibility of different women's experiences. Likewise, the historian Elsa Barkley Brown argues that "we have still to recognize that being a woman is, in fact, not extractable from the context in which one is a woman—that is, race, class, time, and place. We have still to recognize that all women do not have the same gender" (43), or, by extension, the same identity as mothers. Still, the issue of motherhood threatens to seduce the most vigilant anti-essentialist. As the sociologist Evelyn Nakano Glenn observes, "Because the gendered allocation of mothering appears to flow inevitably from the division based on reproductive function, mothering—more than any other aspect of gender—has been subject to essentialist interpretation: seen as natural, universal, and unchanging" ("Social" 3).

Karen Sanchez-Eppler has examined the dangers of such universalizing in the context of the midnineteenth-century abolitionist and feminist movements, concluding that because white feminists appropriated images of black women's oppression for their own political goals, what began as "enlightening and empowering motions of identification" ended by "obliterat[ing] the particularity of black and female experience" (31). Unlike the competing rhetorics of feminism and abolitionism, however, early twentieth-century discourses of maternalism—which held that a mother's responsibility for her children's well-being made her uniquely suited to cultivate other forms of social welfare—provided a theoretical point of connection between black and white women activists. Thus, as Jim Crow violence and disenfranchisement sparked a national black women's club movement, and Progressive Era reform movements defined white middle-class women as the de facto guardians of the less privileged, both groups used the "image, experience, and rhetoric" of motherhood to "forge a new more inclusive definition of the 'political'" (Boris 214). Indeed, if early twentieth-century maternalism "transformed motherhood from women's primary *private* responsibility into *public* policy" (Koven and Michel 2), it also served as a rhetorical link between black and white women's movements, both of which used the figure of the race mother as a powerful symbolic construct.[1]

Certainly, the imbrication of motherhood and race at the turn of the century spurred reconstructions of womanhood on both sides of the color line. Laura Doyle has suggested that the very concept of a race mother depends upon a system of racial patriarchy in which "mothers reproduce bodies not in a social vacuum but for either a dominant or a subordinate [racial or ethnic] group" (5). Doyle associates such reproduction with "subservient procreat[ion]" (21), but this perspective ignores the extent to which early twentieth-century maternalists used rhetorics of racial mothering to support their bids for political power, reproductive autonomy, and racial justice. The formation of National Mother's Congresses in the 1890s; the establishment of the U.S. Children's Bureau in 1912 (the first U.S. agency headed by a woman); the passage of the Sheppard-Towner Maternity and Infancy Protection Act of 1921 (the first federal legislation passed by and for women); and cross-racial efforts on behalf of the Dyer antilynching bill suggest that motherhood provided a powerful platform for middle-class women reformers to effect change in the public sphere. The African American club woman Carrie Clifford, for example, built her case for suffrage in decidedly maternal terms, arguing that it was "the great mother-heart reaching out to save her children from war, famine, pestilence; from death, degradation and destruction, that induces her to demand 'Votes for Women,' knowing well that fundamentally it is really a campaign for 'Votes for Children'" (185).

At the same time, the rhetorical and literary uses of motherhood in the early twentieth century reveal the inherent contradictions of maternalist ideology, which served both to articulate a notion of universal womanhood and to reinforce racial hierarchy. Speeches delivered at the 1893 World's Congress of Representative Women and at the annual meetings of the National Congress of Mothers (beginning in 1897) demonstrate both how central motherhood would be to twentieth-century definitions of American womanhood and the extent to which maternalist discourses depended on racial and class hierarchies. For black and white women alike, serving as municipal mothers involved ministering to those who, by dint of race and/or class, required their elevating influence.

Mothers as Representative Women

As the site of the World's Congress of Representative Women (WCRW), the 1893 World's Columbian Exposition provided an unprecedented opportuni-

ty for American women to articulate their pivotal role in national development as well as their contributions to the greater progress of civilization; indeed, Congress appropriated money for the exposition because it would serve
as "an exhibition of the progress of civilization in the New World" (qtd. in
Bederman 31). Stressing the national and international importance of the
event, May Wright Sewall, chair of the WCRW's organizing committee, called
the weeklong series of meetings "the most remarkable ever convened," not
excluding "the councils of Nice and Trent, the pregnant interview between
King John and his Barons, and the first Continental Congress" (Introduction
1). Because the World's Congress featured 330 "representative" women who
addressed a combined audience of more than 150,000 in a seven-day period,
Sewall's comparisons are slightly less inflated than they at first appear.

Yet the issue of representation was a vexed one for the Board of Lady Managers that organized the World's Congress. Southern white women protested
their relative exclusion from the 115–member board, while African American
women repeatedly petitioned (with no success) for representation. Because
no black man had been appointed to the all-male commission that oversaw
the exposition as a whole, black women seeking representation on the Board
of Lady Managers, one of twenty auxiliary organizing boards, sought to re-
dress both their own lack of voice and the broader exclusion of African Americans.[2] Writing to each member of the Board of Lady Managers in 1892, the
African American educator and elocutionist Hallie Q. Brown voiced the "settled conviction among the colored people, that no adequate opportunity is
to be offered them for proper representation in the World's Fair" (Wells and
Douglass 124).

So deliberate was the exclusion of African Americans from what came to
be called the White City that Ida B. Wells and Frederick Douglass published
and distributed ten thousand pamphlets titled *The Reason Why the Colored
American Is Not in the World's Columbian Exposition*. Appealing first to white
self-interest, Wells and Douglass argued that the absence of black representation both damaged the reputation of African Americans and sullied the
image of the United States as a leader of the civilized world: "The exhibit of
the progress made by a race in 25 years of freedom as against 250 years of slavery, would have been the greatest tribute to the greatness and progressive-
ness of American institutions which could have been shown the world." In
addition to challenging the fair's status as a testament to American progres-
sivism, they made a more material case for why African Americans had a right
to be represented at the fair, arguing that "the colored people of this great
Republic . . . were among the earliest settlers of this continent" and that "the
wealth created by their industry has afforded to the white people of this coun-

try the leisure essential to their great progress in education, art, science, industry and invention" (49). Without such representation, Douglass and Wells feared, visitors to the Columbian Exposition would ask: "Why are not the colored people, who constitute so large an element of the American population, and who have contributed so large a share to American greatness,—more visibly present and better represented in this World's Exposition? . . . Are they so dull and stupid as to feel no interest in this great event?" (49–50)

White women had faced a similar dilemma when their petition to Congress to appoint women to the exposition's organizing commission failed and when male selection committees repeatedly rejected women's proposed exhibits. Forced to display women's accomplishments in the separate Woman's Building, the Board of Lady Managers inadvertently reinforced the notion that the rest of the White City represented wholly male accomplishments. Thus, while the Lady Managers "worked tirelessly to prove that women and men had contributed equally to the advancement of civilization," the Woman's Building "underlined white women's marginality to civilization," not least because it was positioned directly opposite the midway, the "uncivilized" section of the fair where Asian, Native American, and African displays were laid out in descending order of "barbarism" (Bederman 34). The *Chicago Tribune* reported that the proximity of Turkish and Chinese to Native American and Dahomean villages afforded fair goers the opportunity to "descend the spiral of evolution, tracing humanity in its highest phases down almost to its animalistic origins" (qtd. in Rydell 62).

Black women's participation in the World's Congress of Representative Women must be seen through the lens of the racist ideology that dominated the fair as a whole; yet in comparison to black men, and despite their exclusion from the Board of Lady Managers, black women were a significant presence at the congress. Unlike African American men, who were represented only indirectly by Frederick Douglass—present in his role as minister to Haiti—six black women spoke as "representative" women. Yet because five of their six speeches were scheduled as part of a multinational symposium called "The Solidarity of Human Interests," whose goal was to illustrate the "progress of women in Spain . . . Poland, Italy, Siam, Iceland, and Syria" as well as "the progress of women of African descent in the United States" (Sewall, "Prefatory Comments" 632), these women were representative only insofar as they could be classified as foreigners within.

The invocation of motherhood in the speeches at the World's Congress thus served distinct purposes for white and black women. For white women motherhood offered an opportunity to demonstrate women's pivotal role in the advancement of white civilization. Particularly where suffrage was con-

cerned, asserting the political value of women's maternal nature meant up-
holding racial hierarchy. For black women, on the other hand, motherhood
was a means of articulating the universality of women's interests, the intellectual and moral progress of African Americans since Emancipation, and,
despite their segregated position on the program, the quintessential Ameri-
canness of black women.

May Wright Sewall's opening address introduced the congress as a proudly
ecumenical event, yet she responded to black women's dissatisfaction with
the congress organizers by issuing an admonition to forgive and forget: "Glad
as we are to unite in this Congress mistresses of the different arts, we feel it a
gladder if a humbler duty to unite in it the races that are at work within our
own land for liberty. It is a wonderful truth that the capability for forgiveness, that divinest of attributes, is a human inheritance. You will find upon
the list of speakers a descendant of the last hereditary chief of the Cherokees,
and also some descendants of that other more greatly outraged race, import-
ed only to be reduced to servitude, who come to us but one remove from the
generation of their own blood which was sold from the block. Is not this a
magnificent proof of the capacity for forgiveness possessed by these two
races?" ("Introductory Address" 16). But despite Sewall's declaration of races
"united in liberty," white women's speeches articulated the national importance of motherhood by drawing clear distinctions between black and white
womanhood. In arguing for suffrage, for example, many white speakers con-
trasted the potentially salutary effect of women voters with the pernicious
influence of foreigners, a category that, given the positioning of black wom-
en on the program, must be seen as encompassing African Americans. Ignoring the fact that some of these undesirable foreigners were also women,
white women asserted the solidarity of race over gender.

Julia Ward Howe's speech, "The Moral Initiative as Related to Woman,"
invoked two categories of womanhood and intimated that suffrage was to
be only a white woman's prerogative. She began with an encomium to True
Motherhood, proclaiming: "Happy is the man whose mother has been a tow-
er of strength to herself and her family. . . . The mother love has watched at
the gates of his childish Eden with a drawn sword. . . . The nucleus of all that
he is to believe, to aim at, and to do, has been delivered to him, like a sealed
packet full of precious things, by a mother who honors supremely all that
honors humanity" (317). Yet despite the incalculable influence of "mother
love," Howe noted that in politics "the man opens the door for himself and
shuts it against his wife, opens the door for his son and shuts it upon his
daughter," compelling "one-half of the human race to look back toward the
old barbarism, while the other insists on looking forward to the new civili-

zation" (318). Given the association of barbarism with nonwhite populations, Howe's use of evolutionary discourse is implicitly racialized; the woman who, without the vote, is wrongly forced to "look back toward" barbarism is by definition a civilized white woman.

J. Ellen Foster's address, "The Civil and Political Status of Women," was more explicitly racialized, counterposing native white women's potential political influence with the allegedly pernicious effect of nonwhite and foreign populations. Invoking evolutionary language similar to Howe's, Foster asserted that the imminent evolution of "perfected humanity" was "pervaded by woman's presence and influence" (439), but she bemoaned the "mixed populations in crowded cities and [the] colonies of foreigners distributed through the country" who "give rise to apprehension in the minds of intelligent women" (440). Allowing that "some of our foreign-born citizens are of the noblest fiber," she charged that "masses of others are the garbage of oriental and European civilizations" and that "*they all vote*," in marked contrast to American women, the "daughters and granddaughters of Revolutionary heroes, the mothers, sisters, and the wives of a later generation of heroes" (441). Significantly, in distinction to many foreigners, who were "disqualified by heredity and environment for responsible citizenship" (441), a native-born white woman earned political voice through her service as "the mother of citizens" (445).

While many white speakers drew a distinction between white women and women of color, Ida A. Harper drew an analogy between race and sex slavery that seemingly asserted the solidarity of all women's interests:

> When the young people of the present generation read Uncle Tom's Cabin, and the speeches of Garrison and Phillips . . . they are filled with amazement. They are unable to comprehend that the monstrous evil of slavery existed and flourished in this beautiful country, and found its defenders among ministers and church members and the so-called best element of society. . . .
>
> Just like this it will be, a few generations hence, as the youth of that age read of a time when the women of the nation were held in a state of political bondage. . . . "Did the most ignorant and degraded of foreigners, the lowest and most vicious of Americans . . . who happened to be men, have the privilege and the power of the ballot, while the hosts of church women, and the army of schoolteachers, and all the wives and mothers were disfranchised because they were women?" (451–52)

Yet Harper's comparison of women's disenfranchisement with African Americans' access to the power of the ballot takes the black male experience as normative, ignoring black women's continued disenfranchisement.

Helen Gardener, a white woman who frequently spoke on heredity, addressed race in more generic terms, identifying the subjugation of women as the chief impediment to human progress. That Gardener was one of a handful of women to present two speeches at the WCRW—"Heredity in Its Relation to a Double Standard of Morals" and "Woman as an Annex"—underlines how central women's duty to reproduce race was to arguments for female emancipation. Anticipating Charlotte Perkins Gilman's argument in *Women and Economics,* Gardener argued in "Woman as an Annex" that "nowhere in all nature is the mere fact of sex made a reason for fixed inequality of liberty," yet among humans, "maternity under sex subjugation, linked with financial dependence upon the one not so burdened, have fixed [a] subordinate status upon that part of the race which is the producer of the race" (489–90). Such an arrangement accounts for the "slow, the distorted, the diseased, and the criminal progress of humanity," for "subordinates can not give lofty character. Servile temperaments can not blossom into liberty-loving, liberty-breathing, liberty-giving descendants" (490). In short, Gardener argued, women cannot produce good citizens while themselves enslaved.

But Gardener went further, to threaten that "maternity is an awful power. It blindly strikes back at injustice with a force that is a fearful menace to mankind. And the race which is born of mothers who are harassed, bullied, subordinated, and made the victims of blind passion or power . . . can not fail to continue to give us the horrible spectacles we have always had of war, of crime, of vice, of trickery, of double-dealing, of pretense, of lying, of arrogance, of subserviency, of incompetence, of brutality, and alas, of insanity, idiocy, and disease" (493). Gardener's invocation of "insanity, idiocy, and disease" reflected the concerns of the late nineteenth-century social purity movement, which sought to curtail husbands' sexual infidelities to protect innocent wives and children from venereal disease. But her argument that women's continued oppression posed a specifically racial threat drew on the language of the burgeoning eugenics movement, which evaluated the reproductive behaviors of different groups of Americans in terms of their contribution to racial betterment. Still, Gardener questioned the universality of the masculine terminology used in discussions of the race question, noting that when men spoke of the race, "they do not mean the race; they mean men . . . [thus] for the word 'universal' we must read—male; for the 'people,' the 'nation,' we must read—men" (491).

Gardener's dissatisfaction with men's partial use of the term *nation* found echoes in speeches by African American women, including Fannie Barrier

Williams, Frances E. W. Harper, Anna Julia Cooper, and Hallie Q. Brown, who objected to the invisibility of women's contributions to nation building and to the definition of black women as non-American. Williams's speech, "The Intellectual Progress of the Colored Woman of the United States Since the Emancipation Proclamation," described African American women as "daughters of men who have always been true as steel against treason to . . . the republic" and thus "as thoroughly American in all the circumstances of citizenship as the best citizens of our country" (706). Indeed, she argued that "we are so essentially American in speech, in instincts, in sentiments and destiny that the things that interest you equally interest us" (709). She regretfully noted, however, that "there has been no special interest in [our] peculiar condition as native-born American women. [Our] power to affect the social life of America, either for good or for ill, has excited not even a speculative interest" (696). Of course, Williams's decision to focus on black women as "native born" reinforced another boundary, suggesting both her desire to affiliate with white women and her need to distinguish black women from immigrant women, whom the white suffragist Ida A. Harper described as the "lowest and most vicious of Americans."

Taking up the theme of black and white women's solidarity of interests, Frances E. W. Harper suggested that black women would contribute to the progress of humanity by countering the destructive habits of men with the "grandly constructive" work of women, particularly the maternal work of transmitting "influence for good or evil across the track of unborn ages" ("Woman's" 433–34). Such influence, Harper asserted, was an essential part of nation building, for "to grapple with the evils which threaten to undermine the strength of the nation and to lay magazines of powder under the cribs of future generations is no child's play" (437). Harper ended with a plea that the "hearts of the women of the world . . . throb as one heart unified by the grand and holy purpose of uplifting the human race" (437).

Anna Julia Cooper, however, insisted on an essential difference between black and white women, for while "the white woman could at least plead for her own emancipation, the black woman, doubly enslaved, could but suffer and struggle and be silent" ("Discussion" 712). She offered a brief on behalf of the slave mother who "watered the soil with blood and tears" and continued her "self-sacrifice" in the post-Emancipation era, when "many an unbuttered crust was eaten in silent content that she might eke out enough from her poverty to send her young folks off to school" (712–13). Likewise, Hallie Q. Brown began her speech by reminding her listeners that "for two hundred and fifty years the negro woman of America was bought and sold as a chattel. The sacred ties of wife and mother were broken and disdained" ("Discussion" 724).

Yet Brown, like most of the black women who spoke at the fair, complied with May Wright Sewall's presumptive characterization of black women as forgiving by emphasizing that the black woman remained essentially maternal—"patient, sympathetic, and forgiving" (*World's Congress* 724)—despite the horrors of slavery. Thus Sewall could note approvingly that "an Afro-American [Fannie Jackson Coppin] who was herself a slave discusses with temperance and without bitterness the social, intellectual, and industrial status of her race" ("Prefatory Comments" 633). But more revealing than Sewall's self-fulfilling prophecy of black women's forgiving nature is her use of women of color to prove the legitimacy of white feminist causes. Specifically, Sewall interpreted the black women's speeches as evidence that "the woman question . . . can not be regarded as the curious culminating expression of the insane passion for independence characteristic of the Anglo-Saxon race" (632). Pointing out that "Afro-Americans, but one generation from personal bondage, [were] demanding the same freedom of thought and action that is innate in the Saxon," Sewall asserted the "reciprocal dependence of all classes of women" (633). Yet even this strategically inclusive gesture sustained the notion of racial difference by identifying the quest for freedom as innate in white women and merely imitative on the part of black women. Invocations of motherhood at the World's Congress thus served both to affiliate and differentiate various "classes" of womanhood.

Representing the Mother Woman

Notions of inherent racial difference underwrote representations of motherhood even more explicitly at the first annual meeting of the National Congress of Mothers. Organized by Alice Birney and convening in Washington, D.C., in 1897, the congress attracted two thousand participants and was recognized by a White House reception and extensive press coverage (Ladd-Taylor, *Mother-Work* 46). While this assembly of women reflected a strain of maternalism that Molly Ladd-Taylor calls "sentimental maternalism"—its program describes a baby as "a tiny feather from the wing of love dropped in the sacred lap of motherhood" (*Work and Words* 1)—such sentimentality was by no means incompatible with political efficacy.[3] In fact, the National Congress of Mothers received explicit endorsement from Theodore Roosevelt, who spoke at a number of its congresses, and succeeded in securing mothers' pensions, the first social welfare measure advocated by women activists on behalf of mothers and children.

The National Congress of Mothers' program articulated the power of motherhood, proclaiming that "the destiny of nations lies far more in the hands of women—the mothers—than in the possessors of power," as well as its universality: "She is only half a mother who does not see her own child in every child" (*Work and Words* 1, 3). Yet women's power as mothers was increasingly defined, by the National Congress of Mothers and by the child-study movement that it helped to foster, as an indirect power asserted through children on behalf of the race. "How," Alice Birney asked in her opening address to the congress, "can we divorce the woman question from the child question? Is not the one the natural, logical corollary of the other?" (7). The idea that "the child is the hope of the race" (*Work and Words* 4) echoes through a majority of the speeches at the first annual congress and would gain national currency through the popularization of works by the Swedish feminist Ellen Key and the American sociologist G. Stanley Hall. This definition of maternal power in terms of the race—along with the racial segregation of mothers' clubs—reinforced the race and class hierarchy implicit in maternalism.

In her response to Birney's welcoming address, Mary Lowe Dickinson, president of the National Council of Women, attributed women's social reform efforts to the workings of maternal instinct, arguing that "it is the mother heart that has shown itself in the unprecedented growth of philanthropic movements, in the vigorous grip now being felt upon the problem of poverty and pauperism, in the loving sympathy with sickness and suffering, and in its recognition of the starving and blunted aesthetic tastes of the masses." Literalizing the metaphor of municipal mothering, Dickinson envisioned a day when "the outstretched hands of mothers shall make an orphanage for the whole world's childhood" (13).

That this universal ministry represented the natural relation between "advanced" white women and more "primitive" mothers is suggested by titles of other speeches at the National Congress of Mothers—Frank Hamilton Cushing of the Washington, D.C., Bureau of Ethnology spoke on "Primitive Motherhood," while Lucy S. Bainbridge discussed "Mothers of the Submerged World"—and by Dickinson's own fond recollection of the Columbian Exposition as a model for the National Congress of Mothers: "As I went about that wonderful White City during the Columbian Exposition . . . I said softly to myself, 'We women have it in our power to make a white city.' . . . The stones of its buildings will be the white thoughts of white-hearted women. It will be a city that shall glow sometimes with the rose tints of our hope for the race, with the golden glow of our purposes for good, and may be by and by with the purple of our honest pride in the good that we have wrought" (20).

While Dickinson's repeated invocation of whiteness implies a metonymic relationship between color and maternal virtue, Frances E. W. Harper made clear that white women's "pride in the good that we have wrought" would need to be earned through service to their less privileged sisters. In a speech titled "The Afro-American Mother" Harper asserted that white women had the "opportunity of serving the ever-blessed Christ by ministering to his little ones, and striving to teach neglected and ignorant mothers how to make their homes the brightest spots on earth" (68). Harper insisted that she did not seek special favors for black women but wanted only to be "tried by the same rules and judged by the same standards as are other people" (70).

Yet in asking that white women not "class the worthy and worthless [black women] together" (70), Harper revealed her own relatively elite position within an intraracial class hierarchy and called attention to the politics of representation ingrained in the black women's club movement. Like white members of the National Congress of Mothers, black club women defined ministry to the less fortunate as a central part of their maternal duty. Thus Mary Church Terrell, president of the newly formed National Association of Colored Women, applied the NACW's motto, "Lifting as We Climb," specifically to the task of elevating "the masses of our women, through whom the womanhood of our people is always judged" ("What Role" 154). Terrell acknowledged that more than altruism motivated black club women's efforts, for "colored women of education and culture know that they cannot escape altogether the consequences of the acts of their most depraved sisters. They see that even if they were wicked enough to turn a deaf ear to the call of duty, both policy and self-preservation demand that they go down among the lowly, the illiterate and even the vicious, to whom they are bound by ties of race and sex" (154–55). Where Terrell acknowledged the interdependency of elite and working-class black women, Anna Murray, one of the few other black women to address the predominantly white congresses, defined the problems of children and the problems of the race as indivisible: "The children of any race are the hope of that race [and] it is doubly true of all backward races, and especially true of American children of African descent. The problem of a Republic is the problem of childhood, and in America there is a race problem which will be solved aright only when the Republic of all childhood is nurtured and guarded as the jewel of our civilization" (174–75).

Indeed, assertions of maternal rights were increasingly made on the grounds of children's or racial needs. In her speech to the congress on "The Moral Responsibility of Women in Heredity," Helen Gardener argued: "If woman is not brave enough personally to command and to obtain absolute personal liberty of action, equality of status, and entire control of her great and race-endowing function of maternity, she has no right to dare to stamp upon a child and to curse a race with the descendants of such a servile, a dwarfed, a time- and master-serving nature" (135). In the same speech Gardener adopted the language of contamination that would come to typify eugenics discourses, complaining that "ignorant and undeveloped motherhood has been and is a terrible curse to the race. An incompetent artist is merely a pathetic failure. A superficial woman lawyer simply goes clientless. . . . But a superficial, shallow, incompetent, trivial mother has left a heritage to the world which can and does poison the stream of life" (142).

Sallie Cotten's speech proposed a "national training school for women" as a means of curbing such contamination. Drawing on similar metaphors of disease, she noted that "the national Government says to foreign contagion, 'Thus far shalt thou come and no farther,' but contagion of local and internal origin continues to destroy our populations" (215–16). Arguing that "woman's most imperative duty . . . is to supply a population composed of the highest types of men and women," Cotten proposed "the cultivation by women of a scientific motherhood, which shall in time correct the errors of the past and redeem the future by penetrating the mysteries of heredity and learning to control its possibilities" (211). Maintaining that "every true woman will feel her heart leap with joy at the thought of assisting in perfecting her race and in conferring a permanent blessing on the earth" (219), Cotten drew on sentimental ideals of womanhood. Yet she signaled her engagement with more modern scientific debates about motherhood by emphasizing the national and racial importance of maternity: "All the significant portents point to America as the field of . . . the next century of progress, and to the Anglo-Saxon as the dominant spirit of that progress" (210). She ended by defining female, racial, and national advancement as inseparable elements of progress: "Women are called to lead, because America is destined to be the scene of evolutionary activities of the near future, and she must take her place as a factor in that evolution" (219).

But because the revaluation of maternity was based largely on the recognition of mothers' crucial role in evolution, a mother's interests were frequently subordinated to those of the child. As Barbara Ehrenreich and Deirdre English have noted, the child came to be seen as a "kind of evolutionary protoplasm, a means of *control* over society's not-so-distant future" (191). In *Century of the Child* (1909) the Swedish feminist Ellen Key insisted on the vital importance of the child, observing that "the transformation of society begins with the unborn child" (100). Key warned that "vengeance is being exacted on the individual, on the race, when woman gradually destroys the deepest vital source of her physical and psychic being, the power of motherhood" (103). Only by focusing on the child for several generations could woman hope to bring forth the "completed man" (105).

Key's books were best-sellers in America, perhaps because they reinforced a familiar view of the mother even while stretching traditional definitions of womanhood to include a "new reverence for [woman] as a sexual being" (*Century* 12).[4] Certainly, Key's popularity stemmed in part from her argument against Charlotte Perkins Gilman's proposal for collective child rearing, which would have been deeply threatening to the capitalist conception of the nuclear family. Denouncing Gilman as "amaternal," Key defined her own theory as follows: "The maternal as opposed to the amaternal theory is this: that a woman's life is lived most intensively and most extensively, most individually and most socially; she is for her own part most free, and for others most fruitful . . . in and with the *physical and psychic exercise of the function of maternity, because of the conscious desire, by means of this function, to uplift the life of the race as well as her own life*" (*Woman Movement* 200).

Key's dictum was not far from Theodore Roosevelt's proclamation, in his 1908 speech to the First International Congress in America on the Welfare of the Child, that "the mother is the one supreme asset of national life . . . more important by far than the successful statesman or business man or artist or scientist" ("Address" 174). Both defined a woman's value in terms of her potential for motherhood. Indeed, Key supplied the unstated assumption beneath Roosevelt's adulation of the mother: If woman was the nation's "supreme asset," it was primarily because she brought forth the "completed man," or, more precisely, the child who would become this man. Nowhere is the congruence between the "new mother" movement and evolutionary discourse— both of which privilege the child over the mother—more explicit than in Key's *The Woman Movement* (1912), which pictured the modern mother as worshiping her child: "The *new mother,* as the doctrine of evolution and the true woman movement have created her, stands with deep veneration before the mystic depths she calls her child, a being in whom the whole life of mankind is garnered" (200). Similarly, the evolutionary metaphors that dominated discussions of reproduction in the 1910s and '20s suggested that motherhood should be protected and perfected not for women's sake but for the future of the race.

By 1914 the National Congress of Mothers was publishing essays on such topics as "Parenthood and Race Culture," "The Ideals of Eugenics," "The Influence of Heredity and Environment upon Race Improvement," and "The Duty of Recording Family Traits" (Weeks 10–12). While this emerging focus on heredity and eugenics did not foreclose the congress's concern with social reform, by the 1920s the congress had begun to deemphasize "sentimental maternalism" (changing its name to the National Congress of Parents and Teachers) and to embrace instead scientific principles of child rearing (Grant 56–58). With this new emphasis the notion of universal motherhood, while still invoked, paled beside assertions of strict racial hierarchy. In an essay titled "What Constitutes a Good Mother?" Mary Weeks proclaimed that "there is no caste in motherhood. . . . rich or poor, white or black. . . . The name of 'mother' represents a common suffering, a common bond of sympathy" (195). But Charles Davenport, a prominent eugenicist, was more typical when he complained that "at a time when, through prudential restraint, the birth rate of the best blood of our nation barely suffices to replace that lost by death, the unrestrained, erotic characteristics of the degenerate classes are resulting in large families, which are withdrawn from the beneficent operation of natural selection by a misguided society that is nursing in her bosom the asp that may one day fatally poison her" (Weeks 113). Davenport's formulation not only defined class difference in terms of degrees of sexual restraint but also characterized social welfare itself as a misguided and unnatural form of maternalism, carrying the threat of racial poison.[5]

Women's fictional writing about motherhood in the early decades of the century reflects a similar tension between universal and racially specific notions of motherhood. But another tension emerges as well. A mother's racial responsibility—her duty to live for others, and specifically her role as a conduit for racial advancement—plays a central role in works by black and white authors. Yet when maternity becomes the explicit subject of fiction, this perspective necessarily collides with a conception of mothers as subjects and potential agents. Thus, while nonfictional discourses of race and reproduction tend to focus on the "products" of reproduction—a eugenically desirable child or a good mother's moral influence—they also make possible narratives that attempt to represent motherhood from the inside, rejecting both sentimental and instrumental conceptions of maternity.

Indeed, the early twentieth-century scientification of motherhood, along with the trend toward naturalism in American fiction, fostered calls for a thoroughly reformed women's fiction, particularly where portrayals of motherhood were concerned. Literary columns in the *Woman's Era* called for more admirable black mothers in literature (Gere 197), while Charlotte Perkins Gilman demanded whole new "fields of fiction" that would include "the interaction between mothers and children" yet go beyond the "eternal 'mother and child,' wherein the child is always a baby" (*Man-Made* 105). Mary Coolidge, author of *Why Women Are So* (1912), went so far as to trace women's woeful ignorance of reproductive matters to a tradition of women's literature that remained silent on the difficulties of motherhood: "In [the dream world of romance] there were no puzzling and inevitable facts of nature— the lover was always pure and brave and considerate; the heroine beautiful and adored. There was no baby even, as in real life, to precipitate difficulties, except on the last page" (16). Coolidge protested, in particular, nineteenth-century sentimental portrayals of motherhood because they "play[ed] up the emotional and spiritual compensations of motherhood, while ignoring or glazing over its hardships" (43). Coolidge observed that "there is slight need of writing on the compensatory aspects of motherhood, since healthy happy mothers in every age have been satisfied with their lot. . . . [But] without discounting in any degree the beauty or the rewards of normal motherhood, it is necessary to point out how far short, in the past, the actual experience often [falls] short of that ideal so constantly preached" (43–44).

For Coolidge, as for Gilman, realistic portrayals of motherhood in literature could play a pivotal role in fostering "voluntary, conscious, intelligent parenthood" in place of "degenerate procreation" (329). Her simultaneous interest in reforming women's fiction and increasing "racial conscience" so that children might be "better born" (343) suggests that the literary and eugenic projects of reconceiving motherhood were not only contemporaneous but mutually informing.[6] Certainly, arguments for revising literary images of motherhood needed "racial" justification in an era when challenging traditional gender roles seemed to threaten the survival of American literary culture; according to the critic Robert Herrick, the penalty for "overlooking biological distinctions . . . in art as in nature is sterility, extinction" ("Hermaphrodites" 489). But if Gilman's and Coolidge's critiques aptly characterized popular nineteenth-century romance novels, they overlooked two inaugural portrayals of twentieth-century motherhood—Kate Chopin's *The Awakening* (1899) and Pauline Hopkins's *Contending Forces* (1900)—that center on heroines for whom motherhood is a highly ambivalent identity. Going beyond the "eternal mother and child," Chopin and Hopkins (and Wharton, Kelley, and Larsen after them) portrayed the distance between the actual and ideal experience of motherhood, even as they drew on and revised discourses of racial mothering.

2. Reconstructing Motherhood: Pauline Hopkins's *Contending Forces* and the Rhetoric of Racial Uplift

IN HIS FOREWORD to the Schomburg Library of Nineteenth-Century Black Women Writers, Henry Louis Gates, Jr., names Phillis Wheatley the symbolic mother of the black female literary tradition and suggests that "all subsequent black writers have evolved in a matrilinear line of descent" (x). The forty-volume Schomburg collection does much to flesh out this genealogy, for it includes several volumes of fiction and nonfiction from the "woman's era," the period between 1890 and 1910 that saw an unprecedented flowering of African American women's writing.[1] Contemporary black feminist critics have identified the political concerns motivating this generation of writers, whose project of "reconstructing" womanhood depended upon confronting and revising "dominant domestic ideologies and literary conventions of womanhood" (Carby, *Reconstructing* 6).[2] But how was black *motherhood* reconstructed in the fiction and feminism of the woman's era? Given the historical erasure of black mothers as speaking subjects, how could maternity be claimed as a site of literary intervention at the beginning of the twentieth century?[3]

Pauline Hopkins's *Contending Forces: A Romance Illustrative of Negro Life North and South* (1900) provides fertile ground for exploring such questions, for her "romance" functions in large part as a revisionary history of black motherhood. Spanning more than a century (1790 to 1900) and locations from Bermuda to Boston, *Contending Forces* juxtaposes the stories of slave mothers with those of early twentieth-century black mothers, its peripatetic plot suggesting that for black women during and after slavery, motherhood was anything but a "settled" identity. While the novel's plot revolves as much around the reconciliation of a mother and her child as the union of star-crossed lovers, critics of *Contending Forces* have not examined in any detail its complicated representation of maternity.[4] Yet Hopkins's ambivalent, and sometimes contradictory, portrayal of motherhood offers a complicated response to early black women's writing about motherhood, from Harriet Wilson's *Our Nig* (1859) to Frances E. W. Harper's *Iola Leroy* (1892).[5] More important, *Contending Forces* provides a benchmark for examining twentieth-century depictions of black maternity, for it reflects the contested meanings of black motherhood at the turn of the century, when white race theorists attributed the "degeneracy" of the black race to the maternal failings of black women, while black intellectuals lauded the mother's vital role in race progress.

Hopkins's representation of maternity necessarily draws on ideologies of womanhood and motherhood current in the post-Reconstruction era: nineteenth-century white notions of True Womanhood, which emphasized piety, purity, and domesticity, as well as early twentieth-century definitions of the black "race mother," which echoed the tenets of True Womanhood to extol the virtuous mother's role in racial uplift.[6] Yet as Hopkins shows, neither of these maternal ideals took into account the common experience of black mothers, who were victims of racially motivated sexual violence both before and after Emancipation. Her intervention in these ideologies thus involves not only telling the "real" story of black mothers (she claims that "incidents portrayed in the early chapters of the book actually occurred" [147]) but also interrogating contemporary racial and sexual discourses that contributed to black women's subjugation and limited their efficacy as mothers. Thus, while *Contending Forces* draws on racialized constructions of maternity, including the white "true" mother and the black "race" mother, it simultaneously disrupts notions of racial determinism and gender essentialism on which these constructions depend. Indeed, Hopkins's engagement with contemporary racial ideologies is inextricably linked to her revisionary history of black maternity.[7]

Hopkins herself was clearly motivated by the related—yet often conflicting—imperatives of race and gender. As an editor of and frequent contributor to the *Colored American Magazine,* a periodical dedicated rather generically to the "uplift of the race everywhere," she was obviously invested in the goals of the racial uplift publishing industry. But the preface to *Contending Forces* suggests that, as a woman, she had reason to question the much-proclaimed progress of the race.[8] The novel's two-part plot is carefully structured to support her claim in the preface that the atrocity of white violence during slavery was duplicated after Reconstruction; its two central mother figures endure similar fates—including literal or symbolic rape and separation from their children—though they respond in strikingly different ways.

The romance proper, set in the 1890s, focuses on the trials of Sappho Clark, a new boarder at "Ma" Smith's Boston boardinghouse who, with her light-skinned beauty and impeccable manners, soon wins the approval of the black middle-class society over which Ma Smith presides. Earning her living as a stenographer and participating actively in the community Sewing Circle, which is Hopkins's fictional version of the black women's club movement, Sappho carefully conceals her painful past in the South, which includes an incestuous rape (by a white half-uncle) followed by sexual slavery in a New Orleans brothel and an eventual escape to Boston. Here the apparently respectable Sappho pursues a romance with an equally exemplary hero, Will Smith. But her hope of marrying him is jeopardized by the threatened revelation of her most devastating secret, that she is an unwed mother. Her agonized decision to renounce romance in order to reclaim her son, whom she has left in the care of a relative, forms the climax of the novel, setting in motion Sappho's return to the New Orleans convent where she gave birth, Will's chivalrous pursuit of Sappho and her son, and finally a joyful reunion and marriage.

Sappho's story is preceded by that of Grace Montfort, the apparently white wife of Charles Montfort, a slaveholder who transports his plantation from Bermuda to North Carolina in the 1790s. Incensed by Montfort's "liberal" treatment of his slaves, the Montforts' neighbor, Anson Pollock, kills Charles and attempts to take possession of Grace, who, because she is rumored to have black blood, can be claimed as his property. Grace eludes Pollock through suicide but not before she is whipped by his overseers.

Hopkins's description of Grace's whipping—the novel's earliest and most extended depiction of racial violence—epitomizes the novel's profoundly unsentimental view of maternity as well as its complicated representation of race. Hazel Carby has rightly identified Grace's whipping as a thinly disguised rape, but I am more interested in how this scene of sexualized violence dramatizes Grace's symbolic fall from white to black and, simultaneously, from revered mother to abject slave. Torn from her young son, who is "clinging to her skirts" when her attackers seize her, Grace is doubly violated—as a woman and as a mother—when she is "bound to the whipping post as the victim to the stake, and lashed with rawhides alternately by the two strong, savage men" (68).

The scene as a whole bears quoting at length, for it both evokes the historical "difference" of black mothers—who, unlike white mothers, could be violated with impunity—and challenges the premise of innate racial differences. For while the whipping proceeds from Grace's putative definition as black, Hopkins's imagery suggests that racial membership is neither intrinsic nor obvious but the product of historical definitions enforced through violence. As Hopkins describes it,

> The air whistled as the snaky leather thong curled and writhed in its rapid, vengeful descent. A shriek from the victim—a spurt of blood that spattered the torturer—a long, raw gash across a tender white back. Hank gazed at the cut with critical satisfaction, as he compared its depth with the skin and blood that encased the long, tapering lash. It was now Bill's turn.
>
> "I'll go you one better," he said, as he sighted the distance and exact place to make his mark with mathematical precision. . . . Again the rawhide whistled through the air, falling across the other cut squarely in the center. Another shriek, a stifled sob, a long-drawn quivering sigh—then the deep stillness of unconsciousness. Again and again was the outrage repeated. Fainting fit followed fainting fit. The blood stood in a pool about her feet. (69)

Taking turns in a whipping that also serves to brand Grace as a slave, Pollock's overseers lay claim to Grace by marking her with visible lines of blood. Her allegedly black blood externalized and literalized—the racial privilege suggested by her "tender white back" overwritten by marks testifying to her racial difference—Grace becomes wholly identified with the "contaminated" bloodline that both motivates and justifies their actions. That Grace's formerly white son Jesse is subsequently "absorbed into the unfortunate [black] race" (79) underscores the arbitrariness of a color line defined not by the essence of "black" mother's blood (as in legal fictions of race) but by the assertion of white male power. Even more significant, Grace "becomes" black at the same moment that she is disempowered as a mother, so that black womanhood is associated with a lack of maternal agency, as well as with a loss of domestic sovereignty.[9]

While Grace's story is formally segregated in the early chapters of *Contending Forces,* where Hopkins provides a "retrospect of the past," the novel's frontispiece, which shows the bleeding mother lying at the feet of two white men, serves as a constant reminder of black women's continued subjugation. Indeed, this early image of a mother—marked with blood lines and surrounded by a pool of blood—introduces a trope that Hopkins used throughout the text, where blood functions variously as an internal measure of race and an external sign of sexual violence. Hopkins's contradictory references to "good" and "bad" blood undermine the racial determinism of social Darwinism, which defined black mothers as counter-evolutionary forces. At the same time, her repeated depictions of violated blood bonds—particularly those between mother and child—complicate the idealized image of race mothers promoted in the work of her black feminist contemporaries.

Racial Uplift and the "Literary Worker"

Hopkins's need to demonstrate race progress while simultaneously protesting present conditions reflects a larger tension in the racial uplift movement,
a tension that she negotiated daily in her role as literary editor of the *Colored American Magazine*. From its inception in May 1900 the magazine—
which announced itself as "An Illustrated Monthly Devoted to Literature,
Science, Music, Art, Religion, Facts, Fiction and Traditions of the Negro
Race"—set forth a dual program. First, it would compensate for the negative representation of "citizens of color" in "Anglo Saxon" magazines; by
providing a venue for black citizens to "demonstrate their ability and tastes,
in fiction, poetry, and art," it would force white readers to "recognize our
efforts, hopes, and aspirations" ("Editorial" 60).

The desire for white recognition was secondary, however, to the magazine's
goal of cultivating a collective self-recognition among its black readers. "Above
all," the editors wrote, the magazine "aspires to develop and intensify the
bonds of racial brotherhood, which alone can enable a people to assert their
racial rights as men, and demand their privileges as citizens." Exhorting their
readers to contribute as well as to subscribe to the magazine, the editors noted that "a vast and almost unexplored treasury of biography, history, adventure, tradition, folklore, poetry and song, the accumulations of centuries of
such experiences as have never befallen any other people, lies open to us and
to you" ("Editorial" 60). The editors further emphasized the collective and
participatory nature of their venture (published, after all, by the Colored Co-
Operative Publishing Company) by issuing calls for manuscripts by "young
composers," photographs by "amateurs and professionals," and articles by
"ladies of social and literary prestige" (63–64).

Yet despite such populist calls for mass participation, and despite its invocation of an apparently classless "racial brotherhood," the magazine's
demonstration of race progress depended in part on its representation of
black elites' difference from the masses. As Kevin Gaines argues in *Uplifting
the Race*, black elites' "contradictory position as both an aspiring social class
and a racially subordinated caste" led them to disprove notions of biological inferiority by asserting intrarace class distinctions, so that "the very existence of a 'better class' of blacks [served as] evidence of what they called race
progress." At the same time, black elites' efforts to rehabilitate the image of
the race depended upon their ability to demonstrate respectability, which
could be enacted most persuasively through "an ethos of service to the masses" (xiv).

As a magazine that sought both to educate the newly literate black "mass-es" and to demonstrate the success of black elites to white readers and to them-selves, the *Colored American Magazine* embodied the tension between racial solidarity and class stratification inherent in racial uplift ideology. Serving as literary editor and eventually chief editor, and contributing more writing than any other single author, Hopkins played the most influential role in determin-ing the magazine's direction between 1900 and 1904, when the magazine came under the control of Booker T. Washington (Johnson and Johnson 8). In March 1904, just before she resigned, Hopkins articulated her own vision for the magazine by reporting approvingly the advice of John Freund, the editor of the *New York Evening Post,* who advised the editors of the *Colored American Magazine* that "your magazine can appeal to the individual member of your race, inspire him with hope for the future . . . raise his aspiration and give him much valuable knowledge. It can do as much also by informing the people of this country, the whites, as to what you have already done, [and] what you all purpose to do, in the future" (Hopkins, "How" 155). Significantly, Freund emphasized that the white public had to be "educated to the fact that you have already risen and that you are using brave efforts to uplift your race and bring it to a higher plain" (154). Thus it was not enough to demonstrate individual elites' achievements; a collective commitment to racial uplift, a tacit promise that the masses would soon join the elite on a "higher plane," was necessary to secure the sympathy and support of the white reader.

Many articles in the early years of the magazine assumed a distance be-tween writer and reader, reflecting a missionary-like zeal to cultivate taste and discernment in readers presumed to be uncultured. W. W. Holland's May 1902 essay, "Photography for Our Young People," asserted that "it is a character-istic of our people to love pictures and music, but our taste along these lines has not been cultivated. Most of us admire flashy, red, or otherwise brilliant pictures, as we also like the 'Cake walks' and 'Ragtimes,' but when we look upon Raphael's masterpieces or hear the 'Messiah,' only the select few can see the beauty or appreciate the harmony and realize the handiwork of the almighty" (5). Likewise, in her own essay on female artists Hopkins noted that it is "the office of art to educate the perception of beauty, and to devel-op our dormant taste" ("Famous Women" 363).

But if these and many other didactic statements implied clear class distinc-tions between elite author and common reader, functioning both to impart "valuable knowledge" and to "raise [middle-class] aspirations," Hopkins's representation of the black female writer as a "literary worker" downplayed the class difference between the literary author and her readers. In an essay titled "Some Literary Workers," part of Hopkins's series on "Famous Women of the Negro Race," she begins by emphasizing the uplifting influence of the educated black woman, who is clearly set apart from, though devoted to, the masses: "Women who have enjoyed the 'higher education' with its broadening culture [and] aesthetic influence . . . are doing much for the masses among their own people" (277). Yet Hopkins's portraits of individual black women authors emphasize not their exemplary difference but their solidarity with, and service to, other workers. Thus Hopkins writes that "the story of Phillis Wheatley's life is common history with all classes of people, yet, we love to rehearse it, renewing our courage, as it were, for the struggle of life, with live coals from the altar of her genius" (278). In the next month's installment Hopkins likewise notes that as a young child Frances E. W. Harper was "deemed fit for labor" and "put out to work in order that she might earn her own living" and that at the height of her career "Mrs. Harper was not contented to make speeches and receive plaudits, but was ready to do the rough work, and gave freely of all the moneys that her literary labors brought her" ("Literary Workers" 366, 368). Defining the role of the "literary worker" as analogous to that of the common laborer, Hopkins elides the class difference implicit in racial uplift endeavors.

Indeed, like the educators and club women whom Hopkins honors in other installments of this series, the ideal literary worker sought not individual fame but collective advancement. As Hopkins notes in her piece entitled "Club Life Among Colored Women," "While women have by individual effort done much for the progress of society, and the names of illustrious women adorn the pages of literature, art and science . . . these personal efforts [can] best be centralized by co-operation" (273). Hopkins's emphasis on writing as eminently practical work—as respectable work akin to club work—is in part her answer to continued proscriptions against women's writing, particularly political writing. "We know," she writes, "that it is not 'popular' for a woman to speak or write in plain terms against political brutalities, that a woman should confine her efforts to woman's work in the home and church" ("Some Literary" 277). Like her contemporary, Gertrude Mossell, who, in *The Work of the Afro-American Woman* (1894), described the black woman journalist as a "lamp in the pathway of the co-laborer, a guide to the footsteps of the generation that must follow" (102), Hopkins sought to defend black women's professional writing by deeming it integral to racial uplift.

But Hopkins's definition of the literary worker as a public servant also reflects her specific vision of popular fiction as a political tool. According to a biographical sketch in the *Colored American Magazine*, Hopkins's ambition was "to become a writer of fiction, in which the wrongs of [the] race shall be so handled as to enlist the sympathy of all classes of citizens, in this way reaching those who never read history or biography" (Elliott 47). Hopkins's populist bent, her self-definition as a popular writer, is equally evident in the preface to *Contending Forces,* where she argues that "the colored race has historians, lecturers, ministers, poets, judges, and lawyers,—men of brilliant intellects who have arrested the favorable attention of this busy, energetic nation. But, after all, it is the simple, homely tale, unassumingly told, which cements the bond of brotherhood among all classes and all complexions" (13).

According to Hazel Carby, Hopkins's black readership was indeed heterogeneous, comprised not only of "those in professional service . . . [predominantly] teachers and clergy" but also of "male and female tobacco factory operatives, male blacksmiths, wheelwrights . . . butchers, carpenters and joiners," as well as "female dressmakers, milliners, seamstresses . . . [and] domestic workers (Introduction xxxiv). If we add to this diverse readership the dual purpose that Hopkins assigned to her fiction—namely, to "preserve manners and customs" and to provide a "record of growth and development from generation to generation" (*Contending* 13–14)—we can begin to account for the internal inconsistencies of her first published novel. The former purpose, to "preserve manners and customs," casts Hopkins in the role of native folklorist, salvaging and preserving folk speech and customs for an appreciative "inside" audience. The second purpose, to "demonstrate growth and development from generation to generation," casts her in the role of cultural apologist, demonstrating to an external white readership how far the black race has come from these humble roots.

For Hopkins, as for many of her black female contemporaries, the intergenerational perseverance of the black mother was largely responsible for racial growth and development. But Hopkins's portrait of black mothers in *Contending Forces* radically revises Gertrude Mossell's 1894 tribute, which defines black women as essentially and instinctively maternal. Mossell notes that "many of our women have turned aside from laboring for their individual success and given thought to the condition of the weak and suffering classes. They have shown that the marvellous [*sic*] loving kindness and patience that is recorded of the native women of Africa . . . [and] the 'black mammies' of the Southland was not crushed out by the iron heel of slavery but still wells up in their bosoms and in this brighter day overflows in compassion for the poor and helpless of their own down-trodden race" (28). While Mossell credits black women's instinct for helping the helpless to an intrinsic, African-derived maternalism, Hopkins insists that maternal instinct was neither natural nor limitless. Inscribing the history of black mothers in eighteenth- and nineteenth-century America as constitutive of their identity in the twentieth century, Hopkins counters dehistoricized representations of black mothers in both social Darwinist and racial uplift discourses.

Blood Ties

Hopkins's repudiation of racial determinism depends on her redefinition of the black mother's role in evolution. To appreciate Hopkins's revision of contemporary evolutionary discourses, it is useful to recall the proliferation of social scientific and popular writing that explained the supposed regression of the black race after Emancipation in pseudo-Darwinian terms.[10] The title of Charles Carroll's diatribe, *The Negro a Beast,* published the same year as *Contending Forces,* exemplifies the common view of African Americans as natural beasts who, left to their own devices, would "revert to type."[11] Theories of inherent racial traits, and the related idea of tainted blood, held a particular fascination for authors and readers of white race fictions, including Thomas Dixon's novels, *The Leopard's Spots* (1902) and *The Clansmen* (1905), later immortalized in D. W. Griffith's film *Birth of a Nation.* Like Dixon's negrophobic texts, Robert Lee Durham's best-selling *Call of the South* (1908) traced the essence of black identity to primitive, indeed evil, blood: "An occasional isolated negro may have broken the shackles of ignorance, measurably and admirably brought under control the half-savage passions of his nature . . . yet beneath all this creditable but thin veneer of civilization there slumbers in his blood the primitive passions and propensities of his immediate ancestors, which are transmitted to him as latent forces of evil to burst out of his children and grandchildren in answer to the call of the wild" (180). The collective message of these texts—captured in the title of Benjamin Rush Davenport's 1902 novel, *Blood Will Tell*—depended upon the assumption of racial essences transmitted through biological inheritance.

Against the racial determinism of such novels, Hopkins offers a theory of racial evolution based on family environment—and particularly maternal influence—rather than genetics. She notes, for example, that despite severely limited employment opportunities, a black "genius in a profession, trade, or invention [is commonly] evolved from the rude nurturing received at the hands of a poor father and mother engaged in the lowliest of service" (Hopkins, *Contending* 86). Attributing the production of racial genius to the salutary influence of the home sphere, Hopkins envisions an evolutionary process that, far from dooming the black race to extinction (as some white theorists predicted), helps in its struggle to advance. In Hopkins's description of natural selection nature itself redresses manmade wrongs, for "the mighty working of cause and effect, the mighty unexpected results of the law of evolution, seem to point to a different solution of the Negro question than any worked out by the most fertile brain of the highly cultured Caucasian" (87).

While Hopkins thus reinterprets the "law of evolution," she seems to rely on the notion of inherited race traits to account for the relative virtue of her characters. Assigning conventional meanings to white and black blood, she gives her heroine fair skin and "aquiline" features and credits black accomplishments to the "infusion of white blood" during slavery, noting that "the Negro race must be productive of some valuable specimens, if only from the infusion which amalgamation with a superior race must eventually bring" (87).

Hopkins's critics have tended to read such passages as evidence of her unconscious investment in racist ideologies, yet her selective use of such ideologies suggests a more conscious manipulation of racial signifiers.[12] While her comments quoted earlier uphold the myth that superior white blood elevates inferior black blood, Hopkins's portrayal of other "mixed" characters upsets this equation and calls into question the idea of innate racial traits. She attributes the debased character of the novel's chief villain, for instance, not solely to biology but to the institution of slavery: "Langley's *nature* was the *natural* product of such an institution as slavery. *Natural* instinct for good had been perverted by a mixture of 'cracker' blood of the lowest type on his father's side with whatever God-saving quality that might have been loaned the Negro by pitying *nature*. This blood, while it gave him the pleasant features of the Caucasian race, vitiated his moral *nature* and left it stranded high and dry on the shore of blind ignorance" (221, emphasis added). Here, even as she points to the corrupting influence of slavery as the source of Langley's nature, Hopkins traces his "moral nature" to biology, that is, to his cracker blood. Hopkins's excessive and contradictory use of the word *nature* calls attention to its ambiguous and shifting meanings. Using what Gates has called "motivated repetition" (*Signifying* 66), Hopkins signifies on *nature* in order to rob the term of its significance. For if nature has so many meanings—referring at once to instincts and the effects of institutions, to physiological and moral qualities—any easy equation of blood and character becomes impossible.

Instead, Hopkins credits any racial deficiencies to the material effects of slavery, particularly its destruction of the home. To demonstrate the historical contingency of so-called racial qualities, she asks her readers to imagine the effects of slavery on whites: "Subject the Anglo-Saxon to the whip and scourge, grind the iron heel of oppression in his face until all resemblance to the human family is lost in the degradation of the brute, take from wives and mothers the sacredness and protection of home in the time before birth, when moral and intellectual development are most dependent upon pre-natal influences for the advancement of generations to come . . . and what have you? classic features and a godlike mind? No! rather the lineaments of hideous despair, fearful and hopeless as the angel forms that fell from heaven to the black gulf of impenetrable hell" (222). Placing the mother at the center of the evolutionary process, Hopkins stresses the catastrophic effects not of "black" blood but of black women's historical oppression. In Hopkins's domesticated version of Darwin home *is* environment, the child's first home its mother's body. The "advancement of generations to come" is thus predicated not on biological essences but on granting black women the "sacred" right of mothers to the protection of the home sphere. The novel's multiple examples of violence against black mothers gain force in light of Hopkins's dire predictions.

Hopkins was not alone in connecting maternal rights with racial destiny; a decade earlier the white sociologist Lester Ward had advanced a "gynocentric" theory of evolution, claiming that "woman *is* the race, and the race can be raised up only as she is raised up" (274–75). But while Ward's generic "race" refers implicitly to the white race, Hopkins deliberately deconstructs racial binaries. Her fictional feminist, Mrs. Willis, instructs the young women of the Sewing Circle that "there is no such thing as an unmixed black on the American continent" and that "we cannot tell by a person's complexion whether he be dark or light in blood" since "out of a hundred apparently pure black men not one will be able to trace an unmixed flow of African blood since landing upon these shores!" (151) Indeed, as Hopkins demonstrates, white men are themselves responsible for blurring the color line. Thus, when Sappho wonders out loud if she is responsible for her sins—that is, for having a child out of wedlock—Willis assures her that black women are not responsible for the "*illegitimacy* with which our race has been obliged, as it were, to flood the race" (149). By incorporating not one but several white rapists into her story line, Hopkins makes it abundantly clear that black women could not be held responsible for the so-called contamination of either the black or white race.

Yet black women's responsibility for reproducing race—for giving birth to and raising children defined as black in the U.S. racial order—received renewed emphasis in the post-Reconstruction era, and Hopkins seems to have been as interested in challenging overly idealized representations of the black mother as she was in exposing white racist stereotypes. In his *History of the Colored Race in America* (1887), William Alexander defined black women's power as inextricable from their heroic self-sacrifice: "It is through her children that a woman rules posterity; that she leaves, for good or for evil, indelible marks on the universe. . . . Just in proportion as Colored Mothers train aright their children, so we will see that the race advance, and not until then. . . . It is the glory of a woman, that for this she was sent into the world, to live for others rather than for herself; to live, yes, and often to die for them" (598–99). Racial and maternal discourses also commingled in the writing of Hopkins's black female contemporaries, whose message of racial uplift outlined an impossibly heroic role for the black mother. Defining the race itself as a child in need of maternal guidance, Anna Julia Cooper cautioned her peers that "a race in such a stage of growth is peculiarly sensitive to impressions" and thus in need of model mothers (*Voice* 144–45). Similarly, Frances E. W. Harper counseled in her 1892 speech, "Enlightened Motherhood," that the "mothers of our race . . . [must be] patient, loving, strong, and true," their homes an "uplifting power in the race" (292).

That the black woman's role in racial uplift was contiguous with her maternal duties is most clearly seen in E. Azalia Hackley's guidebook for girls, which emphasized that "the colored mother . . . carries a heavy burden—the weight of future generations of a handicapped, persecuted people" (181). If, as Hackley claimed, the "privilege to carve the destiny of a race" rested with the black woman, it was because she carried both the biological and cultural responsibilities of maternity. Cooper endorsed both roles in *A Voice from the South* (1892), where she argued that black women would be the "fundamental agency under God in the regeneration, the retraining of the race as well as the groundwork and starting point of its progress upward" (*Voice* 28). For Cooper biological regeneration and cultural retraining fell equally under woman's purview.

Hopkins herself praised the redemptive power of race mothers in the *Colored American Magazine*, noting in an article about black women's clubs that "our women are proving the salvation of the race in America. True-hearted, fond wives are they to their husbands, and faithful, loving mothers to their daughters and sons who rise up and call them blessed" ("Echoes" 709). Like her contemporaries, Hopkins promoted the image of a supermoral black mother as an antidote to white representations of black women as "morally obtuse" and "openly licentious." When a white male writer could claim that the black man's alleged impulse to rape white women stemmed from the "wantonness of [black] women" (Bruce 84) and a white woman writer could characterize the black woman as a "sinister figure behind the black man, forever dragging him downward" (Tayleur 267), black women writers clearly needed a persuasive counterimage.[13]

To the extent that traditional "legitimate" motherhood signified respectability, black women's focus on the mother as a regenerative force not only countered social Darwinist assertions of racial degeneration but also helped to reform the overly sexualized image of the black woman. Unfortunately, in demonstrating that black women were the moral and maternal equals of white women, racial uplift rhetoric often endorsed the concept of "universal womanhood" and in so doing overlooked the differences between black and white women's experiences. As Evelyn Brooks Higginbotham has shown, race work itself depended on a politics of respectability, "equat[ing] normality with conformity to white middle-class models of gender roles and sexuality . . . [linking] mainstream domestic duties, codes of dress, sexual conduct, and public etiquette with both individual success and group progress" (271). Thus while Cooper could claim in *A Voice from the South* that no one but a black woman could "reproduce the exact Voice of the Black Woman" (iii), a claim to which her book eloquently testified, she argued at the 1893 World's Congress of Representative Women that "woman's cause is one and universal" ("Discussion" 715).

The political necessity of identifying black women with a generic "woman's cause"—despite the persistent racism of white feminists—is evident as well in Fannie Barrier Williams's observation in "The Club Movement Among Colored Women in America" (1900) that "thirty-five years ago [black women] were unsocialized, unclassed and unrecognized. . . . If within thirty-five years they have become sufficiently important to be studied apart from the general race problem and have come to be recognized as an integral part of the general womanhood of American civilization, that is a gratifying evidence of real progress" (382). Thus, while Cooper could offer a theoretical articulation of black woman's unique position—asserting that the black woman was "confronted by both a woman question and a race question and [was] yet an unknown or unacknowledged factor in both" (*Voice* 134)—in practice, focusing on either racial or gender oppression meant agreeing to subordinate the other. As Williams's description of the black women's club movement suggests, in order to be recognized as a separate class within the "general race problem," black women risked being subsumed under the "general [white] womanhood" of America.

A New and Holy Love

The tenuous but vital link between black and white mothers—the strategically useful, if misleading, idea that motherhood is a shared experience—has its literary roots in women's slave narratives. In *Incidents in the Life of a Slave Girl* (1861), for example, Harriet Jacobs solicited white women's sympathy by asserting that the slave mother "may be an ignorant creature, degraded by the system that has brutalized her from childhood; but she has a mother's instincts, and is capable of feeling a mother's agonies" (16). Yet Jacobs was compelled to assert an instinctive similarity precisely because of the profound differences between black and white women's experiences. She thus asked her white female readers to recognize not only similarities but differences between themselves and the slave mother: "Contrast *your* New Year's day with that of the poor bond-woman! With you it is a pleasant season. . . . But to the slave mother New Year's day comes laden with peculiar sorrows. She sits on her cold cabin floor, watching the children who may all be torn from her the next morning; and often does she wish that she and they might die before the day dawns" (16). The success of Jacobs's appeal to an "essential" maternal instinct depended, then, upon her simultaneous evocation of difference.

Likewise, in *Contending Forces* Hopkins must demonstrate black women's essential (or "true") womanhood while maintaining the historical specificity of their experiences; she must, in particular, reveal the continued violation of black women's bodies without reinforcing the time-honored association of black women with the body.[14] Hopkins's contradictory images of motherhood reflect these apparently irreconcilable objectives. She responds to the myth of the overly sexual black woman by portraying Ma Smith as a moral matriarch whose obvious maternal instincts are matched only by her unassailable virtue. If black women were excluded from the nineteenth-century definition of True Womanhood, Ma Smith fits squarely within its boundaries. Enjoying privileges historically accorded to white women, principally the "privacy of a humble home," Smith fondly recalls the joys of motherhood, counting as "precious jewels" her "honest husband and two beautiful children" (176–77) and continuing to mother not only her own children but also the adults who board at her lodging house.

Indeed, Ma Smith's impeccably ordered lodging house, at once a private home and a public accommodation, illustrates the domestic and political harmony that Hopkins associates with unviolated black motherhood, much as images of the undefiled (white) female body stood metonymically for the health of the Republic in nineteenth-century nationalist discourses (Berlant 23). Devoting an entire chapter to describing the physical space that embodies and literally houses a black community, with an emphasis on the female labor that sustains it, Hopkins constructs what Claudia Tate would call an "allegory of political desire" in which an idealized domestic space signifies the desire for an "equitable political system that distributes rewards on the basis of personal integrity, commitment, and hard work" (*Domestic* 101). She also defends black women's homemaking skills against nativist claims that superior housekeeping—and the racial purity for which it stood—was a uniquely Anglo-Saxon talent.[15] Hopkins introduces Ma Smith's daughter, Dora, for example, as an industrious apprentice homemaker: "She had been upstairs the best portion of the day preparing a room for an expected lodger. There had been windows to wash, paint to clean, a carpet to tack down, curtains to hang and furniture to place in position—in short, the thousand and one things to do that are essential to the comfort of the lodger and the good reputation of the house" (*Contending* 80). The satisfaction with which Dora and her mother survey the results of their labors is well deserved, Hopkins notes, for "even in palatial homes, a more inviting nest could not be found" (88). Fittingly, it is within their "cosy [*sic*] kitchen," outfitted with "spotless white" linens, that Ma Smith entertains her children with a story of her father's vigilant defense of his daughter's reputation, underscoring the relationship between domestic probity and female purity.

Affirming the cultural work of mothers like Ma Smith, Mrs. Willis—herself a mother—teaches the young women of the Sewing Circle "the place which the virtuous woman occupies in upbuilding a race," through both biological reproduction and cultural rehabilitation. Willis thus admonishes these potential mothers to "fill the positions now occupied by [their] mothers" in refuting charges of "moral irresponsibility and low moral standards" (148). Such work is amply repaid, Hopkins suggests, in the unsurpassable joys of motherhood, for although Ma Smith "knew what it was to bake and brew, to mend and make over, to minister to the needs of childhood with increasing maternal cares near at hand," she looks forward to reliving, as a grandmother, the "joys which had been hers when [her firstborn son] lay within her arms a soft morsel of humanity, with sweet brown face and melting black eyes that mirrored themselves within the citadel of her heart" (176).

Apart from this rosy portrait of Ma Smith, however, black mother-child relationships in *Contending Forces* are consistently characterized by separation and loss and frequently are subject to violence that renders literal mothering, much less race mothering, impossible. Indeed, in the early chapters of the novel Hopkins uses the trope of violated maternity both as plot—she recounts horrors of slavery, including a child forced to "whip his mother until the blood ran" and "women in the first stages of their accouchement" subjected to "terrible things . . . too dreadful to relate" (19)—and as setting. Thus Hopkins describes the antebellum American South, which is unguided by the "mother-hand" of England (25), as a decidedly "barren" environment (30). It is within this hostile and unmaternal environment that the symbolic rape of Grace occurs.

Grace's fate, based on the mere rumor of black blood, points up the arbitrary and contingent nature of racial definitions. But it also invokes—and then undercuts—notions of universal womanhood. Grace's trauma seems to underscore woman's cause as "one and universal," for although Grace's alleged race triggers her victimization, suggesting that women of color were particularly vulnerable to sexual exploitation, Hopkins warns her white female readers that white skin provides no immunity from sexual violence. Indeed, the villainous Anson Pollock makes no distinctions between white and black women, for Hopkins reveals that "he had not hesitated to whip [his white wife] by proxy . . . in the same way he did his slaves" (50). Engaging white women's fear of white male violence, Hopkins asks them to identify with Grace along gender, rather than race, lines. As her cautionary tale makes clear, only the former category is certain.

But if vulnerability to male violence is an experience all women share, Hopkins depicts two different responses to this violence that point up the limitations of True Womanhood and thus true motherhood. While Grace is defined as biologically black, by virtue of the "one-drop" theory of race, her response to her victimization follows the white code of True Womanhood: When she realizes the loss of her husband-protector, she kills herself to avoid becoming Pollock's mistress. According to the cult of True Womanhood, her suicide testifies to her purity (and thus her "whiteness"), proving her constitutionally unable to withstand assaults on her virtue. Yet paradoxically, this virtue, the sine qua non of femininity, prevents her from performing woman's highest function, that of the mother.

Grace's suicide leaves her former slave, Lucy, to raise Grace's orphaned children, now defined as black. Taking care of children to whom she is not biologically related, the darker-skinned Lucy is an early instance of the black "othermother" who, as Patricia Hill Collins has demonstrated, often assists a blood mother in raising a child (119). Hopkins's description of the "ample breasted" Lucy unfortunately replicates the stereotype of the mammy who, according to Barbara Christian, plays the "tougher, less sensitive" complement to the "delicate, ornamental" Southern lady (8). Yet while the mammy was typically portrayed as sexless—her sexuality and thus her sexual vulnerability beneath notice—Hopkins notes that in taking over Grace's maternal responsibilities Lucy inherits her sexual role, for "Pollock elect[s] to take Lucy in the place he had designed for Mrs. Montfort" (*Contending* 71). Pollock's easy substitution of Lucy for Grace suggests that America's sexual economy mirrors its slave economy, that women, regardless of race, are interchangeable.

Hopkins's substitution of Lucy for Grace suggests that, despite her attempts to blur the color line, she was more comfortable identifying the historical race mother as unambiguously (that is, visibly) black. Lucy, not Grace, performs a mother's most vital roles: in caring for Grace's children, she ensures the survival of future generations—on whom the romance plot depends—and, much like Nanny in Zora Neale Hurston's *Their Eyes Were Watching God,* she "saves the text" of the past (Hurston 16). When Lucy reappears as a centenarian in the final pages of the novel, she is the only witness to the events of the past and the only living link between the mothers of the nineteenth and twentieth centuries, whose stories Hopkins insists are connected. Hopkins reveals at the end of the novel that Will and Dora are the grandchildren of Grace Montfort's son Jesse, whom Lucy cared for after Grace's murder. Perhaps more important, Lucy's persistence as a mother, despite the sexual violence she inherits from her white "sister," provides a model that Sappho will eventually follow.

Like Grace and Lucy, Sappho is victimized by a white villain convinced of the natural promiscuity of black women; her rapist justifies his act by asking "What does a woman of mixed blood, or any Negress, for that matter, know of virtue?" (*Contending* 261) But Sappho's story embodies even more fully than theirs the novel's theme of maternal loss, for her abduction and rape at the age of fourteen simultaneously separate her from her mother and make her an unwilling mother. Denying her own son out of shame, Sappho is at once a motherless child and a childless mother.

Hopkins suggests, however, that only by acknowledging her son can Sappho rise above the stigma of Alphonse's birth. Fleeing from Boston to New Orleans to avoid exposure, and reluctant to take her son with her (for, as Hopkins notes, she "had felt nothing for the poor waif but repugnance"), Sappho nonetheless vows to "do her duty without shrinking" (342, 345). Recalled to her maternal duty only through guilt, Sappho would seem an unnatural mother, but Hopkins demonstrates the contingency of maternal "instincts" when she observes that only Sappho's "feelings of degradation had made her ashamed of the joys of motherhood, of pride of possession in her child." Like the slave mother described by Jacobs, this twentieth-century mother has been deprived of maternal joy. Yet as Sappho commits herself to a future with Alphonse, "all that feeling [of shame] was swept away . . . her shipwrecked life about to find peace" (345).

Indeed, while the ideology of True Motherhood (which necessarily excludes the unwed mother) induces Sappho's "feelings of degradation," the experience of mothering—described in a chapter entitled "Mother-Love"— exerts a healing influence on mother and child. As Sappho embraces Alphonse, "something holy passed from the sweet contact of the soft, warm body into the cold chilliness of her broken heart. The mother-love chased out all the anguish that she had felt over his birth" (346–47). This highly sentimental passage seems to deny the violence through which Sappho became a mother, as if the experience of mothering her now-eight-year-old son overrides the conditions of his birth. Yet in ascribing Sappho's psychic transformation to the powers of mother love, Hopkins does not merely repeat a cultural cliché. Read through the historical lens provided by Grace's rape and subsequent abnegation of motherhood, Sappho's decision to resume her role as mother represents an assertion of black female power through a revised and reclaimed maternity.

Certainly, Sappho is amply repaid for her earlier struggles as a mother: The "chastening influence" of sorrow has made her worthy of a noble future as a race mother, and the "new and holy love that had taken possession of her soul" provides "compensation for all she had suffered" (*Contending* 346–47). Possessed by this holy love—an amalgam of mother love and love for the race—Sappho also gains a measure of self-possession that allows her to own her child. "Mamma couldn't claim you then," she explains, "but now she's going to take you away, and you will always live with her" (346). Promising what the slave mother could not, Sappho asserts her maternal rights as inviolable.

Yet even as she reconstitutes Sappho and Alphonse as a family (without the legitimating presence of a husband), Hopkins takes pains to absolve her heroine from her apparent sexual sins. Arriving at a New Orleans convent, Sappho unburdens herself to the sympathetic mother superior. Not only is she forgiven by her maternal confessor but her trials have turned her into a saint, for as one nun comments, "She is like the angels in the picture of the Crucifixion, so sweet and sad" (349). Sappho's apotheosis is complete when Will—upon learning her secret—dreams of a "great cathedral" where "upon the altar before him appeared the Virgin and Child . . . the face of the mother was Sappho's, the child by her side was the little Alphonse" (387). Rewriting the myth of the bad black woman, Hopkins presents Sappho as the Madonna, the epitome of white ideals of female virtue.

Curiously, having affirmed Sappho's right to motherhood outside marriage, Hopkins defends Sappho's virtue by invoking the very paradigm she has attempted to reconstruct. The image of a virginal mother suggests, after all, that a woman can be a mother while remaining sexually pure; it thus gratifies the contradictory desires behind the cult of True Womanhood. Having explored the implications of this contradiction for black women—for whom motherhood was often not chosen but compelled—Hopkins apparently felt obliged to balance her portrayal of motherhood as an embodied identity with an icon of spiritualized maternity. The image of Sappho as the Madonna serves her well in this regard, for given her white readers' prejudices,

Hopkins cannot merely assert her unwed mother's virtue but must make it visible and memorable. Will's vision of Sappho as a virgin mother effectively erases the body, veiling the sexual act—in this case, an act of violence—that necessarily precedes motherhood.

But Hopkins's final representation of Sappho as a transcendent mother does not outweigh the text's counterimages of Grace's whipping or Sappho's rape; Hopkins's eventual revelation of family ties between Grace and Will is but her final reminder of slavery's informing presence. That Hopkins meant to stress Sappho's physical as well as psychic suffering is clear when Dora laments the "crucifixion" of Sappho's spirit (330). Comparing Sappho not only to the Virgin Mother but also to the crucified Jesus, Hopkins makes literal what Elizabeth Ammons has called the nineteenth-century "dream of the mother-savior" (158). For when Hopkins describes the "Negro plod[ding] along bearing his cross—carrying the sins of others" (332), the most obvious referent (despite the generic male pronoun) is Sappho, who in bearing Alphonse has literally and metaphorically carried the burden of the white father's sexual sins.

While not in itself unique, Hopkins's image of a maternal Christ is particularly well suited to a novel that signifies constantly on motherhood. The ironic juxtaposition of black and white mother figures throughout *Contending Forces*—from Grace to Ma Smith, from the mother superior to the Virgin Mary—makes a normative notion of motherhood as difficult to sustain as an essential theory of race. What is most striking about Hopkins's reworking of maternal ideologies, however, is her characterization of the mother savior as being in need of the redemptive powers of maternity. "Won't you love your poor unhappy mamma?" Sappho asks her child, even as she sets about her task of "carrying comfort and hope to the women of her race." Concerned equally with the survival of the race and with the survival of a mother who, "but for the child . . . would've broken down" (347), Hopkins inscribes her heroine's maternal desire as well as her duty, rejecting a purely sacrificial model of motherhood. Significantly, Hopkins specifies that Sappho's ministry will be to the women of the race, suggesting that individual mothers both depend upon and help sustain black female community.

Not surprisingly, the reunion of mother and child overshadows that of hero and heroine as the dramatic climax of this matrifocal novel. Rewriting a historical legacy of loss as an enabling fiction of maternal power, Hopkins ends by depicting motherhood as the triumph of black womanhood—at once a site of personal agency and an indispensable element in race progress—but she does not allow her reader to forget the black mother's painful trials during and after slavery. Indeed, Hopkins explicitly associates racial uplift with the pain of childbirth when she has one of her "race men" exclaim: "This new birth of the black race is a mighty agony. God help us in our struggle for liberty and manhood!" (244–45) This maternal metaphor—ironically appearing in a call for black manhood—makes eminently clear that women are indispensable to race progress, that female labor undergirds male efforts to secure liberty. By remembering the mothers whose agonies during slavery were too often reproduced after Emancipation, Hopkins dramatizes what Anna Julia Cooper called, in a phrase equally evocative of childbirth, the "long dull pain" of the "hitherto voiceless Black Woman." Surveying the accomplishments and struggles of black women at the turn of the century, Cooper concluded that "the race cannot be effectually lifted up till its women are truly elevated" (*Voice* 2, 42). Hopkins's fiction inserted a similarly cautious note into the optimistic rhetoric of racial uplift, insisting that as long as black women did not hold title to their own bodies and those of their children, they could not be emancipated—and emancipating—mothers.

3. The Romance "Plot": Reproducing Silence, Reinscribing Race in *The Awakening* and *Summer*

PAULINE HOPKINS'S IMAGE of an unwed black mother as the Virgin Mary was perhaps the most daring, but certainly not the most commented upon, literary revision of True Motherhood at the turn of the century. In 1899, just one year before the *Colored American Magazine* introduced *Contending Forces* as "the most powerful narrative yet published of the wrongs and injustice perpetrated on the race," the latest novel of a popular local color writer received considerably less favorable press. Of course, reviewers of Kate Chopin's *The Awakening* did not object to Adele Ratignolle, the contented "mother-woman" described as a "faultless Madonna" (54), but to Edna Pontellier, the woman who casts off the obligations of marriage and motherhood to pursue not one, but two, extramarital romances. "It is not a healthy book," wrote one reviewer, while another regretted that a "writer of so great refinement and poetic grace [should] enter the overworked field of sex fiction" (qtd. in Culley 146).

Chopin's novel, which presents Edna's sexual awakening in some detail while deemphasizing (and deflating) her role as a mother, takes precisely the opposite approach of *Contending Forces*. Indeed, *The Awakening* explicitly rejects the romance plot, particularly its resolution in marriage and contented motherhood, that Hopkins claims for the wronged Sappho Clark. For Edna children do not offer the "compensation" of a "new and holy love" (Hopkins, *Contending Forces* 346) but threaten to "drag her into the soul's slavery for the rest of her days" (Chopin, *Awakening* 175). To Chopin's contemporaries, however, more shocking than her satiric view of the "mother-woman" was her daring representation of female sexual desire. Her frank depiction of Edna's awakening would be matched only by Edith Wharton's *Summer,* published eighteen years later. Far from being "overworked," the subject of women's sexuality was largely unexplored fictional territory in the first two decades of the twentieth century.[1]

That Chopin and Wharton, perhaps the most respected (and respectable) women writers of their era, should attempt such representations belies the assumption that they were uninterested in, even hostile to, the "woman question."[2] Current reassessments of Chopin's short fiction, much of which depicts women struggling against the constraints of marriage, complicate the popular image of Chopin as a contented mother-author who dashed off short stories with her six children gathered around her in the parlor. Emily Toth's biography of Chopin gives us a woman who "refused to be a conventional mother" (20) and, like her most famous heroine, engaged in a scandalous extramarital affair. Similarly, the discovery of Wharton's "Beatrice Palmato" fragment (a graphic depiction of father-daughter incest), and a more general reconsideration of how profoundly Wharton's sexual awakening at the age of forty influenced her life and work, call into question her reputation as the wholly proper grande dame of American letters. Moreover, as Elizabeth Ammons has suggested, while Wharton expressed doubts about the feminist and suffrage movements, she nonetheless saw the "position of women in American society [as] the crucial issue of the new century" and devoted much of her fiction to depicting the "waste, crippling, and curtailment" of even her boldest female protagonists. According to Ammons, "Typical women in her view—no matter how privileged, nonconformist, or assertive—were not free to control their own lives" (*Edith* 3).

In *The Awakening* and *Summer* Chopin and Wharton present transgressive heroines whose sexual awakenings promise to release them from conventional female roles, yet in each case the sexually rebellious woman exercises little power over her fate; indeed, both novels end by putting their "awakened" heroines back to sleep. In texts filled with references to speech and silence, the failure to awaken fully is linked simultaneously to the limits of what Dale Spender has called "man-made language," a system of communication that reproduces patriarchal social and sexual relations, and to the apparent inevitability of childbearing. Thus, while Edna Pontellier and Charity Royall push the boundaries of nineteenth-century womanhood by attempting to satisfy their sexual desires, their stories begin and end in the silence appropriate to women's traditional place.

Although several critics of *The Awakening* have examined linguistic aspects of the novel now credited with inaugurating twentieth-century literary feminism, *Summer* has not been subjected to similar analyses, nor has it received its fair share of scholarly attention among Wharton's works.[3] Yet the relationship between language, sexuality, and maternity is equally stressed in the novel that Wharton was fond of calling her "hot Ethan." Considering *The Awakening* and *Summer* in tandem demonstrates how central the question of language was to reimagining women's place in early twentieth-century U.S. culture, as well as how consistently issues of linguistic agency were linked to issues of race. If, as Michael North argues in *The Dialect of Modernism,* "dialect became the prototype for the most radical representational strategies of English-language modernism," allowing expatriated white artists like Gertrude Stein and T. S. Eliot to inhabit the paradoxically liberating role of "racial outsider" ("Preface" n.p.), how might the dialect of silence that pervades Chopin's and Wharton's sexual awakening novels reflect a similar liberatory impulse? Such a question is germane to these texts because of their mutual emphasis on linguistic dynamics as they structure relations between men and women, as well as between dominant and nondominant social groups. What makes these texts intriguing for this study is the way in which the racial imperative of maternity derails their shared feminist project of linguistic critique, highlighting the apparent incompatibility of female emancipation and racial advancement.

In *The Awakening* and *Summer* sexual emancipation proves illusory precisely because it is linked to maternity, which is associated with linguistic paralysis, physical confinement, and death. In endings that rewrite the happy conclusion of *Contending Forces,* the heroines of *The Awakening* and *Summer* experience not an ascension to motherhood—a passage into adult womanhood and the domestic power that it confers—but a descent into the powerlessness of childhood, represented in both cases by silence. Their sexual awakenings leading inexorably to harsh reproductive realities, Edna and Charity become increasingly infantilized, deprived of both voice and agency, as they confront the possibility of motherhood. Yet despite maternity's abortive effect on their heroines' growing autonomy, Chopin and Wharton uphold the notion that motherhood is woman's most enduring contribution to "the race."[4]

Chopin's and Wharton's representations of white middle-class women not as producers of children but as children echo Charlotte Perkins Gilman's analysis of the stultifying and racially harmful construction of womanhood at the turn of the century. Indeed, while contemporary critics of *The Awakening* in particular have tended to rely on second-wave feminist theories, the first-wave evolutionary feminism of Charlotte Perkins Gilman provides a more fully historicized framework that allows us to consider why *The Awakening* and *Summer* uphold racial hierarchy even as they challenge gender hierarchy. Gilman's fiction and nonfiction consistently focus on the relationship between female empowerment and racial evolution; indeed, her argument that the infantilization of women had negative racial consequences was persuasive at the turn of the century precisely because it tapped into widespread fears of white racial degeneration. She also evinced a lifelong interest in the ways in which language shaped woman's place in culture. In *The Man-Made World; or, Our Androcentric Culture,* for example, she complains that woman occupies the "place of a preposition in relation to man. She has been considered above him or below him, before him, behind him, beside him, a wholly relative existence—'Sidney's sister,' 'Pembroke's mother'—but never by any chance Sydney or Pembroke herself." Gilman concludes that "all our human scheme of things rests on the same tacit assumption; man being held the human type; woman a sort of accompaniment and subordinate assistant, merely essential to the making of people" (20). Gilman's sarcastic final phrase, which traces women's linguistic subordination to her "mere" role in the "making of people," suggests how central reproduction was to all her arguments about culture, not least her arguments about language.

Extending Gilman's quasi-anthropological observations, while drawing on the local color tradition of using dialogue as an index to culture, Chopin and Wharton document conversational dynamics that both reflect and produce women's place. At the same time, their critique of women's sociolinguistic subordination depends, as does Gilman's, upon a reproduction of racial and cultural difference. "Other" women in their texts are endowed with a variety of characteristics, from unfettered sexuality to maternal promiscuity, but they function always as a measure of the white heroine's exceptionality, her necessary distance from the Nature they represent. Where Chopin and Wharton represent Edna and Charity as overpowered by "man-made" language, they render other women as naturally mute, their deeper silence serving as a foil for the white heroine's gradual loss of voice, even as their darker bodies, which appear to lodge no complaint against the "ways of nature," register the eugenic imperative of white maternity. Thus, although Chopin's and Wharton's portrayals of romantic love denaturalize the conventions of romance, exposing it as a plot (in both senses of the word), they simultaneously naturalize and enforce racial difference. Their mutual critique of patriarchal language as a culturally enforced limitation on women's agency is accompanied by their concession to biological determinism as a necessary element in the reproduction of race.

"A Sex Specialized to Reproduction"

Chopin's and Wharton's preoccupation with speech and silence anticipates much second-wave feminist theory, in which voice has become a popular metaphor for female agency; yet few contemporary feminists would have the audacity to posit, as Gilman did, an all-encompassing theory of female oppression relating women's social, political, and economic subordination to proscriptions against female self-expression. Moreover, while contemporary literary critics have only recently begun to factor race into their analyses of white-authored literature, the recurring emphases of Gilman's work make clear the extent to which race was integral to white feminist theorizing at the turn of the twentieth century. Although Gilman's voluminous nonfiction and fiction covered a range of feminist concerns, from suffrage to child care, from housekeeping to sexual violence, she repeatedly stressed the reciprocal relationship between female emancipation and racial advancement; indeed, she consistently predicated "race" progress on the elevation of women's social status.

The culmination of more than a decade of lecturing on women's issues, *Women and Economics* (1898) condemns a social arrangement that made women "oversexed," which, in Gilman's terminology, means not so much overly sexual as overly feminine. Her analysis connects women's passivity and stunted growth to their dependence on the heterosexual marriage contract, which had disastrous consequences not only for women but for the future of civilization. Adopting Darwin's theory of sexual selection and drawing on the "gynaecentric" theories of the sociologist Lester Ward, Gilman speculates on the causes of the "maladjustment of the sex-relation in humanity" (*Women* 25).[5] Like Ward, Gilman opposed those social Darwinists who took a deterministic view of history, believing instead that by working to improve social institutions, human beings (unlike lower species) could influence the workings of natural selection; as Gilman observes in her autobiography, "We are the only creatures that can assist evolution" (*Living* 42).[6] In *Women and Economics* she identifies the conditions that most need addressing in order to advance the evolutionary process:

> Man, in supporting woman, has become her economic environment. Under natural selection, every creature is modified to its environment, developing perforce the qualities needed to obtain its livelihood under that environment. Man, as the feeder of woman, becomes the strongest modifying force in her economic condition. Under sexual selection the human creature is of course modified to its mate, as with all creatures. When the mate becomes also the master, when economic necessity is added to sex-attraction, we have the two great evolutionary forces acting together to the same end; namely, to develope [*sic*] sex-distinction in the human female. For, in her position of economic dependence in the sex-relation, sex-distinction is with her not only a means of attracting a mate . . . but a means of getting her livelihood. (38)

Like Margaret Sanger, who would argue that women should have access to birth control if only because of its benefits to the nation and "the race,"

Gilman emphasizes that the chief evil of the "abnormal sexuo-economic relation" is that it acts as a "check to individual and racial progress" (59). The "entire race" is hindered, she warns, when women are constructed as "parasitic creatures" (62). Thus, even in a society where the "whole field of human progress has been considered a masculine prerogative" (52), man's progress is retarded by woman's subjugation, which not only makes her an inferior creature but also, in Gilman's Lamarckian view, passes on undesirable characteristics to the next generation. For "the female segregated to the uses of sex alone naturally deteriorates in racial development, and naturally transmits that deterioration to her offspring" (183).[7]

Yet despite her belief in the inheritability of acquired traits, Gilman (like Pauline Hopkins) stresses the cultural, rather than biological, underpinnings of evolution, asserting that in each generation woman is "re-womanized by her traditional position" and has to "live over again in her own person the same process of restriction, repression, denial; the smothering 'no' which crushed down all her human desires to create, to discover, to learn, to express, to advance" (70). Indeed, according to Gilman, "The position of women, after their long degradation[,] is in many ways analogous to that of the freed slave. He is refused justice on account of his inferiority. To reply that [that] inferiority is largely due to previous injustice does not alter the fact" ("Educated Bodies" 178).

Unfortunately, in light of Gilman's persistent racism, her comparison of white women's condition to that of newly emancipated slaves must be seen as a convenient appropriation of terms rather than an instance of identification. On the issue of lynching, for instance, Gilman identified with white women and against black men. Apparently unfamiliar with the work of Ida B. Wells, Gilman accepted the idea that lynching was a response to black men's attacks on white women and advocated the following solution: "If the dangerous negroes of the black belt knew that every white woman carried a revolver and used it with skill and effect there would be less lynching needed" ("Should" 217). Thus, while Gilman frequently uses the term *race* to refer to a putatively universal human race, her own racial attitudes suggest that the race she had in mind was the white race. Gilman's analysis of women's oppression is thus inextricable from a racist ideology that made enhancing evolution not merely a self-evident good but a specifically white racial imperative.[8] She notes disapprovingly in *Women and Economics* that "the lower social grades bear more children . . . than the women of higher classes" and expresses the sentiment that any woman who ignores the "racial duty of right selection" helps to "exterminate her race" (201).

Though inextricable from her feminism, Gilman's investment in white racial advancement produced a number of contradictions in her work. For example, while Gilman argues repeatedly that optimal racial evolution depends upon expanding women's opportunities outside the home, she also recognizes that "the human female [is] denied the enlarged activities which have developed intelligence in man" (*Women* 195) chiefly because of her culturally enforced role as mother, the one role essential for the "racial" reproduction that Gilman advocates elsewhere. According to Gilman, "As a sex specialized to reproduction, [women give up] all personal activity, all honest independence, all useful and progressive economic service for [their] glorious consecration to the uses of maternity" (*Women* 198–99). Gilman sees the "psychic manifestations" of women's exclusive association with maternity as particularly destructive, for a "morbid, disproportioned, overgrown home life" cannot help but produce a "degrading abnegation in woman" (*Home* 178–79). Her 1912 article "Our Brains and What Ails Them" offers her most extended analysis of women's acculturation to passivity. Titling one section of the article "The Effect of the Position of Woman on the Race Mind," Gilman characteristically makes her plea for women's emancipation by emphasizing the racial results of their subjugation. Asserting that there is no female mind, just a human brain that has been "denied normal use and exercise in the female," Gilman warns that "the race brain . . . has been steadily robbed and weakened by the injury to the mother-half" (228–29).

Indeed, Gilman's abstract pleas on behalf of the race frequently pale beside her depictions of individual women denied the opportunity for intellectual interchange but, in her sardonic view, "kept alive at least long enough for reproduction, else the race perish" ("Our Brains" 227). Grant Allen, author of *The Woman Who Did* (1895), saw nothing wrong with such an arrangement, arguing that women, like drones or male spiders, are naturally "sacrificed to reproductive necessities" (qtd. in Gilman, *Women* 172). For Gilman, however, the consequences of such an arrangement are not only unnatural but horrifying: "If one wishes to gather a sense of pain to last throughout life, cast one shuddering look down the ages at the condition of women's brains. Each girl born with as much brain as her brother. Each woman, throughout her entire life, denied the use of it, suffering her life long the gnawing of an unappeasable appetite—a wholly natural and righteous appetite, the strongest appetite in human life—that of the soul, as we call it" ("Our Brains" 247).

Typically reticent about sexuality, Gilman makes no mention of it here. Yet in her assertion of women's intellectual "appetite," and particularly the "unappeasable" appetite of the soul, she acknowledges a form of female desire integral to the awakening of Chopin's and Wharton's heroines. Like Chopin,

Gilman imagines women's emancipation from the "soul's slavery," but for Gilman, disturbed not only by the state of the generic "race mind" but also by the particular waste of female minds, true freedom could come only from intellectual, as well as sexual, liberation. Indeed, Gilman explains the lure of romance as deriving from women's intellectual deprivation, for in the absence of other activities woman "pours her whole life into her love. . . . With her it is a deep, all-absorbing force, under the action of which she will renounce all that life offers, take any risk, bear any pain. It is maintained in her in the face of a lifetime of neglect and abuse" (*Women* 48).

Such self-abnegation was, for Gilman, consistent with the "required virtues of a subject class: obedience, patience, endurance, contentment, humility, resignation . . . and unselfishness," precisely the virtues sought in the ideal mother (*His Religion* 134). Yet Gilman's own postpartum experience led her to conclude that "the human female, modified entirely to maternity, become[s] unfit for any other exertion, and a helpless dependent" (*Women* 19). Indeed, her most disturbing representation of women's childlike dependency as constructed through maternity is her autobiographical fiction, "The Yellow Wallpaper" (1892), a now-canonical description of her own experience of S. Weir Mitchell's infamous rest cure.

While most of Gilman's short stories and novellas meet her own criteria for fiction, which she believed should chronicle the "increasing individualization of women" (*Women* 151), "The Yellow Wallpaper" portrays a woman who, far from individuated, imagines herself literally blending into the wallpaper. Scattered references to "the baby" suggest that the apparently mad narrator is suffering from postpartum depression (Gilman herself underwent Mitchell's treatment a year after becoming a mother), yet Gilman's horror story focuses not on the psychological strain of becoming a mother but on the enforced infantilization of this mother. Here, maternity represents not a "glorious consecration" but a hideous incarceration: locked in a room that she believes to be a nursery, the unnamed protagonist is forced, as Gilman was, to sleep for much of the day. For to return women to their "natural" state, the rest cure demanded that they live "as domestic a life as possible" and "never touch pen, brush, or pencil" ("Why I Wrote" 52).

Equally interesting in light of Chopin's and Wharton's representations of women's silence is Gilman's depiction of the narrator's husband, a doctor who attempts to suppress her writing, speech, and thoughts. Confessing that she is hungry for "more society and stimulus," the protagonist notes that her husband "says the very worst thing I can do is to think about my condition." She is also expressly forbidden to write and keeps a journal only under "heavy opposition" (4). Her "imaginative power" and "habit of story-making" are

deemed manifestations of her lack of "proper self-control." Yet, as many critics have noted, it is precisely because she is denied self-expression that the
narrator sees "so much expression in an inanimate thing," namely, the yellow wallpaper. Her madness must be attributed, then, not to the "hysteria"
for which she is ostensibly being treated but to the suppression of her voice.
Eventually, the narrator becomes the "crawling" woman she sees in the wallpaper, reduced to endless creeping around the room. While this behavior is
certainly a sign of her increasing insanity, it is also a mark of her infantilization. Indeed, her childlike crawl is consistent with the desired outcome of the
Mitchell treatment, which aimed to instill in unruly women more appropriately feminine qualities, to make them docile, domestic, and, above all, quiet. Gilman's final image suggests that the crawling child-woman has returned
not only to the dependent state of a toddler but also, presumably, to the infant's prearticulate state.[9]

However horrifying her fictional depiction of the rest cure, Gilman's own
experience of total confinement clearly gave her insight into the obstacles
faced by intellectual and artistic women. Six years later, in *Women and Economics,* Gilman used an image from "The Yellow Wallpaper" to argue that
woman's confinement to the home, which differed only in degree from the
virtual incarceration advocated by Mitchell, limited not only her knowledge
of the outside world but her ability to express herself to this world. She notes
that "the freedom of expression has been more restricted in women than the
freedom of impression, if that be possible. Something of the world she lived
in she has seen from her *barred windows.* Some air has come through the
purdah's folds, some knowledge has filtered to her eager ears from the talk of
men. . . . But in the ever-growing human impulse to create, the power and
will to make, to do, to express one's spirit in new forms, here she has been
utterly *debarred*" (66–67, emphasis added).

Indeed, in the "The Yellow Wallpaper" Gilman represents the extremely
narrow range of women's sanctioned activities in the space of a single room
outfitted with barred windows. As the logical extreme of women's domestic
confinement, this setting provides a baseline against which to measure the
pronounced disregard for domestic boundaries in *The Awakening* and *Summer. The Awakening* not only suggests that the social formalities of New Orleans society contrast unfavorably with the relative freedoms of Grand Isle and
the limitless expanse of the sea but also locates Edna's sexual awakening not
in the domestic space she shares with her husband but in a small "pigeon
house" she claims as her own. The claustrophobia of *Summer's* domestic
spaces is suggested by its setting in North Dormer, a town whose name suggests that the entire municipality is as constricting as a house and whose an-

nual celebration of "Old Home Week" underscores its investment in traditional domesticity. Fittingly, Charity's sexual awakening occurs in an abandoned shack (well outside the town's boundaries) whose decrepit walls define it as a liminal space between nature and culture.

Gilman's presentation of women as symbolically imprisoned—excluded from "the talk of men" and "debarred" from expression and creation—makes explicit issues that Chopin and Wharton addressed indirectly from their earliest attempts at fiction. Chopin's "Emancipation: A Life Fable" (1869), for example, represents women's psychic entrapment through the metaphor of a cage, while one of Wharton's earliest works, "The Valley of Childish Things" (1895), explicitly links arrested female development to a lack of linguistic prowess.[10] In Wharton's parable a young girl leaves a safe valley to explore a land beyond the mountains, where she learns "many useful arts" and "grows to be a woman" (58). Unfortunately, when she returns with her intended mate, she learns that her former playmates have "remained little children" and that even her worldly companion prefers a "dear little girl with blue eyes" to an independent woman adventurer; significantly, the preferred love object is "too young to speak articulately" (59).

In their sexual awakening novels Chopin and Wharton would represent the infantilizing rules of womanhood through the trope of speech and silence. In *The Awakening* and *Summer* sexuality seems to provide a means of self-expression not available in language, but sexual emancipation cannot be truly liberatory because sexual activity leads inevitably to maternity, which they depict as the ultimate limitation on (white) women's freedom. Recall that Gilman could imagine full emancipation for women only in a utopian world. In *Herland* (1915), her fictional world without men, women are both freed from the demands of traditional child care and, by reproducing parthenogenically, relieved of what Gilman saw as the burden of sex. Chopin and Wharton were not as willing to offer utopian solutions, nor were they content to conceive of female sexuality as fulfilling only reproductive needs. Sandra Gilbert, describing Edna as a "resurrected Venus," argues persuasively that Edna embodies "the erotic liberation that turn-of-the-century women had begun to allow themselves to desire" ("Second Coming" 62), whereas Cynthia Griffin Wolff describes *Summer*'s subject as "the never-to-be-repeated period when sexual love seems to be 'everything'" (xvii). But for Chopin and Wharton women's erotic liberation had distinct limits, among the most important of which were the needs of the race. It is easiest to discern the tensions inherent in their white feminist projects by first analyzing their explicit critique of the romance "plot" as it helps to sustain female silence and then examining their implicit endorsement of racial hierarchy.

An Indescribable Oppression

Acknowledging female sexual desire, Chopin and Wharton addressed a sub-ject that Pauline Hopkins necessarily avoided. Where Hopkins countered cul-tural representations of black women as overly sexual by creating a virtuous, if violated, True Woman, Chopin and Wharton rejected the image of white women as naturally nonsexual by creating heroines who refuse to apologize for their physical desires. In *The Awakening* and *Summer* sexuality (and not marriage, for one heroine experiences her awakening before, and one only after, marriage) marks the initiation into womanhood, much as sexual en-counters define manhood in the traditional bildungsroman. In "The Novel of Awakening" Susan J. Rosowski describes a parallel tradition in literature by women in which a female protagonist "attempts to find value in a world defined by love and marriage." Unlike her male counterpart, the female pro-tagonist gains self-knowledge, only to become aware of "the disparity be-tween that self-knowledge and the nature of the world." Her awakening is thus an "awakening to limitations" (49), for she cannot reconcile her newly acquired sense of self with the conventional roles she is expected to play.

As a story of a specifically sexual awakening, Wharton's *Summer*, like Chopin's better-known novel, belongs to a subgenre of the awakening nov-el. Wharton's protagonist, Charity Royall, spends a summer discovering her sensual and sexual selves and, like Edna, must deal with the limitations she discovers once awakened, chiefly the limits of her own pregnant body. Far from offering a "hymn to generativity and marriage," as Wolff suggests, *Sum-mer* depicts Charity's physical generativity as an obstacle to her desires. Both novels explore the lure and the danger of romantic love, and in each case the heroine's incomplete development of self is tied to her inability to express herself in language. Their progressive speechlessness might serve as an illus-tration of Charlotte Perkins Gilman's theory that woman's relationship to language, particularly her stunted capacity for self-expression, replicates and reinforces her position in society.

Depicting women overpowered by words even as they discover their own sexual power, *The Awakening* and *Summer* suggest that romantic relation-ships provide but a superficial freedom of expression. Not only do Edna and Charity become less audible as the novels' plots advance but their loss of voice and agency coincides with their recognition of the "awakened" woman's seemingly inevitable reproductive fate. Chopin and Wharton suggest, in fact, that in the process of producing a child (or, in Edna's case, in the mere re-membrance of this process) a woman becomes like a child: silent, passive, and, like the new mother in "The Yellow Wallpaper," utterly dependent. In all three narratives the natural and cultural laws of reproduction—the social conventions of romance as well as the biological process of maternity—serve to reproduce women's silence.

If, as Sandra Gilbert and Susan Gubar have argued, the "female linguistic project" in the twentieth century was to "renovate the entire process of verbal symbolization" that has "historically subordinated women," the dismal endings of *The Awakening* and *Summer* suggest that Chopin and Wharton were not hopeful that women could possess an alternative "mother tongue" (*War of the Words* 228). Significantly, neither Charity's nor Edna's mother is living; even more telling, confronting a maternal body—for Edna, Adele's body in labor, and for Charity, the dead body of her own mother—only hastens their mutual descent into silence.[11] Dramatizing the connections between language, sexuality, and reproduction, *The Awakening* and *Summer* address the complex relationship between what Gilbert and Gubar call the "sexuality of linguistics and the linguistics of sexuality" (228) by suggesting the incompatibility of woman's voice and her reproductive fate.

Lacking mothers, Edna and Charity have no maternal models for their sexual and reproductive experiences.[12] Their reticence as young girls reflects a dearth of opportunities to speak within their families, foreshadowing their sense of isolation as adults. As a girl, Edna is not "given to confidences" (57) and is "not accustomed to an outward and spoken expression of affection, either in herself or in others" (61). Her adolescent girlfriends are similarly "self-contained," presumably models of the female reticence expected of young ladies. Edna's mother has died and she feels no particular connection with her father, to whom she has "not much of anything to say" (122). Thus she has "all her life long been accustomed to harbor thoughts and emotions which never voiced themselves" (96). A similar lack of conversation marks Charity's relationship with her male guardian: at mealtimes "they [face] each other in silence" (*Summer* 40). Nor is there any occasion for female conversation: Charity "always thought of her mother as so long dead as to be no more than a nameless pinch of dirt" (60), and she remembers Lawyer Royall's deceased wife as "sad and timid and meek" (24). Reinforcing the silence of this household is the deafness of its only other occupant, a housekeeper who otherwise might have functioned as a surrogate mother for Charity. Not surprisingly, as Charity matures into a young woman, she "holds herself aloof" from the "sentimental preoccupations" that form the basis of friendship among the village girls (61).

The stressed absence of female (particularly mother-daughter) conversation is telling, given that Chopin and Wharton populate their novels with male characters who represent a wide range of public discourses, from commerce and medicine in *The Awakening* to law and religion in *Summer*. If, as Mikhail Bakhtin argues, novelistic dialogue, particularly the specific "manners and styles" of characters' speech, must be read as "symbols for sets of social beliefs" (357), Chopin's descriptions of conversations between men and women make clear the nineteenth-century belief that women's proper role was silence. Certainly, Chopin's own experience taught her the female "art of making oneself agreeable in conversation." She learned never to "take the liberty of talking about [her]self," for as she remarked in her commonplace book, "Strange as it may appear it is not necessary to possess the faculty of speech; a dumb person, provided he be not deaf, can practice it as well as the most voluble. . . . Lead your antagonist to talk about himself—he will not enter reluctantly upon the subject, I assure you—and twenty to one—he will report you as one of the most entertaining and intelligent persons" (Toth and Seyersted 83).

The *Awakening*'s Adele Ratignolle, in all ways the model of appropriate female behavior in Creole society, has adopted these very principles, taking care to be "keenly interested in everything [her husband] said." Adele's nurturing "mother-woman" role defines her conversational duty to her husband, so that when he speaks she "lay[s] down her fork the better to listen" (107). Similarly, at Edna's dinner party Mrs. Highcamp is "full of delicate courtesy toward her husband" and addresses the bulk of her conversation to him (128), while Miss Mayblunt pretends to be "greatly amused" by Mr. Merriman (144). Even the relatively sympathetic Dr. Mandelet expects Edna to "entertain him" while he attends Adele's labor (170). He is a kinder, gentler version of Edna's dictatorial husband, but he shares Edna's father's belief that "authority [and] coercion" are "the only way[s] to manage a wife" (125).

Edna's lack of linguistic agency, her "unthinking" yielding to such domination (78), is equally evident in her patterns of thought. Unaccustomed to speaking, Edna cannot achieve an internal dialogue that might allow her to understand her own awakening. Thus, as she feels the first stirrings of discontent with the role defined for her, she is unable to articulate, even to herself, the source of her feelings. Twice in the opening chapters Chopin remarks that Edna "could not have told why" (49, 56). Later, when Edna is "casting aside [her] fictitious self" and "becoming herself" (108), she shows remarkably little self-knowledge. Experiencing emotions that she cannot understand or control, she is alternately happy and unhappy "without knowing why" (109). Thus Edna remains at the mercy of a "vague anguish," an "indescribable oppression" (49), indescribable because, despite a superficial "freedom of expression" (53), there is no real candor in Creole society.

With Madame Ratignolle, however, Edna begins to "loosen the mantle of reserve that had always enveloped her" (57) and to question the discrepancy between the "realm of romance and dreams" and the "world of reality" (63). Chopin shows that Adele is "the most obvious influence" on Edna's mental awakening, for Edna articulates with Adele her previously unspeakable thoughts arising from the "inward life which questions" (57). Unlike conversations with her husband, which require her silence, those with Adele leave Edna "intoxicated with the sound of her own voice and the unaccustomed taste of candor" (63). Significantly, such intoxicating talk stops abruptly when Robert, her youthful admirer, appears.

Yet male intrusion is not the most important obstacle to female conversation, for as Sandra Gilbert notes, Grand Isle is essentially a "female colony" (Introduction 25); if female conversation can be successful anywhere, it should be here. But Chopin suggests that women so internalize gendered discourse—Adele will not "consent to remain with Edna [while] Monsieur Ratignolle was alone" (88), for example—that opportunity for female conversation is sacrificed to maternal and spousal responsibilities. Because she so faithfully adheres to social rules, particularly those governing gender relations, Adele cannot see them as conventions; thus, when she cautions Robert to uphold the gentleman's code of honor in his relationship with Edna, she does not claim to express her own views but "what she believed to be the law and the gospel" (65). She justifies the selfless mother-woman role to Edna with no less authority: "The Bible tells you so. I'm sure I couldn't do more than that" (97). Edna's rejection of the maternal sacrifice ideal leads to a "heated argument" in which the "two women did not appear . . . to be talking the same language" (97).

Thus, as Edna begins to "look with her own eyes" (151), she necessarily "stands alone" (145). Certainly, Edna's developing consciousness is at odds with her desire for conversation with other women, for female conversations remain devoted to women's traditional concerns. Edna has little interest in Adele's favorite topic of conversation, her "condition," but the subject she wants most to avoid is that most cherished by the women of Grand Isle. Indeed, maternity is the one topic that encourages women's verbal self-display, for Chopin notes that "no one would have known a thing about [Adele's pregnancy] but for her persistence in making it the subject of conversation" (52) and that in "relating to old Monsieur Farival the harrowing story of one of her *accouchements*," she "withhold[s] no intimate detail" (53).

If Edna is limited by the social conventions governing male-female conversations, as well as by a lack of sustained female community, Wharton's Charity Royall feels alienated from language itself. An amateur librarian with a strong antipathy to books, Charity recalls with distaste her visit to a neighboring town, where "a gentleman [said] unintelligible things before pictures that she would have enjoyed looking at if his explanations had not prevented her from understanding them" (*Summer* 10). Describing books as "deadening," Charity is a confident reader only in nature, perceiving the world most keenly through her body: "She was blind and insensible to many things, and dimly knew it; but to all that was light and air, perfume and color, every drop of blood in her responded" (21).

By contrast, Charity's guardian, Lawyer Royall, identified by his profession rather than by a given name, is explicitly associated with law and history, two forms of public discourse that are dependent upon a mastery of words. His mastery of Charity herself is overdetermined, for he is not only her guardian and father figure but, having brought her down from the mountain, her savior. Despite Charity's rebellions, Royall maintains control of her fate, largely by what he says, throughout the novel. He is the "biggest man in town" (22), and, though Charity is at times verbally rebellious, Royall never cedes the power to define her history. Her life is both a story told about her—she has to overhear Royall telling Lucius in order to learn the truth of her origins (73)— and a tale turned against her, when Royall later denounces her as a whore.

Having literally named her, and with a name that forever recalls her debt to him, Royall claims the right to define Charity according to his own purposes. Thus he can call her a "whore" when she defies him (151) yet pronounce her a "good girl" when she marries him (276). At such moments Charity is noticeably silent; the phrase "she made no answer," and variations of it, runs like a refrain throughout the novel. At the end of the novel it is Royall's commanding voice, not the reason of his argument, that seems to silence Charity. Preempting her speech, he asks and answers the question that determines her fate: "Do you know what you really want? I'll tell you. You want to be took home and took care of. And I guess that's all there is to say" (271).

While Edna experiences limited self-revelation with Adele, Charity is completely without allies, for the women in the novel are either powerless or hostile. Though she seeks out Miss Hatchard after Royall's sexual overture, Charity soon realizes that "she would have to fight her way out of the difficulty alone." Because talk about sex is prohibited, Miss Hatchard can offer no counsel, and Charity feels "incalculably old" as she realizes that Miss Hatchard has "got to be talked to like a baby" (31). A proper spinster who affects total ignorance of sexual matters, Miss Hatchard is a perfect example of the child-woman that Wharton satirized in "The Valley of Childish Things." Ironically, the one apparently maternal woman whom Charity encounters is the abortionist, who fusses over Charity and calls her "my dear" (224), only to demand her brooch as payment for her advice.

Only when Charity realizes that "she herself had been born as her own baby was going to be born" (240) does she recognize in her estranged mother a precedent for her own experience and a potential source of advice. Unfortunately, her mother's death just before Charity arrives on the mountain deprives her of the opportunity to discover an empowering "mother tongue." As Minister Miles intones the last rites over her mother's body, the language of religion, like all other official languages, proves irrelevant to Charity's experience, for she cannot reconcile the minister's lofty phrases with her all-too-earthly vision of her mother. As he reads, "In my flesh shall I see God," Charity stares disbelievingly at her mother's rotting flesh (251).[13] Yet she is cowed by the minister's "mighty words," which master her "as they mastered the drink-dazed creatures at her back" (253). His is the "voice of authority" in this scene (256), and his presence inhibits Charity's ability to make sense of her experience. After the funeral Charity's "bewildered brain labour[s] with the attempt to picture her mother's past," (258) but like her own, her mother's remains inaccessible.

The Lure of Romance

If *The Awakening* and *Summer* portray typical conversation as dominated by male voices, their depictions of failed (or nonexistent) female conversation suggest little optimism about the nurturing potential of female community. Elaine Showalter has traced the dissolution of women's community to a "gender crisis of the turn of the century" ("Death" 134). She argues that as patterns of gender behavior were being redefined at the turn of the century, women were caught between two worlds of female experience. The first, a homosocial world of "intense female friendships and mother-daughter bonds characteristic of nineteenth-century American women's culture," was gradually replaced by the second, in which single-sex relationships were dissolved "in the interest of facilitating more intimate friendships between women and men" (134).[14] Without mothers, sisters, or other homosocial ties, Charity and Edna place disproportionate emphasis on their romantic relationships; yet because verbal inequality is endemic to male-female relationships in these novels, Edna's and Charity's potentially liberating sexual experiences only recreate the power dynamics at play in their relations with husband and guardian, respectively. Indeed, the white feminist project undergirding these novels can be read most clearly in their unsentimental depictions of romantic love, in which the effects of "awakening" are described, paradoxically, in terms of numbness, sleep, and silence.

From the start of her romance with Robert, Edna feels herself "blindly following whatever impulse moved her, as if she had placed herself in alien hands for direction" (Chopin, *Awakening* 79). Edna's passivity is particularly odd because in the previous scene she has responded to her husband's characteristic commands with unusual verbal assertiveness: "Don't speak to me like that again; I shall not answer you" (78). Her easy acceptance of Robert's courtship seems to negate this linguistic rebellion. Likewise, Alcée Arobin, who is most directly responsible for Edna's sexual awakening, nonetheless has a narcoleptic effect on her: "His presence, his manners, the warmth of his glances, and above all the touch of his lips upon her hand [act] like a narcotic upon her" (132). Edna's response to both men is marked by a lack of will that belies the autonomy suggested by her increasing self-expression with Adele. "Obsessed" with Robert, she is simultaneously "assailed" by hopelessness, which comes over her "like something extraneous, independent of volition" (145). With Arobin, Edna wears a "dreamy, absent look" and he leaves her in a "sort of stupor" (161).

Of her many male interlocutors, Edna speaks most freely to Dr. Mandelet, who appears best able to perceive the true nature of her awakening. Significantly, only Mandelet imagines that Edna's new self might be an intellectual one (118). More important, he perceives Edna's transformation as a change in voice, observing at Edna's emancipatory dinner party that "her speech was warm and energetic. There was no repression in her glance or gesture" (123). Yet Dr. Mandelet's choice of dinner tales suggests that his advice to Edna is bound by conventional ideas of romance, making it difficult to believe his promise to Edna that they will discuss things she has never "dreamt of talking about before" (171). Mandelet tells "the old, ever new and curious story of the waning of a woman's love," which, as he imagines it, "[returns] to its legitimate source after days of fierce unrest" (123).

Edna, of course, imagines a more radical conclusion to her tale, in which a woman goes off with her lover and "never [comes] back" (123). Her story revises conventional notions of female sexuality and so is potentially threatening to patriarchal order.[15] Signaling her recognition that such an ending is unrealizable outside the boundaries of fiction, Chopin describes Edna's story as "pure invention," a "dream she had" (124). Certainly, the three men who hear her tale—her father, husband, and doctor—do not dream that her words signal Edna's own (as-yet unconscious) intentions. Thus, while Mandelet later insists that he understands Edna, whom he calls "my dear child," she has already moved beyond the limits of his imagination. Yet even in their final encounter, when she attempts to articulate her desires, Edna perceives their failed communication as her fault: "She felt that her speech was voicing the incoherency of her thoughts and stopped abruptly" (171).

Given her constantly aborted attempts at thought, the "awakened" Edna remains, in her ability to conceive of her situation, a "new-born creature" (175). Such an image is consistent with the gestational pacing of the narrative, which ends one chapter shy of forty, the number of weeks in a typical pregnancy. But Edna is not so much reborn as she is returned to an earlier childlike state in a process of regression rather than liberation, so that immediately preceding her suicide she thinks of the "blue-grass meadow that she had traversed when a little child" (176). Completing her return to childhood, Edna is "enfold[ed]" in the "soft, close embrace" of the sea (176), whose ceaseless "whispering, clamoring, murmuring" (175) seems to offer an alternative discourse. But wrapped in the sea's maternal waters, symbolically returning not only to infancy but to the womb, Edna has no need for speech.

Like Edna, Charity chooses a sexual partner who rarely allows her to speak. Intimidated by Harney's sophistication, which exposes her own "ignorance of life and literature" (39), Charity, like Edna, doubts the validity of her own thoughts. Believing that she could never understand the workings of Harney's urban world, she imagines his lifestyle as "so far beyond her understanding that the whole subject hung like a luminous mist on the farthest verge of her thoughts" (Wharton, *Summer* 197). Her perception of herself as powerless leads her to accept Harney's will unconditionally: "She could imagine no reason for doing or not doing anything except the fact that Harney wished or did not wish it. All her tossing contradictory impulses were merged in a fatalistic acceptance of his will" (175).

Wharton represents Charity's diminishing agency chiefly through her decreasing ability to express herself verbally. In one scene Charity has difficulty telling Harney about Lawyer Royall's unwelcome sexual overtures: "You don't know," she says. When he answers, "What don't I know?" Charity is "silent" and he continues speaking (167). Later, when Charity tries to explain her reticence, she is cut off: "'I know the way you must feel about me,' she broke out, 'telling you such things.' But once more, as she spoke, she became aware that he was no longer listening" (169). Finally, when Charity becomes pregnant, she does not feel the authority to speak, even through a letter, in order to assert a claim to Harney. By this point "she [feels] herself too unequally pitted against unknown forces" and accepts "the uselessness of struggling against the circumstances" (220–21). Her linguistically induced resignation, like Edna's persistent "lack of volition," suggests a version of literary naturalism in which the operations of language, rather than heredity or a generalized environment, shape the predetermined outlines of each character's fate.

The relationship between Charity's lack of voice and her lack of agency is similarly stressed when Royall interrogates Harney at the lovers' abandoned house. Here, Wharton writes that there is "an immense and oppressive silence" in which "Charity, quivering with anger, start[s] forward, and then [stands] silent, too humbled for speech" (206–7). When Royall leaves, "there [is] a long silence" during which Charity waits for Harney to speak (208), and when he does, she does not answer (209). Charity's inertia in this scene (and again when she marries Royall) is explicitly tied to a loss of voice: "Her hand lay inertly under [Harney's], and she left it there, and raised her head, trying to answer him. But the words died in her throat" (210).

Given her gradual loss of will, Charity sleepwalks through her wedding to Royall. As they approach the church, Charity welcomes his "silent presence," for seeking "refuge from the torment of thought," she now wants only "warmth, rest [and] silence." Like Edna's, Charity's silence represents a regression to the dependent state of childhood; relieving herself of the burden of thinking, Charity "follow[s] Royall as passively as a tired child" (274). Given the fate of other "fallen women" in the novel—Julia Hawes, for example, becomes a prostitute—the security that Royall offers is perhaps Charity's best option, but it is bought at a high price. Indeed, Charity's wedding is funereal, for as the minister reads the marriage service, his words have the "same dread sound of finality" as those read over her dead mother (278). During the ceremony the "drowsy warmth" of the room lulls Charity into a "heavy sleep," much as the sea lulls Edna. Briefly recovering, Charity feels an "impulse of flight," but it is "only the lift of a broken wing" (280).

This final image of Charity recalls Edna's vision, immediately before her suicide, of a "bird with a broken wing . . . beating the air above, reeling, fluttering, circling disabled down, down to the water" (Chopin, *Awakening* 175). The only flights that Wharton and Chopin can imagine for their heroines are severely limited, circumscribed not only by social convention but also by the limits of language. "One of these days," Edna vows, "I'm going to pull myself together for a while and think—try to determine what character of a woman I am; for, candidly, I don't know. By all the codes which I am acquainted with, I am a devilishly wicked specimen of the sex. But some way I can't convince myself that I am. I must think about it" (137–38). Edna fails to achieve the critical consciousness necessary to articulate new "codes" of womanhood, in large part because, according to Chopin, the only socially sanctioned thoughts for women are thoughts of their children. Thus in the midst of her own labor Adele admonishes Edna, "Think of the children. . . . Remember them!" (170).

Apparently complying with Adele's command, Edna remarks that "one has to think of the children some time or other; the sooner the better" (171). When she does, "the children [appear] before her like antagonists who had overcome her; who had overpowered and sought to drag her into the soul's slavery for the rest of her days" (175). Similarly, Charity's unborn child is a "bodily burden" and a "load that held her down." Yet this child is also "like a hand that pulled her to her feet" (Wharton, *Summer* 265). Having encountered the "savage misery" (259) in which her own mother lived—for upon giving up her child, Charity's mother finds no home except in the marginal mountain community—Charity determines to "get up and struggle on" (265) and, finally, to accept Royall's proposal. Respectable society has no place, Wharton suggests, for the unnatural woman who would refuse to be a mother. Thus, given her pregnant state, Charity finds "in the established order of things as she knew them . . . no place for her individual adventure" (235).

Between Chopin's satiric image of a "mother-woman" (revered for her selfless devotion to her children) and Wharton's representation of a degenerate mountain mother (scorned for abandoning her child), these texts offer no viable model of motherhood. No wonder, then, that confronting the inevitability of maternity—Edna vicariously through Adele's labor, and Charity through the weighty "burden" of her own body—leads directly to literal or symbolic death. In each novel the "established order" of reproduction, an order at once institutional and biological, emerges as the most obvious limitation to white women's freedom. Like Chopin's earlier story of Athénaïse, Edna's underscores the "futility of rebellion against a social and sacred institution" like marriage ("Athénaïse" 235). Even more futile is a revolt against nature. Watching Adele's labor, described as a "scene of torture," Edna feels a "flaming, outspoken revolt against the ways of nature" (*Awakening* 170), but any flames of revolt are squelched almost immediately when she immerses herself in the ocean, which likewise silences her new outspokenness. Equally resigned to the futility of rebellion, the pregnant Charity "passively await[s] a fate she could not avert" (Wharton, *Summer* 214).

Reproducing Race

Although Chopin and Wharton expose the destructive effects of romantic love, a largely social invention that, as Gilman notes, exerted an "all-absorbing force" on women, they find no alternative to the apparent biological imperative of maternity. Indeed, their plots would seem to endorse Dr. Mandelet's suggestion, at the end of *The Awakening,* that the illusions of romance are a necessary "provision of Nature," providing a "decoy to secure mothers for the race" (171). Certainly, neither Chopin nor Wharton questions the value of reproducing racial hierarchy. Even as their heroines become increasingly associated with the body—as a function of their sexual awakening and their attendant reversion to a preverbal childlike state—they remain distinct from other female characters who, by virtue of their color or class, provide examples of "naturally" animalistic nonwhite womanhood. Such characters, who occupy the periphery of each text, serve as a comforting reminder of the heroines' inherently superior racial qualities, but they also highlight the more troubling implications of "uncivilized" white female desire, which appears incompatible with dutiful reproduction.

Cynthia Eagle Russett notes that the Darwinian revolution prompted a number of compensatory rationalizations on the part of educated Victorians, for "if human beings could no longer lay claim to being a separate creation just a little less exalted than the angels, then a human hierarchy of excellence was needed more than ever. Women and the lesser races served to buffer Victorian gentlemen from a too-threatening intimacy with the brutes" (14). In *The Awakening* and *Summer* Other women serve as foils who lack the heroines' more desirable "civilized" qualities yet appear untroubled by woman's "natural" reproductive role. They thus register a eugenic anxiety about the repercussions of white middle-class feminism (particularly the New Woman's alleged aversion to childbearing), even as they embody an enviable freedom from social constraints. Michele A. Birnbaum has argued that Edna's awakening in fact depends upon both the model and the ministrations of black women who play the role of "sexual coaches" and whose homes serve as sexual "safehouses" (309). Birnbaum astutely observes that Edna's identification with socially marginalized women "both affirms her class position and allows her to critique the sexual constraints associated with it" (304), but I would add that such identification plays an equally important role in Chopin's critique of reproduction. Certainly, *The Awakening*'s final image of Edna's children as the "antagonists" who lead her into "soul's slavery" appropriates a racial metaphor particularly suited to her argument that motherhood weakens and infantilizes women, so much so that Edna's children overpower her.

But the racial metaphors that surface in the final chapters of *The Awakening* only make explicit a schema of racial signifiers at play throughout the novel. Most obvious is Chopin's careful observation of her characters' racial classifications: from the "quadroon" who cares for Edna's children (104) to the "griffe" nurse who attends Adele's labor (169), not to mention innumerable "black" figures who hover at the periphery of most scenes. Chopin's attention to racial designations can be explained, in part, by the local color writer's faithful attention to detail. Yet given local color's interest in dialect as a crucial aspect of regional atmosphere, we might expect snippets of dialogue from some of these characters. Strangely, in only three instances does Chopin attribute speech to any of these characters and then indirectly, as when "Old Celestine" lingers to "talk patois with Robert" in a conversation alluded to but not reported (158–59).[16] The absence of such speech is all the more remarkable given the heteroglossia of Creole society, in which remarks are offered "simultaneously in French and English," leading Madame Lebrun to lament the linguistic "Bedlam" of island conversation (89–90). If, as Toni Morrison argues in "Unspeakable Things Unspoken," "some absences are so stressed, so ornate, so planned, they call attention to themselves" (11), the lack of any speech attributed to women of color in a novel preoccupied with women's speech is one such absence.

The effect is to naturalize the silent service of these "other" women, rendering them inanimate aspects of the setting, as when Edna, entering a cafe, observes with equal indifference "the slumbering *mulatresse,* the drowsy cat, and a glass of milk" (Chopin, *Awakening* 164). Edna's essential difference from such women can be observed through her physical distinction from Mariequita, whose "broad and coarse" feet show evidence of "slime between [the] toes," and whose conversation in Spanish with Robert, which "no one present understood," suggests a candor impossible within the Creole code of female reticence (80). Because Chopin takes pains to emphasize Edna's own "white feet" as well as her "white body" (175), readers are clearly to understand that Edna is no more like Mariequita than she is like "the quadroon [who] sat for hours before [her] palette, patient as a savage" (108); indeed, Edna's impatient desires are what most clearly differentiate her from Madame Ratignolle, who has "no regret, no longing" (107), and from the darker women who serve.

Yet Edna longs for the sexual license that she attributes to "backwards" races. Indeed, after her nap on the "snow-white" bed at the Chênière Caminada, she fantasizes that she belongs to a race that has been superseded: "'How many years have I slept?' she inquired. 'The whole island seems changed. A new race of beings must have sprung up, leaving only you and me as past relics. How many ages ago did Madame Antoine and Tonie die? and when did our people from Grand Isle disappear from the earth?'" (85) Her fantasy rests on popular interpretations of Darwin that posited a progressive evolution of races from barbarism to civilization and assumed that only Anglo-Saxons and other "advanced" white races had reached the pinnacle of this progression. The assumption that darker races represented stages supplanted by the Anglo-

Saxon was accompanied, however, by a fear of the weakening effects of "over-civilization" and an effort to recapture the untrammeled vigor of less civilized peoples. Thus, for example, in the same year that *The Awakening* was published, the sociologist G. Stanley Hall, who promoted the primitive as an "antidote to the effeminizing qualities of modern civilization," was enjoining kindergarten teachers to treat little boys like "savages" in order to produce more manly men (Bederman 78).

Edna's desire to "go primitive" can thus be read in two ways: as an attempt to possess the "transcendently seductive" qualities she attributes to nonwhite women (Chopin, *Awakening* 161), as well as to claim their apparent sexual freedom, and as an acknowledgment of her own membership in the culturally transcendent race. For as much as Edna chafes under the "civilized" construction of womanhood, she remains the novel's preeminent representative of culture; thus Mariequita models her own behavior after Edna's civilized, if decadent, example, reasoning that "[if] it was the fashion to be in love with married people, why, she could run away any time she liked to New Orleans with Celina's husband" (173).

Ultimately, Edna's racial difference from other women in *The Awakening* is maintained even at the expense of her own liberation. While Chopin depicts Edna's erotic desire sympathetically, she does not condone her lack of maternal instinct, which would seem to be one example of the dangers of overcivilization. That Chopin recognized and upheld the racial necessity of reproduction can be adduced not only from Dr. Mandelet's somewhat sardonic comment at the end of the novel but also from an apparently insignificant remark made by Edna's sons, who learn the facts of life while staying with their grandmother and report with awe the "ten tiny white pigs all lying in a row beside Lidie's big white pig" (162). Edna's "congratulat[ing] them upon their happy find of the little pigs" is ironic, because she demonstrates neither the natural reproductive instinct of animals nor the fierce attachment to children that Chopin elsewhere attributes to "less advanced" races. In her short story "La Belle Zoraïde," for instance, Chopin describes Zoraïde as responding "instinctively" to childbirth, commenting that "there is no agony that a mother will not forget when she holds her first-born to her heart, and presses her lips upon the baby flesh that is her own, yet far more precious than her own" (198).[17]

The repugnance that Edna experiences when she witnesses Adele in childbirth suggests that she will be inclined neither to forget such agonies nor to willingly endure further childbearing. Thus Edna is "the woman who stands alone" (145) in several senses: she defies sexual codes that support the patriarchal family, and she places herself dangerously outside the "natural" round of reproduction. In Chopin's evolutionary vision such behavior sets Edna apart from both animals and dark-skinned people, who are in fact lumped together in the stories that Edna's children tell about life at their grandmother's farm, where they mingle freely with "the pigs, the cows, the mules" and "Lidie's little black brood" (151). Choosing to (literally) farm out her own "precious brood" (51), the overcivilized Edna is a striking image of the willfully nonmaternal woman who would be upbraided by Theodore Roosevelt and who is revealed by *The Awakening*'s own ending to be an untenable model of white womanhood.

Wharton's investment in the reproduction of race is equally striking. Significantly, Wharton took her heroine's name from a "newspaper account of a crime committed by 'Charity Royall,' a black girl descended from a slave." According to Wharton's friend Elisina Tyler, it was Charity Royall's "fine" name that appealed to Wharton's imagination (Benstock 327). Perhaps it is not coincidental, however, that the novel that Wharton would dub the "hot Ethan" took its inspiration, at least indirectly, from a transgressive woman of color. Though Wharton describes Charity as "swarthy" (8), her difference from the community of North Dormer is not, strictly speaking, a distinction of race. Yet by the second decade of the century the distinction between racial and class difference was blurred by the growing interest in family studies, which attempted to prove the hereditary origins of crime and disease by tracing "dysgenic" traits to particular families.

Dale Bauer has demonstrated Wharton's interest in such studies; Wharton was familiar, for example, with Vernon Kellogg's *Darwinism Today* (1907) and with Robert Heath Lock's *Recent Progress in the Study of Variation, Heredity, and Evolution* (1906). Bauer concludes that *Summer* is a "critique of hereditary family studies and their ideas about sexuality," particularly their tendency to hold mothers chiefly responsible for their children's "defects" (29). But while Bauer opens up an important avenue of inquiry, her conclusion that *Summer* demonstrates the "fitness" of Charity's mother is puzzling, given the profoundly dysgenic image that this mother presents. Moreover, while Charity indeed attempts to rewrite her mother's story, her reinterpretation suggests that maternal sacrifice—and silence—are necessary for evolutionary progress.

Wharton's engagement with the debate about eugenics is most obvious in her juxtaposition of the "civilized" town of North Dormer with the "passive promiscuity" of the mountain community and in her interest in what joins the two: She describes Liff Hyatt, for example, as a "sort of link between the mountain and civilized folk" (55), and much of the novel's plot revolves around Charity's efforts to learn the "history of her origin" (73). Charity's initial encounter with a "weak-minded old woman," "cowed children," and a "ragged man sleeping off his liquor" (85) gives her little incentive to claim as family these "poor swamp-people living like vermin in their lair" (86). Later, when Charity returns to the mountain seeking a connection with her mother, Wharton, like Chopin, freely mingles images of animal and "lower" human reproduction to describe a clearly dysgenic mountain mother, who sleeps on a bare floor with children "rolled up against her like sleeping puppies" (258).

It is from such "stock" that Liff Hyatt comes. Examining his physiognomy, which includes "feverish hollows below the cheekbones" and the "pale yellow eyes of a harmless animal" (56), Charity wonders disdainfully whether she is related to him. Significantly, Hyatt appears just after Charity has indulged in an extended sensual reverie, in which she imagines that "every leaf and bud and blade . . . contribute[d] its exhalation to the pervading sweetness in which the pungency of pine-sap prevailed over the spice of thyme and the subtle perfume of fern, and all were merged in a moist earth-smell that was like the breath of some huge sun-warmed animal" (54). Since Charity responds to "all that was light and air, perfume and colour" with "every drop of blood in her" (21), Liff's intrusion on her reverie seems to serve a monitory function, his undesirable physical appearance warning against indiscriminate couplings. For while comingled plants produce a "pervading sweetness," Charity's following the dictates of nature over the necessary restrictions of civilization will lead, in Wharton's vision, to hereditary misery.

Indeed, while Charity eventually exonerates her mother's careless breeding, Wharton rejects this mother's maternal model as fundamentally flawed. What makes Charity's mother dysgenic is not, primarily, the sexual promiscuity that leads to her pregnancy but the lack of maternal instinct that leads to promiscuity of another sort. Recalling his trip to rescue Charity from the mountain, what Lawyer Royall recalls most contemptuously about Charity's mother is that "she'd have given [Charity] to anybody. They ain't half human up there" (73). Charity, however, recasts her mother's actions as a laudatory instance of maternal sacrifice, asking, "What mother would not want to save her child from such a life?" (260). Charity's positive reinterpretation of her mother's story influences her own decision to marry Royall and raise her child within a "civilized" patriarchal family. Indeed, her selfless decision to raise her child as if it were Royall's not only resembles her mother's choice but literally duplicates it. Yet even as she follows her mother's example, Charity repudiates her maternal promiscuity, demonstrating her superior instincts by twice refusing to give up her child: once when she instinctively recoils from the abortionist and again when she determines that "it was impossible to tear asunder strands of life so interwoven" (231).

What Charity does inherit, and agree to reproduce, is her mother's silence. Like her mother, who dies the very picture of silence, "with lips parted in a frozen gasp above the broken teeth" (250), Charity is finally able to speak only through her now maternal body. Noticing physical "marks of her [pregnant] state," Charity knows such signs will speak loudly to the "watchful village" and that "even before her figure lost its shape . . . her face would betray her" (235–36). Paradoxically, Charity demonstrates that she is a "good girl" (290)— that is, unlike her mother—by allowing her body to announce her pregnancy, while she remains silent about its illicit origins. By choosing to raise her child in the "civilizing" environment of North Dormer, Charity acknowledges the town's salutary effect on her own life, endorsing the law of the father over the unspeakable story of her mother.

Ultimately, both *The Awakening* and *Summer* suggest that sexual transgression is far less threatening than maternal irresponsibility. Chopin's and Wharton's shared feminist project of representing women's lack of reproductive agency through their literal and symbolic lack of voice is thus limited by their capitulation to the necessity of reproducing race. Where Gilman's evolutionary rhetoric predicated racial advancement on women's prior emancipation, Chopin and Wharton concede the primacy of race as an ineluctable limitation on white women's freedom. In the 1920s, as more women appeared to reject the call of romance, and the increasing availability of birth control allowed them to sever the link between sex and reproduction, an intensified need to "secure mothers for the race" breathed new life into the image of the mother-woman. For, according to the prevailing discourse, only "mother-love," that quality in women that allowed them to devote themselves tirelessly not only to their children but to the race, could redeem a nation beset by challenges to the racial and reproductive order.

4. Hard Labor: Edith Summers Kelley's *Weeds* and the Language of Eugenics

"THERE IS NO FORM of life lying nearer Divinity than mere protoplasmic animation, but in some manner is imbued with the sentiment of mother love . . . the human heart knows no higher sentiment. Husbands may turn against wives, and wives may give up husbands; children may repudiate parents and fathers disown sons—but the mother love abides forever." So wrote Hamilton Mercer in *Overland Monthly*'s May 1920 tribute to Mother's Day. In less ecclesiastical but no less certain terms, the child-care expert Dr. William Emerson, a frequent contributor to women's magazines, argued in the January 1922 issue of *Woman's Home Companion* that "the ambition of the normal woman to be an ideal mother is the greatest influence for good that we have." In the early 1920s, despite the ascendancy of the New Woman and the sexual freedom she represented, the cult of True Motherhood was alive and well. If, as the psychologist Phyllis Blanchard believed, sex literature had "come out into the market place," giving Americans "articles about the new sex ethics" and stories of the "psychopathology of sex" (541), America's popular journals—from *Ladies' Home Journal* to the *Pictorial Review,* from *Good Housekeeping* to *Scribner's*—continued to extol the virtues of the "mother-woman."[1]

Even Margaret Sanger invoked the appealing rhetoric of "mother-love" to further her campaign for birth control. Every month Sanger's *Birth Control Review* featured letters from overworked mothers asking for the secret of contraception. Capitalizing on a sort of "mother knows best" philosophy, Sanger captioned the August 1923 section of readers' letters "The Guiding Power of Mother Love: Letters Showing That Mother-Love Points the Way to True Morality." The testimony of Sanger's readers, who asked for more information about birth control not in order to refuse motherhood but in order to become better mothers, offered a seemingly unassailable argument for contraception, one advanced by and for the traditional mother.

Certainly, Sanger did not question the naturalness of the mother instinct; she merely hoped to release motherhood's full power by giving women control over the number and spacing of their children. Indeed, Sanger argued that, far from neglecting her maternal duties, a woman freed from reproductive "slavery" would be all the more motherly: "The bloom of mother love will have an opportunity to infuse itself into her soul and make her, indeed, the fond, affectionate guardian of her offspring that sentiment now pictures her but hard facts deny her the privilege of being. . . . She will want children with a deeper passion, and will love them with a far greater love" (*Woman* 180–81). Sanger at once critiqued and reinscribed the nineteenth-century ideal of consecrated motherhood, concluding that "being the most sacred aspect of woman's freedom, voluntary motherhood is motherhood in its highest and holiest form."

While Sanger presented the goals of her birth control campaign in somewhat romanticized terms, social scientists in the 1920s were more explicitly interested in the practical rewards of scientifically controlled reproduction. "If America does not produce a great race what else matters?" asked Albert Edward Wiggam, a popular lecturer on heredity, whose best-seller, *The Fruit of the Family Tree* (1922), typifies popular interpretations of eugenics. Wiggam stressed the particular importance of women to the eugenic goal of improving the (white) race and, with it, the nation: "It is peculiarly to woman that America looks for the realization of this ideal. She is the natural conservator of the race, the guardian of its blood. Eugenics means the improvement of life, and if we can improve life, produce better human beings, they will themselves improve everything else. Only a noble race will or can build noble institutions" (280). Because birthrates among white, native-born, middle-class women reached an all-time low in the 1920s, the mandate for such women to reproduce was intensified in this decade.

Yet if both birth control and eugenics discourses extolled the power of motherhood, the mother herself was strangely effaced by their mutual focus on the child as the "product" of their efforts. Thus, even as Margaret Sanger broadcast women's pleas for birth control in the *Birth Control Review* (which she edited from 1917 to 1929), her own analysis came to focus on birth control's effect on future generations, defining reproductive freedom in terms of its evolutionary potential.[2] Her profoundly conflicted rhetoric at once insisted on women's right to birth control—drawing on the particularly moving stories of poor women worn out by maternity—and justified this right in terms of the middle-class imperatives of race progress and national advancement. In the 1920s the cause of reproductive freedom, as defined in Sanger's work and in popular representations of eugenics, was underwritten by the still-compelling rhetoric of racial betterment.[3]

Edith Summers Kelley's *Weeds*, published in 1923, told a different story, one that drew on and extended Kate Chopin's critique of the self-effacing "mother-woman" ideal. For Kelley's heroine, Judith Pippinger, the wife of a Kentucky tenant farmer, children are economically as well as psychologically crippling. Rejecting a eugenic view of mothers as evolutionary vehicles, Kelley depicts the material conditions under which reproduction becomes a form of bodily colonization. Thus Judith, worn out by the simultaneous demands of tenant farming and child raising, comes to view her children, one born and one unborn, as "two little greedy vampires working on her incessantly, the one from without, the other from within . . . bent upon drinking her last drop of blood" (208). Where Sanger portrayed the maternal relationship as mutually enhancing to mother and child, Kelley imagined the life of the child as literally feeding off the mother. Focusing on a working-class woman's reproductive plight, *Weeds* is concerned with the relationship between production and reproduction and (like *Contending Forces, The Awakening,* and *Summer*) with the extent to which nature—and cultural constructions of the "natural"—determine women's lives. The very title of *Weeds* highlights Kelley's desire to interrupt the tendency to conceive of reproduction as a natural resource, as when M. S. Iseman complained in his 1912 treatise, *Race Suicide,* that "prolific inferior races invariably drive out the superior, as the weeds of the garden overwhelm the plants" (131). Self-consciously positioning her novel against portrayals of "inferior" mothers in social scientific and popular writing of the 1920s—her first chapter invokes the common perception of "backwoods corners of America, where the people have been poor and benighted for several generations and where for as many generations no new blood has entered" (*Weeds* 13)—Kelley reveals the limitations of the white middle-class birth control movement, as well as the distance between the ideals of scientific motherhood and the experience of working-class mothers.[4]

But the most noteworthy contribution of Kelley's novel is its extended and detailed description of childbirth, which is without precedent in American literature. Intended as the central chapter of *Weeds*, Kelley's groundbreaking portrayal was cut from the novel when it first appeared in 1923. It was not restored in 1972, when the Lost American Fiction series reprinted the novel and thus did not see print until the Feminist Press reissued *Weeds* in 1982. Yet even since the Feminist Press reprinting, *Weeds* has received remarkably little scholarly attention, though its few critics have concurred that it is aesthetically accomplished as well as historically significant. Barbara Lootens has suggested that because the novel fits uneasily into literary categories, it might fare better with women outside the university, particularly women who "circumscribed by poverty, tradition, and biological demands . . . must confront the reality of lives little different from those of their mothers and grandmothers" (105). It is not surprising that, as a working-class novel, *Weeds* remains underappreciated by mainstream literary critics; yet given its groundbreaking portrayal of childbirth and maternity, feminist critics' failure to reclaim *Weeds* as a central text of the American women's literary tradition is inexplicable. The novel's import becomes even more apparent when set against the language of eugenics that dominated discussions of motherhood in the 1920s.

The "Rising Tide" and the "Civilizing Force"

By the 1920s Margaret Sanger had become the most visible spokesperson for the birth control movement and had allied her cause with the male medical establishment and with leaders of the eugenics movement. Sanger's first American Birth Control Conference (1921), for example, featured several prominent eugenicists, as well as Lothrop Stoddard, author of the negrophobic treatise, *The Rising Tide of Color against White World-Supremacy.* That Sanger came to deny her own socialist and anarchist roots—so evident in the radical message of her short-lived journal, *The Woman Rebel* (1914)—in order to attract prominent members of the medical profession has been well documented and often bemoaned.[5] Sanger's decision to back a "doctors only" bill, for instance, kept birth control in the hands of the middle class, for whom it had long been unofficially available. Angela Davis points out the unfortunate repercussions of birth control's professionalization; in the hands of the medical establishment the fight for women's reproductive freedom soon changed into an argument for population control, and "what was demanded as a 'right' for the privileged came to be interpreted as a 'duty' for the poor" (210).

Yet Sanger's capitulation to the goals of the medical and eugenics establishments was perhaps inevitable, given that the cause of reproductive freedom had come to be inextricably linked to the middle-class rhetoric of racial and national advancement in both scientific and popular writing.[6] Just as birth control advocates were dependent for practical reasons on physicians, the cause of women's reproductive freedom was symbolically dependent on the biological importance that eugenicists attributed to the mother. Certainly, eugenicists were among the minority of Americans who publicly endorsed birth control. Against continuing objections that birth control would lead to race suicide, Albert Wiggam enthusiastically trumpeted: "The truth is that birth-control may be the greatest instrument for race progress ever attained by any species" (324). Similarly, Dr. William J. Robinson, an early champion of women's sexual freedom, argued in his *Eugenics, Marriage, and Birth Control* (1922) that "the first means for the improvement of the human race [is] a knowledge of the means of prevention of conception, of regulating the number of one's offspring" (33).

Not all eugenicists were as enthusiastic about birth control; many of the most prominent favored other means of "improving the race." Some, like Dr. Charles Davenport of the Eugenics Records Office, endorsed "positive" rather than "negative" eugenics, arguing that eugenic goals would be better met by encouraging the "good stock" to have more children than by providing the means by which they, as well as the poor, might avoid children (M. Haller 91). Even Wiggam acknowledged that birth control could be a "two-edged sword." Wiggam quelled his own doubts by positing a form of natural selection through which "women of the right sort—the women whose natures we want transmitted through the blood of the race—find a vaster 'freedom,' a deeper knowledge of life and its great mysterious beauties in a home filled with children than the gadabout ever finds with all her sophistication and so-called 'freedom'" (324). Wiggam thus obviated the problem of women's self-selection for motherhood by suggesting that the offspring of women deviant enough to reject maternity would, by definition, be undesirable.

Given such reservations within the eugenics movement, Sanger had good reason to emphasize the "racial" benefits of birth control. Still, her own rhetoric was deeply conflicted in the 1920s. On the one hand, Sanger continued to champion birth control as a means to women's emancipation, arguing that "women in the past have been confronted with the empty victories of political freedom, of economic freedom, of social freedom" and that only "biological freedom" would bring about an era of true emancipation ("Civilizing Force" 537). Indeed, she went so far as to claim that "eugenics without birth control [is] a house builded upon the sands. . . . It cannot stand against the furious winds of economic pressure which have buffeted into partial or total helplessness a tremendous proportion of the human race. Only upon a free self-determining motherhood can rest any unshakable structure of racial betterment" ("Birth Control" 12). On the other hand, maternal freedom and (white) racial advancement were tactically linked in works such as *Woman and the New Race* (1920), where Sanger states baldly that "birth control . . . is nothing more or less than the facilitation of the process of weeding out the unfit, of preventing the birth of defectives or of those who will become defectives" (229). Here she begins by protesting woman's role as "incubator and little more," arguing that access to birth control will give a woman time to develop "other faculties than that of reproduction." Yet these other faculties are valuable chiefly because they can be "transmit[ted] to her offspring" to "make for a greater race" (227). As Sanger pictures the evolutionary process, what is good for women is "naturally" good for the race: "Womanhood shakes off its bondage. It asserts its right to be free. In its freedom, its thoughts turn to the race. Like begets like. We gather perfect fruit from perfect trees. The race is but the amplification of its mother body . . . beautified and perfected for souls akin to the mother soul" (233).[7]

Sanger's genetic metaphors reflect an increasing interest in the "mother body," in part a holdover from the nineteenth-century social purity movement and in part a response to increasingly frank discussions of sexuality in the 1920s.[8] Alongside traditional encomiums to mother love, Sanger inscribes an idealized image of the mother body, differentiating the impure from the pure in search of the "perfected" mother. If the nineteenth-century republican mother was to harness her innate morality to the task of raising better citizens, the twentieth-century mother's most important duty was to keep her body pure for racial reproduction. This shift from the moral essentialism of the cult of True Womanhood to the biological cult of the mother body effectively diminished the maternal role from that of moral agent to that of physical vessel.

It is in this context that Sanger's 1928 collection of letters, *Motherhood in Bondage,* defines "two classes of women," differentiating good blood from bad. Sanger devotes one chapter of this collection to "The Struggle of the Unfit," offering a sampling of letters from mothers unsuited for maternity, ostensibly because of their unusual frailty but often for no reason other than their extreme poverty. Yet Sanger defines working-class mothers' need for birth control not on the basis of their economic oppression—exacerbated by too many children—but on the basis of their physical inferiority, applying to class differences a version of the biological determinism invoked in contemporary discussions of race. Introducing letters from economically impoverished mothers, Sanger writes: "Here is an almost endless series of cases which demonstrate that certain women ought to be totally exempt from the ordeal of maternity. If indeed there is a certain class of women predestined by Nature to the high calling of motherhood, it is no less evident that there are others completely unfit for it" (60). Sanger's use of the term *class* to distinguish women not by economic position but by biological "fitness" suggests how far the birth control movement had strayed from its radical roots.

Sanger does not hold this latter class of mothers responsible for its own relentless, and seemingly irresponsible, reproduction. Rather, she observes, in a remarkable backhanded compliment, that "despite their limitations, their lack of education, these mothers reveal themselves strangely conscious of their duty to the race, of the sacredness of their maternal function, of their realization that the life-stream must be kept clean and fresh" (*Motherhood* xvii). Sanger strategically interprets these women's desire for birth control not as an attempt to preserve their own health or better their economic condition—which, in comparison to the eugenic "race work" to be done, might appear selfish—but as a noble desire to abstain from motherhood in the name of eugenics. Those who might persist in denying birth control to those in need would certainly compare unfavorably to these high-minded, if "low-class," mothers.

While Sanger's own published work had enormous influence—she claimed in her autobiography to have received more than a million letters from women eager to learn more about birth control—by the 1920s the conjoined issues of reproductive rights, maternal responsibilities, and racial advancement found expression not only in birth control and eugenics propaganda but also in the most popular women's magazines. Not surprisingly, these concerns were intertwined with issues of political power during the first decade of women's enfranchisement. Maternal and infant care was one of the first causes for which women used their newly won power as voters; even before the Nineteenth Amendment was ratified, women lobbied for the Sheppard-Towner Maternity and Infancy Protection Act. A feature article by Anne Martin in the February 1920 issue of *Good Housekeeping* solicited support for this bill by reminding its female readership that "our enfranchisement has been urged not only because it is just, but because the weapon of the vote will arm us more effectively to protect women and children, to improve the race." It asks: "Now that American women are practically enfranchised, will they use their political power for this purpose?"

Entitled "Everywoman's Chance to Benefit Humanity: An Everlasting Benefit You Can Win in a Week," this article points out indignantly that, in the previous year, the federal government had allotted $47 million to protect farmers against the loss of hogs, corn, and cattle, while "to prevent the avoidable loss of mothers and babies [it spent] just $47,000,000 less" (Martin 20). Such comparisons were in fact commonplace, reflecting the prevalence of eugenic reasoning in a variety of venues. Margaret Sanger argued that "no civilization worthy of the name can permit the perpetuation of a system of disastrous breeding upon human beings which would be condemned immediately by the federal government if it were practiced by breeders of livestock" (*Motherhood* 62). Albert Wiggam complained that "the United States Government knows exactly how many pedigreed pigs were born in America in the last twelve months, but does not know how many babies were born;

that the government knows officially the quality of its best hogs, mules, horses, sheep, cattle and goats, but does not know officially the quality or ancestry of its best or worst human beings . . ." (293).

The *Good Housekeeping* article demonstrates how women might use their reproductive labor as a political lever in response to such apparent devaluation of motherhood. Observing that "the service to the state that women render in bearing children has received a new emphasis" (Martin 20), in part because World War I had depleted the male population, this article describes women as wielding an inestimable untapped power. Thus Julia Lathrop, head of the recently established Children's Bureau, tells readers that "as women now emerge into joint control of the resources of the world, they will find themselves forced to insist that mothers shall no longer make bricks without straw, that the scientific means for safeguarding her children must be at the command of every mother." Lathrop emphasizes the power that women accrue by bearing children for the state as well as their attendant duty to become scientifically educated: "In the new partnership between men and women which now supplants the ownership, the headship of men, the first and simplest duty of women is to safeguard the lives of mothers and babies. . . . Motherhood has too long suffered from sheer sentiment and has not been treated with common sense. . . . As true sentiment and respect for motherhood develops, we shall depend upon scientific knowledge and make it universally available" (Martin 147).[9]

Yet even as *Good Housekeeping* sought to replace "sheer sentiment" with science, the magazine invoked the reassuring qualities of True Motherhood to win over skeptical readers. Its May 1920 article by Anne Monroe, "Adventuring in Motherhood," sings the praises of public health nurses and doctors, focusing on the work of female doctors trained in science but nonetheless amply maternal. Readers are invited to follow the reporter into the office of Dr. Maud Wilde, of Los Angeles's Mothers' Educational Center, to observe her eugenic efforts, which are seemingly an extension of her maternal instincts:

> I am going to take you straight into her laboratory for perfecting human life, that you may see for yourself the work going on under the small, tender, womanly hands of a tender, womanly woman who realized long ago—when her own babies were born—that the miracle of enlightenment did not take place with the miracle of birth, and that women needed to be taught how to be mothers.
>
> For Dr. Wilde discovered that it isn't merely the babies of uncared-for foreigners who die like flies in a trap, but the babies of the good old stock, often still-born, often lost during the first month, often needlessly sacrificed to the early ideal of false modesty that has hedged our best families about with a wall

of ignorance regarding the most important work that will ever be put into woman's hands. It was this good American blood that she especially wanted to perpetuate, and these good American mothers that she especially wanted to help. (Monroe 130)

Mother love meets eugenic science in the person of this manifestly maternal physician, who is above all a warden of "good American blood."

Continuing its praise of women's contribution to race progress, the same article credits Dr. Margaret Clark of Waterloo, Iowa, with reforming the typical baby beauty contest by devising the "first score card ever used in judging a baby, based on score cards used by stockmen" (137). The explicit analogy between breeding cattle and babies exposes the product-oriented ideology of scientific motherhood. The image of the commodified baby (and of the mother as producer of this child) in this white middle-class journal uncannily resembles an image familiar from the slave narrative, that of the slave mother and child on the auction block (though, of course, these white babies are merely "graded" and not sold).

Most interesting, however, is the article's conclusion, which invokes at once the language of progressive reform and the logic of racial evolution:

> And now, having seen the practical work of all these far-visioned physicians, we must see that though they differ in method, they are moving in one general direction toward a better race through better birth. Scientists, philanthropists, and social workers have been steadily creeping back, and back, and back in an effort to get in behind the trouble. . . . They left the adult to work on the adolescent, the adolescent for the younger child; then they went back to his first five years, till they at last reached the moment of his birth. . . . Now, at last, they have gone clear back to the original source, to the child's very conception—yes to the mother before his conception. How crablike our growth seems; how we go forward only by going back! (Monroe 138)

Paradoxically, precisely because it focuses on the child, the pursuit of racial perfection ends with the mother, who assumes importance by virtue of her womb. For if the child represents a seed of evolutionary hope, the mother's body is its first soil. Indeed, the mother's role is overdetermined, for as Sanger argued in "The Civilizing Force of Birth Control" (1929), "whether we be partisans of heredity or of environment as the chief factor in the life of an individual, there can be no denying this [mother] factor—since the mother is both environment and heredity" (536). A persistent tension in social Darwinist thought (and in progressive reform movements) regarding the relative influence of environment and heredity is here reconciled in the all-important body of the mother, the "original source" of the race. Yet in the evolutionary logic of this analysis, the mother can only be conceived of as an antecedent, a step backward, a skin to be shed.

Was woman to bring forth the "completed man," as Ellen Key argued as early as 1909? Or was she to give birth to herself? Would birth control be championed primarily for the good of the race or for the feminist cause of women's sexual and reproductive agency? While the answer of the now-allied birth control and eugenics movements was clear, two critical literary depictions of motherhood in the 1920s offered different formulations of the problem. Drawing on the heightened interest in the mother body, and on the cultural interest in desentimentalizing maternity, Edith Summers Kelley and Nella Larsen both depicted the physical realities of childbirth in greater detail than their predecessors and wrote beyond the ending of the sexual awakening novel to explore the economic and psychological consequences of maternity.

A Tool of Nature's Cunning

While the inevitability of motherhood is central to Chopin's and Wharton's plots, the experience of motherhood remains at the margins of each novel; in *The Awakening* Edna's own experience of childbirth is "recalled faintly," while Wharton banishes the only mother figure in *Summer* to a remote mountain community and ends her narrative before Charity gives birth. Kelley, on the other hand, continues her heroine's story well beyond the birth of her first child and calls attention to the crucial difference between her novel and what she calls "roseate fiction" by having her heroine reject books that "never tell what happens after [marriage]" and end with "happy ever after" (120).

In *Weeds* the ending is all too clear: children come at the rate of one per year, exhausting Judith's physical and emotional health. The letters that Margaret Sanger received from mothers during the twenties suggest that the pace of childbearing in *Weeds* is not exaggerated. Despite the proliferation of discourse about birth control in the media, reliable methods of contraception remained out of the reach of most women. Public dissemination of birth control information would remain illegal until 1936; meanwhile, working-class women were unlikely to have access to the private physicians who were allowed to prescribe contraceptives.[10]

Kelley's novel extends Sanger's efforts to make the physical realities of motherhood an integral part of the public debate about reproduction and birth control. While Sanger's argument for birth control increasingly reflected the goals of the medical establishment, she nonetheless recognized the unique power of the stories that she collected from women who had no access to doctors. The case histories of economically oppressed mothers were, she knew, particularly powerful ammunition against those who opposed birth control. "These documents," Sanger wrote of the letters collected during her career, "give us something that we cannot obtain from any number of 'maternity surveys' or 'biometric computations' of vital statistics—the secret, never-told factor of maternal anguish and sacrifice" (*Motherhood* 42). Sanger believed that the mother's story was the stuff of literature and that literature—because it had the potential to reveal the personal—might effect change where tracts could not. Motivated by a desire to tell the unvarnished truth about motherhood, Kelley adopts and adapts the language of American literary naturalism—particularly its emphasis on biological and environmental determinism—to examine women's seemingly inevitable reproductive fate. In *Form and History in the Naturalist Novel* June Howard describes the "documentary logic" of American naturalist fiction, which centers on a "plot of decline or fatality" that "structures the narrative as the anatomy of a progressive deterioration" (142). For the artist-heroine of *Weeds,* as well as for the heroine of Nella Larsen's *Quicksand,* which I discuss in the next chapter, this deterioration is precipitated by the act of giving birth, suggesting that, for women, biology is destiny in a more fundamental way than for the male protagonist of the naturalist novel. Yet embedded in both novels is a critique of the social conditions that make motherhood an insurmountable obstacle to artistic creation.

Kelley's critique is limited, in part, by her audience. That the reading public or, at any rate, the publishing industry was not prepared for a critique of reproduction—for unsentimental depictions of maternity in general and of childbirth in particular—is nowhere more evident than in the editorial response to Kelley's depiction of her heroine's first labor. Kelley asks her readers to witness childbirth firsthand, and her depiction of Judith's unremitting anguish is a powerful antidote to false sentimentality about motherhood:

> All the time Judith paced up and down the kitchen floor like a wild tigress newly caged. When the terrific spasm of pain would grind through her body, she would grasp the nearest object and utter, again and again, the strangely unhuman shriek, a savage, elemental, appalling sound that seemed as though it could have its origin nowhere upon earth. . . . As she stiffened, she trembled violently with terror of what was to befall her. . . . But there was no saving her. In the iron grip of the demon, she grew first rigid as a statue, then bent, twisted, writhed in a hopeless, yet desperate, attempt to wrench herself away from his hold. . . .
>
> For her there was no longer any return from the ghastly No Man's Desert of pain into which she had been snatched by a strong, pitiless hand again and again for so many long hours. . . . Stretched out on the bed as on some grisly rack of

torture, she still gasped, strained, ground her teeth and uttered again and again the growl of struggle ending in the fierce snarl of agony. (338–39, 344–45)

Kelley's depiction of childbearing as a terrifying torture that makes women unhuman; her personification of nature as a treacherous demon; and her image of labor as a "No Man's Desert of pain" make this scene the centerpiece of her analysis of reproduction, crucial to her deliberate revision of the "mother-love" myth. Certainly, Kelley was determined to spare her readers no detail in her graphic seventeen-page account of childbirth. Her editors at Harcourt, Brace objected to such realism, however. Scrawled atop Kelley's manuscript is the following advice: "We feel that this chapter should be greatly condensed or cut entirely. It is common to the lot of all women and not to Kentucky alone. It has been done over and over again in modern realistic novels" (Kelley Papers).

While Kelley eventually acquiesced to her publisher's demands, fearing that to leave the scene in would cause some readers to dismiss her entire book as "hysterical" (Goodman 361), its absence significantly blurs her intended focus. Indeed, because they did not read this pivotal scene—originally placed precisely in the middle of the novel—reviewers focused on the "local color" aspects of *Weeds*. Kelley received ample praise for her rendering of the dialect, as well as the physical landscape, of rural Kentucky, and some reviewers noted the oppressive conditions under which her white tenant farmers labored. Few, however, put issues of maternity at the heart of the novel.

Yet *Weeds* is chiefly the story of Judith Pippinger, described as a "poppy among weeds" (88), who begins the novel full of life—with the promise of becoming an artist—and ends physically and spiritually broken by the demands of motherhood. The plot alone would seem evidence enough of Kelley's concerns: after her marriage Judith bears one child a year for three years, desperately aborts a fourth, and then—after attempting suicide—refuses to sleep with her husband, determined to have no more children. "But what is remarkable about that?" her editors seem to say. Predisposed to view women writers as regionalists, Kelley's editors could not appreciate an aspect of the plot not directly connected to Judith's geographic origin. Ironically, precisely because Judith's plight is universal—a quality greatly prized in male-authored "classics"—it is deemed insignificant. Indeed, when Kelley resisted cuts in her manuscript, Alfred Harcourt wrote to tell her: "We don't think you need all of the first obstetrical incident. It is a powerful piece of writing and is what thousands of women go through, but—almost therefore—it is not peculiar to the story of Judith or the Tobacco country" (Harcourt to Kelley).

Even more interesting is the perception that childbirth had been done "over and over again." As just the opposite was true, this dismissive response

signals not a fear of redundancy but an unwillingness to cover uncharted
territory. There had been, of course, veiled references to childbirth, generally accounts from outside a closed door (as in Upton Sinclair's *The Jungle*) but
nothing approaching the detail or length of Kelley's depiction.[11] Kelley felt
that only a woman could achieve a realistic portrayal; as she explained in a
letter to her publisher, "I had never read in the works of a woman novelist—
obviously a woman is the only one who could do it justice—an adequate
description of a childbirth, so I concluded that the job was waiting to be done
by me" (Goodman 361). In fact, one of the only forums for literary depictions of maternity was Sanger's *Birth Control Review*, which published short
stories and drama with obvious political aims. While Kelley took care not to
write propaganda, she was familiar with Sanger's work and may well have
taken her novel's title from a 1922 short story in the *Birth Control Review*.[12]
Certainly, she considered the difference that birth control would have made
to Judith's story. At the top of what appears to be an early draft of *Weeds*,
Kelley inserted in longhand: "Mrs. Sanger should send an apostle into these
wilds" (Kelley Papers). Like the childbirth scene, this observation is not included in the published novel.

While Kelley was determined to produce a long overdue literary account
of childbirth, she was equally intent upon widening the purview of women's
fiction beyond its middle-class parameters. Convinced that American readers, weaned on romance, would "not want to know anything about anybody
who is poor, with the exception of the poor young girl who takes the eye of a
millionaire and the poor young man who successfully makes love to his em-
ployer's daughter," Kelley attempts to revise readers' expectations by offering a sympathetic portrayal of an impoverished rural heroine ("Can an Artist Exist?" 4). Kelley, like her mentor, Upton Sinclair, was a lifelong supporter
of labor causes.[13] As Sinclair's secretary from 1906 to 1907, Kelley also participated in his short-lived experimental community at Helicon Hall during the
same years. The forty or so intellectuals who lived in this colony, which featured communal kitchens and nurseries, included Sinclair Lewis, the suffragist
Francis Maule, and Stella Cominsky, a niece of Emma Goldman's (Goodman
354). But Charlotte Perkins Gilman, a visitor to the community in Englewood,
New Jersey, made the strongest impression on Kelley. In her 1934 reminiscence,
"Helicon Hall: An Experiment in Living," Kelley, like Gilman, challenged traditional views of "natural" motherhood, advocating communal child rearing.
Describing the community's separate quarters for children, Kelley wrote: "I
know that many will raise their hands in horror and call these Helicon Hall
mothers unnatural creatures. A little unbiased observation, however, will
convince anybody that even the most conventional and maternal of mothers

likes to be able to eat her meals in peace and quiet and to have her social intercourse with other grown-ups undisturbed. . . . The colony did this for its mothers at the same time that it gave the children a wonderful time and a very desirable training" (11).

If Kelley, who was not yet a mother during her stay at Helicon Hall, recalled its child-care arrangements with particular fondness, it was perhaps because her own experience was to teach her that female artistry was incompatible with traditional motherhood. In a letter to Upton Sinclair, also from 1934, Kelley wrote: "Kids and young people help to keep their parents young; and that has to be my recompense for having raised my three instead of cultivating my gift for writing. Some women seem to manage to do both; but conditions have made it just too hard for me."

The "conditions" of Kelley's life included periods of near-poverty; she and her husband, Fred Kelley, lived in a tenant shack while managing a tobacco farm in Kentucky and later attempted unsuccessfully to farm in California's Imperial Valley. In 1923, after the failure of this farm, Kelley requested an advance from Alfred Harcourt, which, by enabling her husband to stay home from his job at a slaughterhouse, would free Kelley from her child-care obligations and allow her to revise the manuscript of *Weeds*. As Charlotte Goodman notes, given the constraints on Kelley's own artistic life, *Weeds* is at least partly autobiographical; Kelley, who was to write only one other novel, was, like Judith, an *artiste manqué* (359). Yet Kelley's own experience of writing "underneath the same roof with three irrepressible children who had nobody to care for them but me" (qtd. in Goodman 359) made her unusually sensitive to the material conditions of motherhood as they conflicted with those necessary for artistic production. Kelley's depiction of maternity must be seen, then, in terms of the parallels that she sets up between the alienated worker and the unwilling mother, both of whom inevitably suffer under capitalism. At the same time, by questioning the naturalness of unremitting childbearing, *Weeds* critiques the philosophical determinism of the naturalist novel.

Like the male naturalists Stephen Crane, Jack London, and Frank Norris, Kelley emphasizes the influence of environment and heredity on her heroine's "fate." Unlike the heroes of most naturalist novels, however, Judith Pippinger shows the potential to transcend her environment, for while born into an impoverished Kentucky tenant family, something in Judith's "own inherited nature . . . made her different from her brothers and sisters" (Kelley, *Weeds* 13). From her childhood Judith is unusually sensitive to, and in harmony with, nature. Compared to the women of her community, who are "painfully thin, with pinched, angular features and peculiarly dead expressionless eyes," Judith exudes vitality: "Something more than her beauty set her apart from the others: an ease and naturalness of movement, a freedom from constraint, a completeness of abandon to the fun and merrymaking. . . . Somehow, in spite of her ancestry, she had escaped the curse of the soil" (88).

According to the law of "survival of the fittest," which Kelley invokes several times, Judith should prosper, and early in her married life she indeed rejects the circumscribed existence of a farm wife. With "contempt for the decent and domestic" (25) and a dislike for the inside of houses (116), Judith prefers to remain outdoors sketching the landscape. Her true soul mate, and artistic mentor, is old Jabez Moorhouse, the only person in the community with whom Judith can "enjoy the beauty and strangeness of the world" (170). Yet her artistic nature is ill matched to the life of a tenant woman. As a perceptive neighbor predicts, Judith has "too much life for a gal" (14); precisely because she is more sensitive, she will suffer more, for like everyone else in her impoverished community, she is "foredoomed to failure" (17).

Indeed, Kelley suggests that Judith cannot escape woman's lot because, despite her "superior" nature, she has no more control over her body than do the farm animals. Although the "mother feeling" is an instinct "which rarely showed itself" in Judith (18), she becomes pregnant soon after her marriage to Jerry Blackford. Ignorant of biology, she does not recognize the first signs of pregnancy; for her "the beginnings of the strange disease were shrouded in mystery" (141). While Judith experiences pregnancy as a strange pathology, she could not be more in keeping with the "natural" order of reproduction as understood by her community. Appealing to her married neighbor, Hat, for advice, Judith is told that her pregnancy is nothing more nor less than that of a cow, though as Hat ominously predicts, "Wimmin have troubles caows don't never even dream on. You'll find that out afore you're married long" (147–48). Indeed, the early months of Judith's pregnancy are described as a "dismal nightmare" (149).

Apparently defeated by maternity even before her child is born, Judith endures "oppressive" visits from well-meaning matrons, then sits "slackly in the old rocking chair, her long hands hanging limp like dead things" (157). Yet Kelley makes clear that Judith's response to pregnancy is not inevitable but the result of ignorance. Hat, for example, is surprisingly knowledgeable about the early stages of pregnancy, though she has no children of her own; presumably, Hat knows methods of birth control or abortion that she does not share with Judith. Nor can Judith ask her mother, who died prematurely after bearing five children and suffering three miscarriages.[14]

While the similarity of Judith's plight to her mother's suggests an inevitable repetition of female experience, Kelley critiques the conditions, not the essence, of motherhood. By symbolically linking women's maternal work to specific material conditions—here, to the futile labor of the tenant farmers—*Weeds* interrogates the means of reproduction as well as production. Just as capitalism imprisons the worker—Kelley compares Judith and Jerry's daily trips to the tobacco barn to "the factory hand go[ing] to his daily dungeon" (150)—so do pregnancy and motherhood enslave women. As Judith says of her first child (a son): "It was astonishing that so small a creature should make such heavy demands . . . but dislike her bondage as she might, she was his slave" (158–59). The plight of the worker and the mother are not only analogous but intertwined, for Judith's "enslavement" to motherhood has economic as well as emotional repercussions. Her child-rearing labor jeopardizes the couple's chances of a successful tobacco crop, for after the birth of her first child Judith "no longer went with Jerry to the field to hoe or top tobacco. The baby could not be left alone in the house" (158).

Judith's literal confinement deprives the family of her much-needed agricultural labor and dulls her own artistic sensibility. With nothing to sketch for months on end but the the view from her kitchen window, Judith delights in rare trips to town, where she observes "niceties of tone and line and color, things for which she had no words but which were becoming with each year of mental growth more pregnant with suggestion" (181). These "pregnant" artistic suggestions prove abortive, however, for Judith finds that she is already pregnant with her second child.

Not surprisingly, Judith does not welcome this pregnancy, which occurs inconveniently during a drought that ruins the tobacco crop. If Judith's first pregnancy is as natural as a cow's, her second is both unwelcome and unnatural, for Judith's body continues to produce even when the land does not, exacerbating her family's poverty while deadening her own spirit. Judith's second pregnancy "induce[s] in her a state of body and mind in which, in order to endure life at all, she instinctively closed herself up from it as much as she could . . . plodd[ing] through the round of her daily tasks like an automaton" (189). As Kelley details these tasks, in which child care plays a significant part, they appear impossible to accomplish even without the burden of pregnancy:

> Families must be fed after some fashion or other and dishes washed three times a day, three hundred and sixty-five days in the year. Babies must be fed and washed and watched and kept out of mischief and danger. . . . Cows must be milked and cream skimmed and butter churned. . . . Diapers must be washed, and grimy little drawers and rompers and stiff overalls and sweaty work shirts and grease-bespattered dresses and kitchen aprons and filthy, sour-smelling towels and socks stinking with the putridity of unwashed feet. . . . Floors must

be swept and scrubbed and stoves cleaned and a never ending war waged against the constant encroaches of dust, grease, stable manure, flies, spiders, rats, mice, ants, and all the other breeders of filth that are continually at work in country households. (195)

During this pregnancy Judith, worn out by the continuous labor demanded of a farm wife, comes to view her children as vampires. Indeed, Kelley suggests an inverse relationship between the health of the mother and that of her children. As pregnancy drains her vitality, Judith becomes little more than a vessel for future life: "She was heavy with a great lethargy, as if the life within her, in its determination to persist, were slowly and steadily draining her, leaving her body nothing but a shell, a limp, nerveless, irritable, collapsing shell" (208). Her second baby, also a boy, is born "surprisingly fat and healthy," yet "his health and vigor [is] obtained at the expense of his mother" (210).

As Kelley describes Judith's growing awareness of her powerlessness, she makes more explicit her earlier comparison of motherhood and slavery, literalizing Chopin's image of motherhood as a sort of "soul's slavery": "More and more [Judith] chafed against the never relaxing strain of being always in bondage to them. . . . They were so imperious, so rigorously demanding in the supreme confidence of their complete power over her. They were so clinchingly sure of their ascendancy. They gripped her with hooks stronger than the finest steel. If only she could have been a willing victim . . . but she could not. She strained away, and the hooks bit into her shuddering flesh, unalterably firm, enduring, and invincible. She knew that they would never let her go" (217). Judith has as little power over her children as the tobacco farmers have against the American Tobacco Company. As a disgruntled farmer complains: "You damn betcha they got us by the throat" (232).

Yet Kelley saves her most explicit image of bondage, that of "hooks in shuddering flesh," for the mother enslaved not by capitalists but by her own body. Thus when Judith finds that she is pregnant for a third time, "her features [contract] into an expression of mingled rage and horror" (236), and she begins to question whether bearing a child every year is woman's "natural" fate: "She felt that she had neither the courage nor the strength to go through with it all again, and so soon after the last time. Her flesh cringed at the thought and her spirit faltered. And when the child was born it was only the beginning. She loathed the thought of having to bring up another baby. The women who liked caring for babies could call her unnatural if they liked. She wanted to be unnatural. She was glad she was unnatural. Their nature was not her nature and she was glad of it" (240). As in *Contending Forces, nature* is a slippery term. Yet while Kelley implicitly questions a monolithic conception of woman's nature, as defined solely by maternity, she is too much the realist to provide her heroine with an escape from her predicament. Thus Judith's budding rebellion soon changes to resignation, "the thought of her own utter helplessness against her fate settl[ing] upon her like the weight of something dead" (240).

In contrast to the detailed description of Judith's first labor, the birth of this third child, a girl, is reported undramatically: "In October the baby was born." And, while Judith's sons have grown strong at the expense of her own strength, her daughter, Annie, "a skinny little mite weighing not much more than five pounds," is born as weak as Judith has become (246). Certainly, Annie does not inherit any of Judith's exceptional characteristics; rather, Annie will merely take her place in the inevitable, and seemingly futile, reproductive cycle. When Annie later becomes ill, Judith wonders fatalistically: "Of what use after all that this baby should live?" Indeed, she has seen "dozens of just such little girls as this one that had come out of her own body: skimpy little young-old girls . . . who grew into . . . the sordid burdens of too frequent maternity" (321).

Significantly, with the birth of her daughter Judith begins to realize the full price of maternity, for this child born "out of her own body" is finally not hers at all. The conditions of reproduction seem particularly to alienate mother from daughter, for to bear a female child is to produce a self-replicating link in a reproductive chain. Judith has reluctantly borne Annie, only to see her absorbed into an endless cycle of too-frequent maternity. Like Marx's alienated worker, Judith is estranged from the fruits of her labor, for "in every way [Annie] was a product of the life that had brought her into being, and that life would claim her to the end" (321). Annie, in her turn, will presumably live just long enough to bear a daughter who will repeat the cycle. Far from the optimistic rhetoric of the Swedish feminist Ellen Key, who pictured children as the stepping-stones of generational progress, Annie does not represent a step up the evolutionary ladder. Rather, under the impossible conditions of reproduction the race would seem to stagnate, for in Annie's "puny, colorless, young-old face" Judith sees the "accumulated patience of centuries" (280). Certainly, Judith, the novel's only "rare specimen," will be swallowed up by the relentless process of reproduction.

Yet Kelley offers Judith a short reprieve from maternal cares. Borrowing from and revising the plot of *The Awakening*, Kelley explores both the liberating and inevitably limiting consequences of sexual awakening. After the birth of her daughter Judith has a brief affair with a traveling evangelist. While maternity has been a sort of waking death, sexuality offers the promise of rebirth; thinking of her lover, Judith "thrill[s] to the feeling of newness, of life born again, that stirs through a summer dawn" (276). She is again in harmony with nature and keenly sensitive to her surroundings. In sensual language recalling that of *The Awakening* and *Summer,* Kelley describes Judith's heightened appreciation of nature: "The scent of flowering milkweed distilled out into the hot sunshine was heavy and sweet. Heavier and sweeter was the smell of purple alfalfa blossoms blown across the pasture in warm whiffs" (276). If childbirth is a nightmare in which Judith's body is overtaken, this sexual affair is a dream that restores her to possession—and sensual appreciation—of her own body.

Like Chopin, Kelley uses the metaphor of awakening not only to describe Judith's rekindled passion but also her inevitable accommodation to reality. Judith's sexual abandon is thus itself described as a sort of sleep from which she "did not want to be awakened" (276). While her rediscovered sexuality makes her feel "glad, bold, and strong . . . like some primal savage woman" (279), she eventually awakens to the repercussion of her affair: "In September the thing she had begun to dread happened. She found herself with child. To her bodily misery and disgust were added a misery and disgust more deeply seated, more hateful and appalling. How could she bear to bring this child into the world? . . . The whole thing was too horrible and monstrous to think about. . . . She must find some way to keep it from happening" (282). Judith's seeming betrayal by nature allows her to overcome a "powerful physical revulsion" and attempt to "interfere with nature in its course" (282).

When several folk methods of abortion fail, Judith decides to drown herself, in a scene that rewrites the ending of *The Awakening* by rejecting its lingering romanticism. While the limitless expansion of the sea offered Edna liberation through death, Judith meets a far less romantic fate in the horse pond: "She plunged out boldly straight across the swimming mud and filth of the cowlot . . . there was no slackening of her steps as she came near the tawny pool, but rather an increase of speed; and when she reached the edge she flung herself instantly into the water and disappeared as inconsequentially as if she had been a stone or a clod of dung" (286).[15] If Edna was "Venus rising from the foam" (173), Judith, as befits Kelley's realism, is a creature of the earth.

Judith does experience, however briefly, the exhilaration that Edna feels as she swims out to sea. Kelley notes that Judith "had not been in the water since she was twelve years old. Yet now she swam, vigorously and toward the bank. Even above humiliation and despair there rose in her a sense of power and triumph as she realized that she was master of the water" (287). The act of swimming returns Judith, like Edna, to an experience from her girlhood, in this case to a time before she was subject to the oppressive burdens of maternity. Unlike Edna, however, Judith is literally brought back to earth: "When she was within a few feet of [the opposite bank] she remembered suddenly that she had not come to the horsepond to swim. She relaxed her body and tried hard to sink. The next moment her feet touched the slimy ooze of the bottom and she saw that the water was not above her shoulder. Standing there breast high in the muddy water with the ooze welling up between her toes, she caught herself thinking that she was glad she had not put on her shoes, which were nearly new. Suddenly she began to laugh, wildly, hysterically into the rainy night. . . . She waded to the bank, still laughing insanely" (287). The prosaic details of the muddy water and the new shoes replace Chopin's "seductive voice of the sea"; unable to choose even her own death, Judith is no doubt more typical than Edna of women worn down by maternity. Indeed, the story of Judith's subsequent life, which wavers between outbursts of rage and dull monotony, continues the stories of *The Awakening* and *Summer,* which, to Kelley's mind, must have seemed unfinished.

While Judith proves too strong to die, her suicide attempt brings about the desired miscarriage, and when this miscarriage leaves her permanently exhausted, Judith tries one last time to defy nature's rule by refusing to sleep with her husband: "She was through forever, she told herself, with having children and with running any risk of having children. . . . Her flesh recoiled and her spirit rose in fiery protest against any further degradation and suffering. Too long she had been led along blindly. Now her eyes were open and she would be a tool no more of man's lust and nature's cunning. She would see her path and choose it. She would be mistress of her own body" (299–300). Yet this belated assertion of agency proves useless, for "the stimulation that had come to Judith out of her determination to have no more children died away as all stimulation must, leaving her listless and slack" (306).

Eventually reconciled to her husband, she realizes the "uselessness of struggle. . . . Like a dog tied by a strong chain, what hope was there in rebellion for her or hers? Peace was better than struggle, peace and a decent acquiescence to the things which had to be," namely, an endless cycle of "bearing and nursing babies and rearing them as best she could" (330–31). Certainly, the logic of the plot, which details Judith's decline from "a poppy among weeds" to a "dog tied by a chain," overwhelms the revolutionary potential of her unsuccessful rebellion. Given Kelley's determination to write a realistic story of working-class motherhood, and her decision not to send a "birth control apostle" to Judith's aid, the transformation of Judith's "fiery protest" to "decent acquiescence" is perhaps inevitable.

In the closing pages of the book Kelley represents Judith's final defeat through her changed perception of the landscape that once inspired her to draw. As Judith surveys the land, "a weight like a great, cold stone settled itself upon her vitals; and as she gazed out over the darkening country it seemed to stretch endlessly, endlessly, like her future life, through a sad, dead level of unrelieved monotony" (333). Her bleak vision has its immediate cause in the death of Uncle Jabez, the only person with whom Judith has felt an artistic connection, but its deeper cause is the lack of agency, particularly reproductive agency, without which life will be a monotonous round of maternal duties. The "great, cold stone" suggests at once the unwelcome weight of her inevitable future pregnancies and the deadening of sensation that has made any emotion, much less the overwhelming passion of "mother-love," foreign to her being.

No Man's Land

While Kelley implicitly links Judith's physical and emotional deterioration to social conditions—to her ignorance of birth control and to her family's poverty, both of which are remediable—nature itself appears most responsible for Judith's condition. Yet in the expurgated childbirth scene Kelley draws a more complicated portrait of this most "natural" event, presenting the process of giving birth as at once dehumanizing and potentially empowering. Initially, Kelley suggests that Judith's own laboring body betrays her, "driving, driving, driving, with the force and regularity of some great steel and iron monster" (345). Nature becomes a "fiend . . . constantly at her side" and Judith herself is dehumanized, devolving into ever more animalistic states. As Jerry listens with terror, she utters a "deep-toned, guttural, growling sound that ended in a snarl. It was not like that of an ordinary dog; but more as Jerry imagined some wild, doglike creature, inhabitant of lonely waste country, might growl and snarl over its prey. Could it be Judith who was making this savage sound?" (343) Indeed, the atavistic regression so central to the male naturalist text is here effected by childbirth: "Her eyes, wide open, stared at the ceiling with the look of eyes that see nothing; and her gums were fleshed in the snarl like the gums of an angry wolf" (343–44).

Yet between descriptions of Judith's wolflike cries are suggestions that the female body is all powerful, for in the act of childbirth woman becomes at once sub- and superhuman, particularly from a male perspective. To Jerry, Judith takes on "gigantic proportions": "She was no longer Judith; she was something superhuman, immense and overpowering" (345–46). She is the conduit of a "terrific, invincible energy" and hers is a "herculean" and "never-ending" struggle: "It was her fate only to struggle on desperately, blindly, knowing only one thing: that each struggle meant the suffering of anguish that is unbearable and that yet must and will be borne; and to do this endlessly, endlessly, endlessly, without rest, without respite" (345). Judith's efforts are indeed nothing less than heroic; the childbirth scene represents the only point at which Kelley deviates from her own realist imperative. Unlike the futile toil of the tobacco farmers, woman's reproductive labor is elevated to epic proportions, suggesting the latent power of maternity.

Finally, however, the language of industrial production dominates this most intimate human scene; Judith devolves from human to animal to machine as the "drive of some great piston . . . relentless and indomitable . . . drove through her quivering body" (344). In this integral chapter women's lack of reproductive agency is figured through the involuntary process of childbirth that, like a machine, is "incessant as clockwork" (344). Judith's necessary resignation to the physical demands of birthing encapsulates the fatalism attached to motherhood throughout the text: "Through no volition of her own, but following only the grimly pointing finger, because follow she must, as a leaf is drawn upon a downward current, the girl entered between the towering entrance boulders of that silent canyon and passed far away from the life of the world" (345).

"That silent canyon" suggests most immediately the state of nonbeing inflicted by the intense pain of childbirth. As the forces of nature take over Judith's body, she ceases to exist in the "life of the world," eclipsed by the imminent arrival of the child. Yet the silent canyon, with its "towering entrance boulders," is itself a sort of birth canal through which the laboring woman might emerge into an alternative world, one that contrasts markedly with the "little-windowed rooms" (116) that Judith associates with domesticity. Thus, even as Kelley emphasizes Judith's lack of volition, she imagines the potential power of childbirth by which a woman might simultaneously give birth to a child and to herself. She thus anticipates the rhapsodic childbirth scene in Meridel LeSueur's novel *The Girl* (begun in the 1930s but not published as a novel until 1978), in which the laboring heroine, surrounded by a community of women, gives birth to "a girl a woman a mother" (131).

Unfortunately, in the absence of such community the experience of childbirth remains a "sinister canyon through which [a woman] must pass to come back to the world of men" (344). While the labor of birth is a "No Man's Desert of pain," it does not finally remove Judith from an economic and familial order very much determined by a world of men. Under the present conditions of reproduction Judith can only see childbirth—and mother-hood—as nature's betrayal: "Nature that from her childhood had led kind-ly and blandly through pleasant paths . . . had at last betrayed her, treacher-ously beguiling her into this desolate region" (344).

Still, Kelley's childbirth scene seeks to complicate her readers' understand-ing of the natural. Uncle Jabez voices the paradox by which Judith, in all ways a child of nature, is nonetheless denatured by maternity: "You'd otta be out over the hills . . . a-runnin' wild with the res' o' the wild things: grass an' wind an' rabbits an' ants an' brier roses an' woodchucks an' sech. That's where you'd otta be, Judy. But I expect you won't never git back there no more. Waal, I s'pose the world has gotta be kep' a-goin'" (351). His words suggest the dis-crepancy between Judith's individual desires and nature's apparent mandate that women bear children. Jabez's commentary invokes the naturalists' priv-ileging of evolutionary law: "Ah well, it's nater. It's nater, that must have her fun with all of us, like a cat that likes to have a nice long play with every mouse she ketches" (350). Yet given Kelley's consistent attempts to dis-equate hu-man and animal reproduction—as when Judith's husband remarks of her childbirth that "if she'd been a caow, she'd a been dead long ago" (345)—Jabez's resignation to nature is clearly meant to be critiqued.

If Kelley's childbirth scene stops short of voicing a direct challenge to the economic and social conditions under which motherhood remained a curse, she does include a cautionary tale that reflects the latent power of materni-ty. Near the end of the novel, just as the exhausted Judith decides to choose "peace over struggle," another villager chooses to destroy what she cannot escape: "It was in April that they took Joe Barnaby's wife, Bessie Maud, away to the insane asylum. For a long time she had been given to fits of destruc-tiveness, when she would break dishes, smash window panes and try to tear up the furniture. These fits had of late been more frequent and violent. One day in April she was seized with this urge to destroy, and building a bonfire in the yard had thrown onto it chairs, bedding, and clothes. She had done such things before; but this time her mania had taken a worse turn. Joe, see-ing the smoke from the fire and knowing only too well what it meant, had run up just in time to save the baby, which she was about to throw into the flames. That night they took her away to the asylum" (308). In a doubling reminiscent of *Jane Eyre* and other nineteenth-century women's novels that use the "madwoman in the attic" trope (Gilbert and Gubar, *Madwoman*), Bessie Maud enacts the maternal insanity at which Judith's attempted sui-cide only hints. This tale of attempted infanticide is an ominous reminder of maternal power as it might emerge from its long suppression.

Significantly, while Bessie's neighbors attribute her madness to heredity, Judith allows for a more material cause, having noticed that while the neighbors pity Bessie Maud's husband for "having to provide for so many babies, nobody was heard to waste any pity on Bessie Maud" (167). When Bessie Maud is pronounced mad, Judith alone empathizes, knowing how narrowly she has escaped a similar fate. "Perhaps," she muses, "Bessie Maud had not been able to draw comfort out of the sunset and the late twitter of birds, and that was why life had gone so hard on her" (308).

Bessie Maud's story has an even more chilling conclusion in the response of the community: "It was too bad, the neighbors all told each other. But it wasn't as bad as it would have been a few years earlier when the children were all small. Now Ruby, the eldest girl, was eleven and big enough to cook the meals and take care of the baby; and at last Joe would know what it was to have peace in his house, and that was something" (308). For the tenant women of *Weeds* motherhood not only ages and eventually kills women prematurely but for that reason also drafts young girls into maternal duty. In contrast to the eugenicist Albert Wiggam's picture of women's apotheosis through motherhood, *Weeds* shows that, under conditions of poverty, each generation of women is worn out before the "natural" reproductive cycle is finished.

Unfortunately, Kelley's alternative story of motherhood had a limited audience, perhaps because it was neither romantic enough to suit popular audiences nor didactic enough to be valued as muckraking fiction. Only one reviewer was sensitive to the critique of reproduction implicit in *Weeds*. Writing for the *New York World,* Laurence Stallings supplied the novel's missing moral, even as he praised Kelley for avoiding propaganda: "One may not accuse Miss Kelley of having written a pamphlet in a circuitous way to avoid those of the clergy who refuse the women of the poor the knowledge of birth-control. She does not even suggest that a benign Government might issue pamphlets on the scientific breeding of the human race along with its gratuitous information as to the scientific breeding of hogs. She is too good a novelist for that, and she has a story to tell. The reader may draw his own conclusions as he witnesses the gradual disintegration of a woman's soul" (13). By embedding her portrayal of "one woman's soul" in a materialist critique of reproduction, Kelley documents the plight of a whole class of women who were more typically represented as dysgenic breeders. Yet because the white middle-class ideology of "mother-love" was too deeply entrenched to be attacked head-on, Kelley can only gesture toward the possibility of rejecting the maternal imperative.

For black women writers of the 1920s the ability to refuse motherhood would prove a powerful rhetorical weapon in the antilynching campaign. Yet this refusal depended, paradoxically, on a reinvigoration of the nineteenth-century ideal of heroic black maternity, as well as on the assertion of an essential black self. As Nella Larsen's *Quicksand* would make clear, both formulations made the articulation of biracial nonmaternal subjectivity a near impossibility.

5. Fatal Contractions: Nella Larsen's *Quicksand* and the New Negro Mother

PUBLISHED FIVE YEARS after Edith Summers Kelley's *Weeds*, Nella Larsen's *Quicksand* (1928) offers an equally bleak, if less explicit, portrait of pregnancy and childbirth. Like Judith Pippinger, Larsen's heroine undergoes a seemingly endless cycle of childbearing that subdues her will and ends her earlier ambitions. As Larsen describes the perpetually pregnant Helga Crane, "she, who had never thought of her body save as something on which to hang lovely fabrics, had now constantly to think of it. . . . Always she felt extraordinarily and annoyingly ill, having forever to be sinking into chairs . . . waiting for the horrible nausea and hateful faintness to pass. . . . The children used her up. There were already three of them [twin boys and a girl], all born within the short space of twenty months" (123). Larsen's image of maternity as depletion, as a process that "uses [women] up," echoes Kelley's description of children as vampires who feed on their mother's body. For Helga as for Judith, birth pangs are also death knells. Thus, after the difficult birth of Helga's fourth child (a sickly infant who dies some days later), Larsen predicts Helga's own demise in the final lines of the novel: "And hardly had she left her bed and become able to walk again without pain, hardly had the children returned from the homes of the neighbors, when she began to have her fifth child" (135).

While maternity structures the entire plot of *Weeds*, whose birth scene is literally central to the novel, *Quicksand*'s ending signals an abrupt shift of emphasis.[1] Most of the novel focuses on Helga's attempts to define herself in terms that transcend the racial strictures of the color line. Lacking familial connections to either her dead white mother or her missing black father, and feeling equally alienated from black and white communities, Helga journeys from Naxos (Larsen's fictional version of "the finest school for Negroes in the South [2–3]) to Chicago, New York, and Copenhagen before her return "home to Harlem" sets her running yet again. A perpetual refugee, Helga flees each successive locale when she discovers its limitations on self-definition and self-representation.

What she cannot seem to escape is her own gendered body. In the claustrophobic conclusion of *Quicksand* maternity comes to signify—and literally to embody—the psychic entrapment that Helga feels throughout the novel. In a text filled with references to fate Helga's reproductive fate serves as her final inescapable destiny. Thus Helga, who feels "caged" from the beginning of the novel (27), meets her final "asphyxiation" in motherhood (134). Because Helga has described the bearing of black children as an "unforgivable outrage" (75), and met every previous obstacle with an impulse to "flee," the novel's denouement is not only puzzling but seemingly perverse. Several critics of *Quicksand* have noted its prevalent metaphors of constriction, yet none has examined why Helga's pregnancies become the final instance of "suffocation" (134) in a plot otherwise characterized by a nearly frenetic mobility nor considered how Helga's own biracial identity complicates the issue of racial reproduction. Indeed, the few critics who have examined the issue of motherhood in *Quicksand* have focused on Helga's problematic relationship with her white mother rather than on her own, seemingly inexplicable, maternal fate.[2]

Quicksand's ending can be explained, in part, by recalling the proscriptions against representing black female sexuality in the early twentieth century. If, as Hazel Carby has argued, Helga is the "first truly sexual black female protagonist" in African American literature (*Reconstructing* 174), the novel's inconsistencies point up the difficulty of portraying black female desire even in the sexually liberated Jazz Age. Given the persistent stereotypes of black women's sexuality, Helga—a single and sensual black woman who scorns marriage and middle-class respectability—makes a particularly dangerous subject.[3] By consigning her rebellious heroine to marriage and motherhood, Larsen disavows Helga's illicit sexuality, mitigating its implications. Indeed, Larsen undertakes a preemptive censure of Helga, whose unconsummated desire for Dr. Robert Anderson, the principal of Naxos, is punished by a precipitous marriage to the Reverend Pleasant Green and a nearly constant state of pregnancy that both displays and disciplines her sexuality.[4]

But this explanation accounts for only part of the cultural work performed by the novel's ending, for as Larsen censures Helga's sexual desire, she also forecloses the possibilities suggested by her "thousand indefinite longings" (51). These recurring longings, usually interpreted as sexual, are better un-

derstood as artistic. Though Helga, like Edith Wharton's Lily Bart, expresses her artistry chiefly through her selection of clothing and her artful manipulation of her surroundings, her efforts represent a longing for a self-
constructed identity, an imaginative refashioning of the parameters of race.
Wanting to claim membership with her "own people" without experiencing "self-loathing" (55), Helga defines freedom in aesthetic terms; her self-
presentations make what she calls a "plea for color" (18), an unapologetic
assertion of a new black aesthetic that might remove the stigma of her "racial markings" (55). Since Helga's body (which she views as a place to hang
"lovely fabrics") is her only medium, pregnancy proves lethal to her artistic
ambitions. Pregnancy at once destroys the canvas—for Helga's swollen body
is not a suitable vehicle for the "startling" clothes that are the tools of her
art—and, by cutting off the possibility of self-creation, kills the artist.

As in *The Awakening, Summer,* and *Weeds,* maternity nullifies a heroine's
attempt at sexual self-definition. Like Edith Summers Kelley in particular,
Larsen is interested in exploring the material effects of pregnancy and childbirth on the woman artist. But Larsen's representation of motherhood also
responds critically to racially specific constructions of the New Negro mother. *Quicksand*'s plot revises, in particular, the self-sacrificial model of maternity common in the work of her black female contemporaries. In the 1910s
and '20s the familiar plot of mothers separated from children—common to
the slave narrative and persisting through the turn of the century—was adapt-
ed to protest the growing incidence of lynching, which, between 1882 and 1927,
claimed an estimated thirty-six hundred black lives (Perkins 9). In the context of the antilynching movement the act of bearing children, previously lauded as black women's indispensable contribution to the race, was frequently
interpreted as a form of collaboration with white racism: by choosing motherhood, women provided, in Helga Crane's words, "more dark bodies for
mobs to lynch" (Larsen 75). Thus in works by Angelina Weld Grimké and
Georgia Douglas Johnson, among others, the self-inflicted pain of childlessness came to symbolize a politics of resistance. Yet even as they suggested the
possibility of refusing motherhood, these writers assumed that maternity itself was implicitly rewarding. Indeed, far from questioning the self-sacrifice
expected of mothers (particularly black mothers), most depictions of black
women choosing not to bear children presented this choice as a tragic loss.

Larsen, on the other hand, does not allow her heroine to "refuse" motherhood, focusing instead on the damaging effects of culturally enforced maternity. Revising a long literary tradition in which motherhood was seen as at
least potentially empowering, and its absence a deprivation, Larsen makes
maternity the greatest obstacle to black women's self-realization and artistic

production. In Helga Crane, Larsen attempts to disassociate black woman-hood from motherhood, articulating instead the "selfish" desires associated with the New Woman. Her depiction of the uneasy relationship between motherhood and artistry, between nurturing one's children and defining oneself, implicitly asks for a broader definition of black womanhood. Thus, while lynching and eugenics are explicit topics of conversation among *Quicksand*'s characters, Larsen focuses not on the alleged depletion of the black race but on the aborted birth of a black woman artist, who is constrained by both reproductive biology and definitions of race that render her biracial identity an irremediable "lack."[5]

The New Negro Mother

The 1920s saw a cultural and literary revaluation of black motherhood that drew on and revised images of mothering under slavery to articulate women's role in an emerging black nationalism. Jessie Fauset's "Oriflamme" (1920) pays tribute to the heroic slave mother by using Sojourner Truth's recollections as an epigraph: "I can remember when I was a little girl, how my old mammy would sit out of doors in the evenings and look up at the stars and groan, and I would say, 'Mammy, what makes you groan so?' and she would say, 'I am groaning to think of my poor children: they do not know where I be and I don't know where they be. I look up at the stars and they look up at the stars!'" Acknowledging slavery's damaging effects on mothering, Fauset's poem nonetheless pays homage to the "symbolic [black] mother" who, while "reft of her children, lonely, [and] anguished," yet "look[s] at the stars." Fauset testifies to the power of such mothers to inspire heroic black manhood, for the "myriad sons" in her poem "fight with faces set, / Still visioning the stars" (64).

As white women aspired to the mantle of "scientific motherhood"—wedding their "natural" maternal instinct to science in order to create the best child possible—black women and men sought to revise stereotypical images of the mammy in order to define a "New Negro mother." Thus, when the Daughters of the Confederacy asked Congress in 1923 to erect a statue in memory of black "mammies," Chandler Owen, coeditor of the *Messenger*, responded: "Let this 'mammy' statue go. Let it fade away. . . . Let its white shaft point like a lofty mountain peak to a New Negro mother, no longer a 'white man's woman,' no longer the sex-enslaved 'black mammy' of Dixie—but the apotheosis of triumphant Negro womanhood" (670). Yet older ideologies persisted in many tributes to black womanhood that stressed the feminine virtue of sacrifice central to the Victorian ideal of motherhood. Well into the twentieth century many African Americans justified woman's traditional role by reference to her "natural" aptitudes. Describing the "Risk of Woman Suffrage" in an article for the November 1915 *Crisis,* Kelly Miller, dean of Howard University, argued that "as part of her equipment for motherhood, woman has been endowed with finer feelings and a more highly emotional nature than man. She shows tender devotion and self sacrifice for those close to her by ties of blood" (37). Miller—like many white eugenicists—worried that women's "natural" feelings of devotion would be eroded if they were given the vote; along with the black nationalist Marcus Garvey, Miller was also concerned about the possibility of black race suicide (Rodrique 142). Hoping to reverse black women's decreasing birthrate, Miller bolstered his conservative rhetoric with an appeal to nature, arguing that "the liberalization of women must always be kept within the boundary fixed by nature. Tampering with the decrees of nature jeopardizes the very continuance of the human race" (qtd. in Rogers 165). Even Alice Dunbar-Nelson, herself a successful author who never had children, decried that "our educated and intelligent classes are refusing to have children; our women are going into the kind of work that taxes both physical and mental capacities, which of itself, limits fecundity" (73).

Other prominent race leaders sought to free black women from a narrowly defined biological destiny, defining black women's "race work" in other than reproductive terms. In his April 1925 column in the *Messenger* the journalist J. A. Rogers wrote: "I give the Negro woman credit if she endeavors to be something other than a mere breeding machine. Having children is by no means the sole reason for being" (165). Similarly, in "The Damnation of Women" (1921) W. E. B. Du Bois argued that "the future woman must have a life work and economic independence. She must have knowledge. She must have the right of motherhood at her own discretion" (512). Among black male intellectuals, Du Bois insisted most vehemently that the decision to be a mother be left to personal "discretion."

Yet elsewhere in the same essay Du Bois praises the black mother in terms that would make refusing motherhood a sign of inauthentic blackness. For Du Bois motherhood is linked inextricably to Africa and vice versa: "The father and his worship is Asia; Europe is the precocious, self-centered, forward-striving child; but the land of the mother is and was Africa" (513). Indeed, according to Du Bois, "The great black race in passing up the steps of human culture gave the world, not only the Iron Age . . . [but also] the mother-idea" (513). Du Bois's paean to black women includes mention of Phillis Wheatley's poetic achievements, but he goes on to define black women's real glory in terms of their feminine, and especially their maternal, qualities. Indeed, these qualities overshadow black women's artistic potential, for "perhaps even higher than strength and art loom human sympathy and sac-rifice as characteristic of Negro womanhood" (520).

Thus Du Bois, with a slight to the unnaturally childless white woman, sees "more future promise in the betrayed girl-mothers of the black belt than in the childless wives of the white North" and has "more respect for the col-ored servant who yields to her frank longing for motherhood than for her white sister who offers up children for clothes" (525). Significantly, he does not question the black woman's "frank longing" for children. Though Du Bois frequently bemoaned white men's sexual abuse of black women, which often resulted in unwanted pregnancy (as Hopkins's *Contending Forces* at-tests), his somewhat romanticized image of the black mother seems to out-weigh this concern.[6] Coming from the single most influential racial spokes-man, Du Bois's comments on the power of black motherhood provide a measure of the expectation within the African American community that all women would want to bear children.

Black women's desire to mother was assumed, in part, because the very survival of the race seemed to depend on women's fulfilling their maternal role. Marouf Arif Hasian has demonstrated that African Americans' critique of hard-line eugenics rhetoric in the 1920s was accompanied by a partial endorsement of "reform eugenics," which acknowledged the mutual in-fluence of nature and nurture, endorsing "positive eugenics" over more dra-conian measures like sterilization of the "unfit" (55, 64). Albert Beckham's 1924 *Crisis* article, "Applied Eugenics," argued that "eugenics is interested in breeding for tomorrow a better Negro. One more anxious, more capable, and more courageous to assume a larger share of our economic, political and social responsibilities. No one nowadays doubts unusual abilities in the in-dividual Negro. . . . What the Negro needs and needs now is more attention given to the group" (177). As in the white eugenics movement, this racial "need" could be fulfilled only by encouraging the "better" black women to have children. W. E. B. Du Bois underscored the need for such encourage-ment when he wrote in a 1932 "Negro Issue" of Margaret Sanger's *Birth Con-trol Review* that "the mass of ignorant Negroes still breed carelessly and di-sastrously, so that the increase among Negroes, even more than the increase among whites, is from that part of the population least intelligent and fit, and least able to rear their children properly" ("Black Folk" 166–67). In the same issue Elmer Carter, editor of *Opportunity* magazine, suggested, in language reminiscent of Theodore Roosevelt's, that "birth control as practiced today among negroes is distinctly dysgenic. . . . Negroes who by virtue of their education and capacity are best able to rear children shrink from the respon-sibility" (169).[7]

As in white eugenics discourse the black woman was viewed in terms of what she gave to the race; thus, like white women, black women gained a degree of power from their domestic and reproductive roles. Certainly, many black women embraced traditional female duties. The *Messenger*'s 1927 symposium entitled "Negro Womanhood's Greatest Needs" featured the views of leading black club women, most of whom echoed the opinion of the writer Hallie Q. Brown that "woman is by nature a home-builder" (199). Echoing the tenets of nineteenth-century republican motherhood, Brown maintained that the home was of inestimable importance because it provided the "foundation stone for the best and highest government of state or country" (198). Similarly, Bonnie Bogle of Portland, Oregon, advised that the black woman "never forget her tender womanly and great motherly heritage . . . the highest rung in the ladder of perfect womanhood" (109).

Even those who saw that the black woman's sphere was expanding defined her importance chiefly in terms of her influence on black men, particularly her role in supporting a nascent black nationalism. Thus, while the "New Negro Number" of the *Messenger* (1923) included articles on black women in the workplace, its lead editorial, "The New Negro Woman," asserted that "the New Negro Woman, with her head erect and spirit undaunted is resolutely marching forward, ever conscious of her historic and noble mission of doing her bit toward the liberation of her people in particular and the human race in general. Upon her shoulders rests the big task to create and keep alive, in the breast of black men, a holy and consuming passion to break with the slave traditions of the past" (757). Above all, she was to fight anything that would "arrest the progress of the New Negro Manhood Movement." Her "dauntless courage, unrelenting zeal and intelligent vision" could find no greater use than to help the black man "[attain] the stature of a full man" and so create "a free race and a new world" (757). Apparently, unlike her white counterpart, the black New Woman would contribute to, not undercut, black manhood. Her social role, like her reproductive role, would support an emerging pan-African nationalism, explicitly defined as male. As Carla Kaplan has argued, influential works like W. E. B. Du Bois's April 1919 *Crisis* editorial "Returning Soldiers" and Claude McKay's poem "If We Must Die," published the same year, forged a liberatory discourse "drawn directly from combat and warfare and dependent upon a grounding in normative masculinity, often specifically drawn from the riveting martial imagery of the returning, triumphant, black 369th regiment" (124).

This is not to say that black women writers and activists did not engage with such discourses; consider Amy Jacques Garvey's warning to the United Negro Improvement Association: "Mr. Black Man watch your step! Ethiopia's queens will reign again and her Amazons protect her shores and people. Strengthen your shaking knees and move forward, or we will displace you and lead on to victory and glory" (Lerner 579). Still, black women's concerns about gender inequality were frequently muted in the public presentation of the New Negro movement, as when Alain Locke changed the title of the social worker Elise Johnson McDougald's March 1925 essay for the *Survey*, "The Double Task: The Struggle of Negro Women for Sex and Race Emancipation," to the more moderate (and gender-neutral) "Task of Negro Womanhood" before reprinting it in *The New Negro*.

Thus, more often than not, black women's contributions to what the *Messenger* called "a free race and a new world" were envisioned in terms of traditional gender roles. The popular writer and lecturer E. Azalia Hackley, for example, fused eugenics and New Negro discourses to define the black mother's particularly pivotal role in race building. According to her 1916 volume, *The Colored Girl Beautiful*, the black woman had the "privilege to carve the destiny of a race," for "whatever the colored mother is, millions of colored children will be. A colored mother lives not only for herself and for her own children, but she must live for the race. A colored mother is a success as she measures up to her relation and obligation to the race" (182). The following year the *Crisis* ran an article titled "Little Mothers of Tomorrow," which praised a Cincinnati public school for "teaching the little colored mothers of tomorrow what so many, many mothers of today do not know;—just what is best for the little babe;—just how to conserve the infant for the race!" (Koch 289).

It is precisely the allure of such roles—which defined the "New Negro Woman" primarily in terms of the "holy and consuming passion" that she could kindle in the "New Negro Man" or in terms of her reproductive contribution to future generations—that Nella Larsen has her heroine resist. Rejecting the instrumental roles defined for black women, Helga seeks not to "live for" another but rather to discover simply how "to be" (Larsen 81).

Refusing Motherhood

Larsen was not alone in questioning the cult of the New Negro mother. In poetry, plays, and short stories black women writers in the 1920s reconsidered the personal and political implications of maternity. Many of Larsen's contemporaries emphasized the pain of mothering in a profoundly racist society, drawing on the tradition of slave narratives to launch a literary protest against lynching. If infanticide in the slave narrative served as a desperate means of direct action—at once sparing a child the pain of bondage and

depriving the master of "property"—refusing to bear children in the post–
World War I era signified a demand for political and social change.

Black women's literary protest not only critiqued the conditions of black
motherhood but also tempered overly romanticized representations of the
black mother. The contrast between idealized and critical representations of
motherhood is nowhere more striking than in Langston Hughes's and Georgia Douglas Johnson's different images of the black mother. In his dramatic
poem *The Negro Mother,* Hughes has his narrator proclaim: "I am the black
girl who crossed the dark sea / Carrying in my body the seed of the Free."
Unfazed by centuries of struggle, his indomitable mother carries both the
biological seed and the cultural dream of freedom:

> I had to keep on! No stopping for me—
> I was the seed of the coming Free.
> I nourished the dream that nothing could smother
> Deep in my breast—The Negro Mother. (17)

Johnson, on the other hand, acknowledges that post-Emancipation racism could make childbearing an act of cruelty. In her poem "Black Woman"
(1922) an unnamed woman pleads with her unborn, perhaps unconceived,
child:

> Don't knock at my door, little child,
> I cannot let you in,
> You know not what a world this is
> Of cruelty and sin.
>
> Wait in the still eternity
> Until I come to you
> The world is cruel, cruel, child,
> I cannot let you in!
>
> Don't knock at my door, little one,
> I cannot bear the pain
> Of turning deaf-ear to your call
> Time and time again! (43)

Johnson's poem, like Gwendolyn Brooks's "The Mother" (1945)—which
begins, "Abortions will not let you forget"—reflects the pain of deciding not
to bear a child. Shirley Graham's 1940 play, *It's Morning,* presents a more
disturbing image of a slave mother killing her adolescent daughter before she
can be sold down the river. Graham's protagonist, Cissie, takes her inspiration from the legend of an African ancestor, a woman "straight lak tree, an'

tall, / Swift as a lion an' strong as any ox" (216), who killed three of her children to avoid their being taken as slaves. In Graham's play, written partly in verse, the African (and African American) woman's strength resides in her ability to subvert slavery, even if it means destroying her children. After killing her daughter, an unrepentant Cissie proclaims:

> when da saints ob God go marchin' home
> Mah gal will sing!
> Wid all da pure, bright stars,
> Tuhgedder wid da mawnin' stars—She'll sing! (221)

Cissie has the comfort of knowing that because her daughter has been spared the almost certain sexual fate of black women, "huh teahs will nevah / Choke huh song nor will huh limbs grow hebby / wid dispair" (223).

Ironically, *It's Morning* takes place on the eve of Emancipation; carrying her dead child, Cissie meets the shocked faces of Yankee soldiers who have come to free the slaves. Like Pauline Hopkins, Graham no doubt intended to suggest that declaring slaves "free" did little to stop the sexual exploitation of black women. While Hopkins embraced motherhood despite the continuing reality of rape, Graham offers a bold model for female emancipation in this black woman's courageous, if lethal, actions.

But the most extended treatment of a black woman's choice to mother or murder was set not in the distant past of slavery but in the present, when the prevalence of lynching recreated the slave mother's dilemma.[8] Angelina Weld Grimké's didactic play *Rachel* (1916) was both the first full-length play by an African American woman and the first play written, performed, and produced by blacks. Sponsored by the drama committee of the NAACP, *Rachel* was also, according to its playbill, the "first attempt to use the stage for race propaganda in order to enlighten the American people relative to the lamentable condition of ten millions of Colored citizens in this free republic" (Perkins 8). Like Hopkins's *Contending Forces,* Grimké's play focuses on a highly respectable black middle-class family and is meant not only to appeal to white audiences but to provide black audiences with a positive self-representation.[9]

Rachel's heroine, none too subtly named Rachel Loving, positively exudes motherliness, as do the play's stage directions, which call for a reproduction of Raphael's *Sistine Madonna* as part of the parlor setting (139). Because her greatest ambition is to raise children, Rachel passes the time until she is old enough to marry by caring for a young orphan, Jimmy. In the opening scene of the play Rachel tells her mother: "Ma dear, if I believed that I should grow up and not be a mother, I'd pray to die now." Certain that she will become a mother, however, Rachel channels her maternal instincts into vows to protect her future children: "I pray God every night to give me, when I grow up, little black and brown babies—to protect and guard" (143).

Yet when she learns the circumstances surrounding the death of her father and half-brother ten years before, Rachel's ambitions change. As her mother explains, Rachel's father, a newspaper editor, denounced in print the lynching of an innocent black man. When he refused to retract his words, he was lynched along with his son, who attempted to come to his aid. This grim history, along with Rachel's growing awareness of racism (her adopted son, Jimmy, is called "nigger" and pelted with rocks), lead her to renounce her desire to bear children. Clearly, black children have little to look forward to, for as Rachel's brother, Tom, complains: "We're hemmed in on all sides. Our one safeguard—the ballot—in most states is taken away already. . . . In the North, they make a pretense of liberality; they give us the ballot and a good education, and then—snuff us out" (156).

Yet Rachel is more concerned about how racism affects children: "First, it's little, black Ethel—and then it's Jimmy. Tomorrow, it will be some other little child. The blight—sooner or later—strikes all. My little Jimmy, only seven years old poisoned" (161). Listening to Jimmy weep after his humiliation at school, Rachel makes a solemn vow never to have children of her own: "You God!—You terrible, laughing God! Listen! I swear—and may my soul be damned to all eternity, if I do break this oath . . . that no child of mine shall ever lie upon my breast, for I will not have it rise up, in the terrible days that are to be—and call me cursed" (161). Invoking the joys of motherhood even as she denies herself these joys, Rachel rues her decision "never to know the loveliest thing in all the world—the feel of a little head, the touch of little hands, the beautiful utter dependence." In the most melodramatic and most powerful scene of the play, she affirms that death is more desirable than a circumscribed existence. Plucking the heads off rosebuds and crushing them under her feet—symbolically killing her future children—Rachel says defiantly, "But I can be kinder than You. . . . If I kill, You Mighty God, I kill at once—I do not torture" (102).

Reviews of the play were mixed.[10] While one critic compared the play favorably to *Antigone* (Wyman 447), another wrote that "the drama is a morbid sermon on the after-effects of lynching and the innumerable humiliations to which Negro Americans are subjected" (qtd. in Hatch 137). The most telling critique, however, accused *Rachel* of preaching "race suicide" (Perkins 9). That Grimké's depiction of one woman's refusal to bear children should spark this concern suggests how highly charged issues of birth control were for the African American community. As Elmer Carter observed, the "idea of birth control . . . could not find a quick response in a group which has been led to believe that its racial status was dependent primarily on its ability to increase and multiply" (169) and that, he might have added, was being lynched in record numbers. In the face of the seemingly genocidal intentions of white lynch mobs, the trend for middle-class blacks to limit the size of their families was all the more threatening.[11] Because Rachel (who is intelligent and well educated as well as instinctively maternal) would make an ideal mother, it is not surprising that her refusal to bear children sparked eugenic fears that the brightest and best among the black community would despair of raising children.[12]

Yet far from endorsing childlessness for educated black women, Grimké's play protests the conditions that lead to her heroine's choice. Rachel's decision, hardly capricious or selfish, is based on her observation of the systematic and institutionalized oppression of black people. The obvious tragedy of Rachel's decision is intended to spark action to change such conditions. Indeed, responding to accusations that her play preached race suicide, Grimké defended her subject matter as the one topic most likely to effect social change. Like Pauline Hopkins, who used images of violated maternity to ensure identification across race lines, Grimké believed that motherhood would be a means of engaging white sympathy. Responding to her detractors in an open letter published in the *Competitor*, Grimké explained:

> Since it has been understood that "Rachel" preaches race suicide, I would emphasize that was not my intention. To the contrary, the appeal is not primarily to the colored people, but to the whites.
>
> The majority of women, everywhere, although they are beginning to awaken, form one of the most conservative elements of society. . . . For this reason and for sex reasons the white women of this country are about the worst enemies with which the colored race has to contend. My belief was, then, that if a vulnerable point in their armor could be found . . . it [would] be motherhood. . . . If anything can make all women sisters beneath their skins, it is motherhood. ("'Rachel' the Play" 413–14)

Grimké's appeal depended, of course, on a shared cultural assumption that giving up motherhood entailed a tremendous personal sacrifice, one endured only to spare an innocent child the realities of discrimination and lynching. Thus, far from confirming the black woman's lack of maternal instincts, Rachel's choice testifies to a maternal selflessness that exceeds that required of most white mothers.

Grimké was one of several black women writers to use literature as a means of protesting lynching, yet Grimké offers an ingenious twist on the standard story of a black mother's anguished choice to give up her children.[13] Georgia Douglas Johnson's poem "Black Woman," for instance, pictures a mother imploring her potential children not to come, arousing sympathy for a woman fighting her own maternal urge. Rachel, on the other hand, can hear her future children weeping, begging her not to let them be born: "They come to me generally while I'm asleep,—but I can hear them now.—They've begged me—do you understand?—begged me—not to bring them here;—and I've promised them—not to" (111). Like Margaret Sanger, who justified birth control in terms of its salutary effect on those children already born, Grimké knew that sympathy would flow more easily for innocent (here, unborn) children than for their apparently unmaternal mothers. At the same time, Grimké no doubt intended to make Rachel herself a more sympathetic character by attributing her apparently dysgenic decision to an extraordinary maternal sensitivity to the wishes of her potential children.

While the pathos of *Rachel* stems partly from the loss of a potential mother, Grimké's short story "The Closing Door" presents a more radical analysis of the black woman's position vis-à-vis lynching and mothering. Here, a mother not only finds her "natural" role co-opted by racial violence but feels her body colonized as an "instrument of reproduction." Published in two installments in the September and November 1919 issues of Margaret Sanger's *Birth Control Review*, "The Closing Door" confirms that racism, not feminine "selfishness," kills mother love. Told from the perspective of Lucy, a "forlorn, unattractive, homeless girl-woman" of fifteen, the story reveals the tragic fate of Agnes Milton who, like Rachel Loving, seems born to mother. As evidence of this aptitude, Lucy testifies that while there was "no binding blood-tie" between her and Agnes, "[it] was the mother heart of Agnes that had yearned over me, had pity upon me, loved me and brought me to live in the only home I have ever known" (September, p. 10). Lucy recalls with pleasure the moment that Agnes announced her first pregnancy, in delicate but decidedly joyful terms: "What do you think would be the loveliest, loveliest thing for you to know was—was—there—close—just under your heart?" (September, p. 13).

Agnes's seemingly charmed existence in an unnamed northern city changes dramatically when a telegram arrives from her family in Mississippi, informing her that her brother, jailed for insulting a white man, has died at the hands of a lynch mob: "An orderly mob, in an orderly manner, on a Sunday morning—I am quoting the newspapers—broke into the jail, took him out, slung him up to the limb of a tree, riddled his body with bullets, saturated it with coal oil, lighted a fire underneath him, gouged out his eyes with red hot irons, burnt him to a crisp and then sold souvenirs of him, ears, fingers, toes. His teeth brought five dollars each" (November, p. 10). Agnes faints upon hearing this news, and when she regains consciousness, her maternal instinct has disappeared. As if awakening from a deep sleep, she says, "I've had to live all this time to find out . . . why I'm here. . . . I'm an instrument . . . one of the many." Realizing that as a potential mother, she is implicated in her brother's fate, Agnes is driven nearly mad with grief: "Yes!—Yes!—I!—I!—An instrument of reproduction!—another of the many!—a colored woman—doomed!—cursed!—put here!—willing or unwilling! For what?—to bring children here—men children—for the sport—the lust—of possible orderly mobs—who go about things—in an orderly manner—on Sunday mornings!" (November, p. 10). Agnes subsequently loses all interest in her own unborn child and, when he is finally born, asks only, "Is he dead?" While she professes no desire to see her son, she is still vulnerable to her own maternal instincts, begging Lucy to "Take him away! Take him away! He's been cooing, and smiling and holding out his little arms to me. I can't stand it! I can't stand it" (November, p. 12). Unable to bear the discrepancy between her baby's innocent appeals and his certain bitter fate, Agnes smothers her child with a pillow.

Where *Rachel* decried the loss of a good mother, "The Closing Door" suggests that, given the prevalence of lynching, it would have been more merciful to mother and child alike if Agnes's child had never been born. Moreover, the short story makes explicit what *Rachel* only hints at, that fifty years after Emancipation, black women's bodies were still not their own.[14] For while these middle-class "free" black heroines are not compelled to bear the children of white masters, they are nonetheless "instruments" of a senseless reproductive process, bearing children who are "doomed" to become fodder for lynchers. Still, the tragedy of "The Closing Door" stems less from Agnes's inability to control her own fertility than from the lynching of her brother.

Indeed, while both *Rachel* and "The Closing Door" suggest means of controlling reproduction, neither alludes to birth control; Rachel avoids the problem of unwanted pregnancy by refusing to marry, and Agnes asserts "control" only after her child is born. Mary Burrill's birth control propaganda play, *They That Sit in Darkness* (1919), offered another option. Published in the same issue of the *Birth Control Review* as Grimké's "The Closing Door," Burrill's play extends Grimké's concerns by dramatizing the tragic effects of laws preventing the dissemination of contraceptive information.[15] Where Grimké's emphasis on civil rather than reproductive rights suggests that black women had different political priorities than white women, Burrill's direct focus on contraception reflects the shared goals of black and white birth control activists.[16] Like many white birth control advocates, Burrill defined knowledge of contraception as essential to women's success as mothers. Obviously influenced by Sanger's work, Burrill adopts not only the message but the rhetorical strategy of the white birth control leader. In fact, *They That Sit in Darkness,* which features a public health nurse visiting a black family, draws heavily on Sanger's tale of her own conversion to the birth control movement. Burrill merely changes the cast of characters, from white residents of New York's Lower East Side to a black family in the South.

Sanger's famous story, which she told frequently on her lecture tours and later included in her autobiography, concerned Sophie Sachs, a poor mother of three who was weak from childbirth when Sanger first visited her tenement home.[17] Mrs. Sachs's doctor tells her that she will die if she has any more children, but when she begs him to tell her how to avoid them, he says only, "Tell your husband to sleep on the roof." Mrs. Sachs then turns to Sanger for advice, and Sanger, knowing it is against the law to give out birth control information, also refuses. When Sanger next visits the Sachs household, the mother has died from a self-induced abortion. The moral of Sanger's story is clear: Given the extremity of poor women's needs, the only real crime is withholding from them the means to limit their families.

Burrill's play rewrites this legend to further heighten its pathos. Elizabeth Shaw, a public health nurse, visits Malinda Jasper, the mother of ten children—"eight livin' an' two daid"—who takes in laundry. Mrs. Jasper bears the double burden of helping to support her family economically and providing all the child care, for as she observes, "Daddy he gits home so late he cain't be no help" (68).[18] Yet she perseveres, inspired by dreams of her children's future, particularly her daughter Lindy's scholarship to Tuskegee. Worn out with work, Mrs. Jasper feels that God is punishing her with each successive child, but the nurse assures her gently, "God is not punishing you, Malinda, you are punishing yourselves by having children every year. Take this last baby—you knew that with your weak heart that you should never have had it and yet—" (71).

To this Mrs. Jasper responds helplessly, "But what kin Ah do—de chillern come!" Prohibited from revealing the "secret" of birth control, the nurse bemoans her own helplessness: "I wish to God it were lawful for me to do so! My heart goes out to you poor people that sit in darkness, having, year after year, children that you are physically too weak to bring into the world—children that you are unable not only to educate but even to clothe and feed. Malinda, when I took my oath as nurse, I swore to abide by the laws of the State, and the law forbids my telling you what you have a right to know!" (72). While eliciting sympathy for Mrs. Jasper, Burrill, like Sanger, documents the social costs of withholding birth control information: Without adequate clothing and food Mrs. Jasper's children will surely become a burden to the state, the same power that denied her the means to limit her family.

Predictably, Malinda Jasper dies after attempting to resume work too soon after the birth of her last child. In the play's most poignant moment Lindy, who has been packing her trunk to leave for school the next day, abandons her plans in order to care for her younger brothers and sisters. Having no choice but to assume her mother's backbreaking job, she tells her younger brother to "stop in de Redmon's an' tell 'em dey cain't have de wash tomorrer 'cause—'cause Ma's dead; but I'll git 'em out myself jes ez soon ez I kin. . . . An' leave word fo' Sam Jones 'at he need'n' come fo' de trunk" (74). As in Edith Summers Kelley's cautionary tale, which depicts a daughter taking over the household duties after her mother is driven mad by maternity, Lindy is drafted too soon into the responsibilities of motherhood. Lindy's name, a variation of her mother's, underscores the inevitability of her family's fate, a cycle of poverty enforced by a lack of contraceptive information.

Given the significance of education in African American literature and culture, Lindy's need to pass up an education at Tuskegee would have had a particularly powerful effect on black audiences. At the same time, Lindy's sexual innocence would presumably prevent white audiences from attributing black poverty to personal failure, specifically to sexual "weakness." Burrill's play thus makes a powerful appeal to both audiences, emphasizing the cost of ignorance not only to mother and daughter but to the state.

Burrill's depiction of motherhood rejects the sentimental maternalism of *Rachel* and "The Closing Door," in which even the determination to renounce motherhood signifies black women's profoundly maternal nature. If black women's writing before the 1920s sought to demonstrate black women's equality with white women by emphasizing their intrinsically maternal nature, the degree of selflessness demanded of Grimké's and Burrill's heroines would seem to render further proof unnecessary. Perhaps because her literary predecessors had demonstrated the "fitness" of black mothers, Larsen could dare to suggest, a decade later, that motherhood was an inadequate, if not fatal, means of self-definition. By affirming the importance of the black woman artist over that of the black mother, Larsen overturns the Du Boisian hierarchy that valued the black woman's "sympathy and sacrifice" over her art ("Damnation" 520). Like Kelley's *Weeds*, *Quicksand* explores the conflict between artistry and maternity for women lacking race or class privilege. But Helga Crane's inability to produce either authentic art or authentic children testifies not only to the conflict between artistry and motherhood but also to the marginalization of the biracial subject within the racial and aesthetic politics of the Harlem Renaissance.[19]

An Insistent Desire

The narrative structure of *Quicksand* reflects a set of related thematic tensions at play in the novel. The first twenty chapters, which focus on Helga's creation of her self as an aesthetic object, are marked by Helga's explicit rejection of maternity, her restless pursuit of cosmopolitanism, and her preoccupation with exteriors. The final five chapters, beginning with Helga's desire to "sink back into the mysterious grandeur and holiness of far-off simpler centuries" (Larsen 114), are defined by Helga's acquiescence to maternity, her resulting immobility in a premodern South, and her increasing preoccupation with interiors, specifically with her children, who, as "products" of her body, serve as an index to her "essential" self.

The mobility that characterizes the majority of the novel is motivated by Helga's "insistent desire" to escape racial designations. Her revolt against Naxos and her subsequent flight north to Chicago is the first in a series of escapes to what seem to be progressively freer locales. Yet *Quicksand*'s opening chapter suggests that race will continue to circumscribe Helga's ambitions; although Helga believes that a lack of money "block[s] her desires" (6), the social meanings assigned to color will present the most serious obstacles. Brought up to loathe her black heritage—Helga recalls her uncle's "oft-repeated conviction that because of her Negro blood she would never amount to anything" (6)—she is accustomed to feeling an unidentifiable "sense of shame" (7). A perpetual malcontent, Helga can "neither conform, nor be happy in her unconformity" (7) because of a persistent doubleness within herself.

But Helga's dissatisfaction stems not merely from the "peculiar sensation" of double consciousness that W. E. B. Du Bois attributed to all African Americans. Rather, Helga traces her discomfort at Naxos to her mixed racial heritage and specifically to her lack of family ties: "Negro society, she had learned, was as complicated and as rigid in its ramifications as the highest strata of white society. If you couldn't prove your ancestry and connections, you were tolerated, but you didn't 'belong'" (8). Helga's sense that she is an outcast from both black and white society makes her "prefer to flee"; she is kept running—eventually "moving shuttle-like from continent to continent" (96)—not only because she has no family but because she has no race. Doubly orphaned, Helga continually feels "a lack somewhere" (7), though she can never name or confront this lack. Thus, as she attempts to discover and fulfill her own desires, Helga has "the uneasy sense of being engaged with some formidable antagonist, nameless and ununderstood" (10). While she identifies this "ruthless force" as a "quality within herself" (11), Larsen suggests that Helga is trapped between the stifling social mores of the black bourgeoisie and the racism of white America and Europe. Between the two, Helga finds no adequate means of self-definition.[20]

Of course, on one level Helga is right: the "lack" resides in herself, because race (or rather the ambiguity of her racial origin) is written into her identity, can be read, for example, in her "skin like yellow satin" (2). Much as she avoids racial categorization—the absence of family and thus of obvious racial heritage allows her a certain degree of social mobility—Helga is indelibly marked by this duality. Her "lack" of racial membership thus becomes her one defining characteristic. For this child of mixed heritage "there had been always a feeling of strangeness, of outsideness," and once her father deserts her, Helga never loses her sense of being an "unloved little Negro girl" (23). With no ready-made familial or racial identity she must essentially create herself.

Yet Helga is continually foiled in her attempts to construct a transcendent racial identity, first because she finds no adequate role models among black women (and of course her own white mother is dead), and, second, because her attempts to define herself artistically are undermined by the distorted images of herself that she sees reflected in the eyes of both white and black men. The problem that Larsen addresses in *Quicksand,* then, is not only the problem of self-definition but also the dilemma of self-representation, an issue at the heart of the New Negro movement.

Quicksand is nearly encyclopedic in its presentation of black womanhood, yet Helga is equally contemptuous of the "race woman," the modern career girl, and the socialite, rejecting in turn all the roles available to women outside marriage. Significantly, the novel's race women—the "lean and desiccated Miss MacGooden" (12) and the "five-years-behind-the-mode" Mrs. Hayes-Rore—as well as the "nondescript" women at the employment office—seem to offend Helga chiefly through their lack of visual appeal. The socialite, Anne Grey, on the other hand, offers Helga the beautiful surroundings that she has always craved and is herself a picture of beauty. Intensely color conscious, and particularly attuned to the aesthetics of race, Helga finds Anne "almost too good to be true," and indeed, Anne's face suggests an enviable amalgam of black and white features. "Brownly beautiful," Anne reminds Helga of a "golden Madonna . . . with shining black hair and eyes" (45). Yet Helga is disappointed by Anne's too-easily-assumed prejudices, specifically, her disapproval of "mixed" black and white parties. As Helga observes, Anne "hated white people with a deep and burning hatred . . . but she aped their clothes, their manners, and their gracious ways of living" (48). For Helga, who values "individuality and beauty" (18), and thus admires both "alabaster" and "dusky" skin, Anne's hypocrisy is unforgivable.

The only woman Helga admires is the very minor character Audrey Denney, "the beautiful, calm, cool girl who had the assurance, the courage, so placidly to ignore racial barriers" (62). The light-skinned Denney's crime in the eyes of black society is that she gives parties for, and dances with, white men. To Anne Grey, Audrey's behavior is "outrageous, treacherous, in fact," epitomizing the problem of the "Negro race [which] won't stick together." As Anne instructs Helga: "I've nothing but contempt for her, as has every other self-respecting Negro" (61). Anne's criticism of Audrey depends on an essentialized notion of race, which bases membership on solidarity against outsiders. But for Helga, who has no reason to feel especially loyal to either the white or the black race—she has experienced an "unchildlike childhood among hostile white folk in Chicago" as well as an "uncomfortable sojourn among snobbish black folk in Naxos" (46)—Audrey's ability to move back and forth between black and white society represents an admirable freedom from color politics.

Helga admires as well Audrey's disregard for the sexual mores of the black middle class. To the sexually inexperienced Helga, Audrey's lifestyle presents an intriguing alternative to the marriage imperative, especially because she has given up her plans to marry "one of those alluring brown or yellow men" who promise financial security. Like Grimké's Rachel, Helga recognizes "how stupid she had been [to think] that she could marry and perhaps have children in a land where every dark child was handicapped at the start by the shroud of color! She saw, suddenly, the giving birth to little, helpless, unprotesting Negro children as a sin, an unforgivable outrage. More black folk to suffer indignities. More dark bodies for mobs to lynch" (75).

Yet while Grimké implies that Rachel's future holds nothing once she has given up motherhood, *Quicksand* examines the possibilities available to Helga once she has rejected traditional models of womanhood. Not eager to marry, and aware of the "smallness of her commercial value" (35), Helga is fortunately relieved of her financial difficulties by an inheritance from her uncle. She is thus freed to pursue full time the vocation she seems born to: creating herself as an art object. This project is what consumes Helga's latent artistic impulses, channeling her desires into the construction of an aesthetic self.

Unlike Judith Pippinger, who sketches, Helga Crane has no obvious artistic ambitions. Rather, Helga is bent on creating herself as a beautiful object and an object of desire. As Susan Gubar has suggested, "Many women experience their own bodies as the only available medium for their art" (296).

Certainly, Helga, who is "thrilled" at "beauty [and] grandeur, of any kind" (63), has few outlets for her keen sense of color. Yet like Lily Bart in Edith Wharton's *House of Mirth* (1905), Helga imbues her selection of clothing with symbolic meaning, as when she presents herself in a "cobwebby black net touched with orange" to display her desire to "fly" from Harlem (56). Noting the similarities between Lily and Helga, Linda Dittmar argues that "for [Lily and Helga] bodies, clothes, possessions, and even chance locale are the raw materials of fantasy; their sense of color, texture, and line yields arrangements that make those who view them (and their own self-viewing) resonate to implied narratives of pleasure and transcendence. Encoding themselves through dress, motion, prose, and set, they turn life itself into a heightened aesthetic production" (141).

They practice a dangerous art form, however. The manifestations of Helga's "urge for beauty" are consistently misinterpreted. At Naxos her desire for a "profusion of lovely clothes" (11) is interpreted not as a sign of artistry but as personal "pride" and "vanity" (6). Later Helga's art is indistinguishable from its canvas: While in Chicago, she is "accosted" by both white and black men who take her carefully arranged appearance as evidence that her body itself is for sale (34). Their propositions commodify her art, anticipating her experience in Denmark where her uncle and aunt, Herr and Fru Dahl, appropriate her "exotic" beauty and the portrait painter, Axel Olsen, makes a bid for the image that the Dahls construct.

Stressing the perils of this uniquely female art form, Larsen structures Helga's aesthetic life as a series of struggles between her own artistic desires and the desire that she incites in her viewers. In the opening chapter of the novel, for instance, Larsen establishes Helga's creative talents by presenting her luxuriating in "her own attractive room," a room decorated with "many-colored nasturtiums," a "blue Chinese carpet," and "oriental silk" (1). Helga herself is no less artfully adorned: In a "green and gold negligee" and "glistening brocaded mules," her "skin like yellow satin [is] distinctly outlined" (2). Her assertion of an "intensely personal taste" within the "strenuous rigidity" of Naxos testifies to the power of her artistic impulses (1). Yet as Larsen presents Helga, she has created herself as a static and somewhat clichéed specimen of female beauty. Moreover, Larsen positions her readers as spectators and seems to encourage them to view Helga as an exotic creature. Emphasizing Helga's "sensuous lips," "unrestrained" hair, and "penetrating, dark eyes," Larsen calls for a sexualized response that invokes racial stereotypes and foreshadows Axel Olsen's objectifying gaze.

Competing with this externalized and itemized depiction of Helga's beauty, however, is the insistence of Helga's own desire: her "vague yearnings" (50), which lead her from Naxos to Chicago, from Chicago to Harlem, and from Harlem to Denmark, as well as her "passionate and unreasoning protest" (53) against the limits of each locale. Defining herself against the backdrop of each city, and using the limited materials available to her, Helga alternately accepts and rejects conceptions of herself as an art object. From Naxos, where her colleague Margaret Creighton tells Helga, "We need a few decorations to brighten our sad lives" (14), to Denmark, where the Dahls dress Helga up in exotic clothing, Helga's beauty is appropriated to satisfy her viewers' aesthetic tastes. While Helga enjoys such attention, she seeks a means of self-presentation that would satisfy her need for autonomous definition, specifically an identity outside racial designations.

Unfortunately, the "blessed sense of belonging to herself alone and not to a race" (64) is a short-lived sensation, for Helga is a product of the color-conscious 1920s, and despite her desire to stand outside race, she embodies the era's fascination with "racial" characteristics. She attributes her own love of color, for instance, to an "inherent racial need for gorgeousness" (18), a passion "only Negroes and gypsies know" (69). Appropriately, Helga evaluates each new city in terms of its aesthetic appeal, excited first by the "multi-colored crowd" of Chicago (30) and then by Anne Grey's Harlem apartment, which, like the "continuously gorgeous panorama of Harlem" itself, satisfies her "aesthetic sense" (44–45). Envisioning her future in terms of the spectacle that she will make, she fantasizes about Europe's potential to show her off to greater advantage: "With rapture almost, she let herself drop into the blissful sensation of visualizing herself in different, strange places, among approving, admiring people, where she would be appreciated, and understood" (57). Here, Helga takes an almost sexual pleasure in seeing herself as others see her; appropriately, she finds temporary satisfaction in Denmark because she believes it is, at last, "her proper setting" (67).[21]

Yet Helga's Danish relatives appropriate her aesthetic domain by insisting on choosing clothes for her: "You must have bright things," the Dahls insist, "to set off the color of your lovely brown skin. Striking things, exotic things. You must make an impression" (68). Thus in Denmark Helga becomes little more than a "decoration," a "curio" and a "peacock" (73). While the Danes find Helga attractive in an "exotic, almost savage way," they appreciate her beauty in aesthetic, rather than human, terms, analyzing her body piece by piece like a rare art object. The voiceless Helga (who can understand, but not speak, Danish) hears herself described in the shorthand of art critics: "Superb eyes . . . color . . . neck column . . . yellow . . . hair . . . alive . . . wonderful" (71).

Helga at first revels in such attention: "She was incited to make an impression, a voluptuous impression. . . . And after a little while she gave herself up wholly to the fascinating business of being seen, gaped at, desired" (74). Like her earlier pleasure in anticipating her European debut, Helga's willingness to "give herself up" has overtones of sexual thralldom. But the attention that she receives in Denmark also suggests visual, if not sexual, violation, for after appearing in a dress "cut down . . . [to] practically nothing but a skirt" (70), Helga experiences a feeling of "nakedness" and "outrage" (79).

Still, Helga believes she has escaped a uniquely American racial masquerade. Contemptuous of black New Yorkers who "didn't want to be like themselves . . . [but] like their white overlords" (74), Helga enjoys an atmosphere in which "difference" is to be accented (72), where her own darkness is "rated as a precious thing, a thing to be enhanced, preserved" (83). Yet it is precisely this commodification through preservation (as in Axel Olsen's portrait of her) that deprives Helga of artistic agency. Effectively immobilized as an art object, Helga soon loses her infatuation with Denmark.

Helga's first "nagging aching" for America appears when Olsen's artistic attentions become sexual, though his proposition only makes explicit her real status in Denmark. Far from controlling her own representation, she has been an object of barter, for, by proffering her beauty to Axel Olsen, the Dahls mean to "secure the link between the merely fashionable set to which they belonged and the artistic one after which they hankered" (90). Significantly, Olsen feels entitled to possess Helga sexually as well as artistically, for, having laid claim to her body on canvas, he believes she will "sell [her]self to the highest buyer" (87). His assumption reveals the connections between Helga's sexual and artistic value, both of which are defined by a white audience.

When Helga turns down Olsen's proposition, she rejects an objectifying definition of black womanhood that has plagued her throughout her travels. But her refusal to barter her body as well as her beauty does not enable her to control her own image. Rather, she comes to realize the impossibility of constructing either a new image of herself or a less rigidly defined black aesthetic. She perceives the limits of Denmark's conception of racial difference when she visits the Circus, a vaudeville house where black men "prance" on stage to ragtime music. Finally, a "speculative spectator" (83) rather than an object of art, Helga recognizes the distortions of black art created for white audiences. Knowing that the picture that she presents to the Danes is equally false, she feels both "shamed" and "betrayed," precisely her feelings about Olsen's portrait of her.

Certainly, Olsen perceives Helga chiefly as a racial icon, to the extent that when he makes his sexual proposition, he speaks "seemingly to the pictured face" on his canvas. Unable to hear Helga's rejection, he insists: "You have the warm impulsive nature of the women of Africa, but, my lovely, you have,

I fear, the soul of a prostitute" (87). Not surprisingly, Helga does not recognize herself in Olsen's portrait of a "disgusting sensual creature" who happens to have her features. Yet Olsen's portrait has market value, for "collectors, artists, and critics had been unanimous in their praise and it had been hung on the line at an annual exhibition, where it had attracted much flattering attention and many tempting offers" (89).

Rendered two-dimensional as an object (not a maker) of art, Helga is subject indefinitely to a penetrating white gaze. For Helga the art world does not offer a respite from racial definitions; rather, it heightens their constriction. In a novel characterized by increasing claustrophobia and finally by a complete lack of mobility, Helga's incarceration in this static image marks the beginning of the end. As Ann Hostetler concludes, "Helga finds that one cannot escape from cultural constructs of race in a life of the body—for this is where these constructs are the most imprisoning" (44). Indeed, having learned the racial limits of Europe as well as America, Helga has nowhere further to "flee." After all, Africa appears in *Quicksand* only as a source of aesthetic artifacts—evidenced by Robert Anderson's "dissertation on African sculpture" (106)—not as a potential refuge for the black artist. Helga thus has no choice but to return "home" to Harlem.

Before Helga's return to New York, Larsen depicts her increasing sense of doom in terms that anticipate the novel's unusual, and seemingly inexplicable, ending. When Helga refuses the Dahls' advice to marry Axel Olsen— significantly, because mixed marriages bring "trouble to the children" (78)— she has an "intimation of things distant" that "oppresse[s] her with a faintly sick feeling." The sensation is highly localized, for she feels "a heavy weight, a stone weight, just where, she knew, was her stomach" (80). Similarly, when Helga has decided to leave Denmark, she cannot imagine returning to New York without recalling the "absolute horrors" of black life. This memory induces a "quickening of her heart's beating and a sensation of disturbing nausea" (82).

Helga's premonitions of her future morning sickness and the "stone weight" of pregnancy are the first hints of the narrative's abrupt shift of focus. As if abandoning the problem of race—which she has shown to be an arbitrary, but nonetheless intractable, category—Larsen structures the final chapters of the novel around Helga's uniquely female, and undeniably biological, fate. Helga's incessant pregnancies will both prevent her from creating art and relegate her to the traditionally limiting roles of wife and mother. Yet the American South to which Helga returns also promises to fill her perennial "lack" of identity, providing the "embodiment" of the "intangible thing" she has always "craved" (120). Indeed, her subsequent childbearing might be seen as a means of determining whom she "really" is, by finding out, quite literally, what is inside her. But Helga's alienated response to her children suggests that her biracial identity is as inauthentic as her female art.

An Appalling Blackness of Pain

Helga's return to America precipitates a "species of fatalism" linked specifically to sexuality and reproduction (106): Larsen describes the New York air itself as "impregnated" with the "dead Indian summer" (98). It is particularly telling that this juxtaposition of pregnancy and death opens the chapter in which Helga encounters her ex-fiancé, James Vayle, who attempts to convince her to settle down and have children. If Olsen needed Helga as a model for his art, Vayle wants her to fulfill an equally instrumental function. Helga's realization that she was "in but one nameless way necessary to him" (8) is precisely what led her to refuse his first marriage proposal. Yet when Helga meets Vayle for a second time, and he again proposes marriage, she learns that she is "necessary" not only sexually but as a reproductive vehicle. Helga's view of childbearing echoes the sentiments of *Rachel:* "Marriage—that means children, to me. And why add more suffering to the world? Why add any more unwanted, tortured Negroes to America? Why do Negroes have children? Surely it must be sinful. Think of the awfulness of being responsible for the giving of life to creatures doomed to endure such wounds to the flesh, such wounds to the spirit, as Negroes have to endure." Likewise, Vayle's response echoes the eugenic fears sparked by *Rachel:* "Don't you see that if we—I mean people like us—don't have children, the others will. . . . That's one of the things that's the matter with us. The race is sterile at the top. Few, very few Negroes of the better class have children. . . . We're the ones who must have the children if the race is to get anywhere" (103).

For most of the novel Helga's freedom—defined negatively—has consisted of avoiding such sexual colonization, refusing to become white culture's exotic and erotic Other, as well as avoiding maternal service to the black race. Yet a more active assertion of sexuality—like a more autonomous artistic identity—proves impossible. Only in relation to Robert Anderson does Helga become a desiring subject, "desire burn[ing] in her flesh with uncontrollable violence" (109). Unfortunately, he is unable to return her passion because "no matter what the intensity of his feelings or desires might be, he was not the sort of man who would for any reason give up one particle of his own good opinion of himself" (108). His self-control contrasts sharply with Helga's sudden loss of control, for directly after her encounter with Anderson,

Helga becomes "distracted, agitated, [and] incapable of containing herself," wandering aimlessly through a sudden thunderstorm until she is "tosse[d] . . . into the swollen gutter" (110). Apparently enforcing the traditional punishment for the fallen woman, Larsen lands her sexually transgressive heroine literally in the gutter.

The novel's subsequent plot is at once implausible and necessary. Helga's religious conversion is insufficiently motivated—for Larsen has noted that "Helga Crane was not religious" (34)—and her precipitous marriage to the Reverend Pleasant Green belies her earlier attitude toward sex and marriage. Considering Helga's admiration of Audrey Denney's sexual license, Helga has little reason to atone for her own sexual passion by embracing either marriage or the church. But by reversing both the structural logic and spatial movement of the novel, Larsen signals a shift of focus from exteriors to interiors, from surfaces to depths. Helga's tendency to flee, which has led her out of the South and out of the country, is replaced by an insistent impulse drawing her back to the South, much as the "irresistible ties of race" have called her back from Denmark (92). As her quest for racial freedom becomes a bid for racial membership, her restless cultivation of exteriors, so consistent with the aesthetics of high modernism, turns to a contemplation of her inner self.

What Helga seeks in the final pages of the novel is a sense of racial authenticity associated with a premodern South. The correlation between southernness and "real" Negro life, while by no means the only criterion of authenticity during the Harlem Renaissance, surfaced with some regularity, particularly in white criticism of black art. Thus in a 1923 review for the *New Republic* Robert Littell attacked a production by the Ethiopian Art Theatre not only because it was directed by a white man but also because "its members [were] far from being what Granny Maumee called Royal Black; and they had behind them not the South which is the Negroes' true background, but the dancing and vaudeville background of Chicago." He concluded that "we must look for the real thing in other directions" (21). Conversely, at least one white writer was praised for capturing the "essence" of black womanhood; according to the reviewer Robert Herrick, the black heroine of Julia Peterkin's *Scarlet Sister Mary* (1928) "in her fecundity, kindness, health and happiness . . . embodie[d] many essential qualities of all strong women, more frankly because more primitively than would be possible for her sophisticated white sisters" ("Study" 172). By exaggerating both the ruralness and the fecundity of Helga's southern experience, Larsen subtly parodies such associations, simultaneously demonstrating that, within such narrow definitions of race, biracial identity can only be a "quagmire" (*Quicksand* 133).

Redefining her own aesthetic of black womanhood, Helga initially finds the "dark undecorated women unceasingly concerned with the actual business of life, its rounds of births and christenings, of loves and marriages, of deaths and funerals . . . miraculously beautiful" (121). Yet as much as she would like to "sink back into the mysterious grandeur and holiness of far-off simpler centuries" (114), a return to the South requires a "submission and humility" that she cannot sustain. Thus, when she attempts to "sink back" into women's time-honored occupations, Helga sinks instead into a maternal quicksand. Indeed, the novel's circular structure is ultimately mirrored in Helga's own body, which prohibits movement in proportion to its increasing roundness.

In the final chapters of the novel issues of race seem to take a backseat to maternity, which Larsen describes sardonically as women's "natural" condition. Observing her rural peers, Helga wonders: "Was it only she, a poor weak citybred thing, who felt that the strain of what the Reverend [said] was a natural thing, an act of God, was almost unendurable?" (125). Helga's question undercuts the presumed naturalness of perpetual childbearing; she comes to question as well the morality of marriage, which allows for female sexuality but exacts a high price. Like Sanger's legend of Sophie Sachs, *Quicksand* depicts male sexuality as voracious: the Reverend Pleasant Green, described alternately as "fattish" (115) and "rattish" (118), is aroused by the image of Helga's "emaciated" body recovering from childbirth (129), though he arouses in her only "deep and contemptuous hatred" (134). Because Helga experiences only a brief period of "emotional, palpitating, amorous nights" (122) before the experience of childbirth puts "the vastness of the universe" between them, she concludes that marriage, "this sacred thing of which parsons and other Christian folk ranted so sanctimoniously, [is] immoral" (134).

For Helga, as for all women in this community, marriage leads inevitably to the "appalling blackness of pain" that is childbirth (128). In a novel obsessed with color and with art such a description cannot be coincidental; indeed, the phrase encapsulates the novel's interrelated dynamics of gender, race, and artistic production. It suggests, first, the ambiguity of Helga's racial status, for Larsen surely meant to evoke not only the "blackness of pain" but the pain of blackness, the physical stigma that, among other things, leads Helga's white mother to disown her. Even more interesting is Larsen's choice of the word *appalling,* for if childbirth appalls, it not only horrifies but also makes pale. The whitening of childbirth might be read as a metaphor of erasure, for in becoming a mother, Larsen suggests, Helga loses her own identity, abandoning her search for a racially transcendent aesthetic as she discovers the "inherent" fraudulence of her white-and-black body.

Significantly, Larsen stresses the fundamentally uncreative nature of Helga's life as a mother. Helga, who has always taken pleasure in the sensual and the aesthetic, finds in marriage and motherhood only an "anaesthetic satisfaction for her senses" (118), an anesthetized as well as an unaesthetic state of being. Paradoxically, the pain of labor brings Helga to "an enchanted and blissful place where peace and incredible quiet encompass her," yet it does so at the cost of her sanity, for in the process "the ballast of her brain [gets] loose," leaving her in a "borderland on the edge of unconsciousness" (128). Maternity leaves Helga in a state of consciousness resembling Charity Royall's sleepwalking stupor and Edna Pontellier's loss of self in the sea. Like these earlier heroines, Helga struggles briefly, "determined to get herself out of [the] bog into which she had strayed" (134), but finally "[seeks] refuge in sleep" (131).

Ironically, while Helga has resisted ready-made definitions of race and gender, fleeing both Naxos and Harlem because of the limited roles that they offer black women, her desire to provide her children with a sense of familial, and especially racial, membership is what finally impedes her own movement. Contemplating her options as she recuperates from childbirth, Helga determines "not to leave them—if that were possible. The recollection of her own childhood, lonely, unloved, rose too poignantly before her for her to consider calmly such a solution" (135). Yet her sense of maternal responsibility competes with her sense of her own fraudulent identity, for she believes that abandoning her children might benefit them by eliminating the "element of race" and allowing them and their father to be "all black together" (135). Helga's dilemma points up a marked contradiction in racial ideologies: Although she has somehow produced "black" children out of an inadequately black body, her biracial identity means that actually mothering them will reproduce her own "lack."

A unified black family, Helga believes, can solve the vexed problem of racial identity—offering her children a freedom from race that she can never achieve—but only at the expense of her self. Because she is unwilling to abandon her children as she was abandoned, Helga is literally confined to the bed of childbirth. Thus, despite her attempts to avoid traditional definitions of black womanhood, her final "use" is as a mother. By bearing children who will not be stigmatized by color (and whose racial identity will be less ambiguous without the presence of a light-skinned, "citybred" mother), Helga attempts to rewrite her own painful past; thus, as the prevailing discourse of black motherhood stipulated, she agrees to leave her "indelible marks on the universe" through her children.

Indeed, like the ideal nineteenth-century mother, Helga demonstrates the "glory of a woman," which, according to the nineteenth-century historian William Alexander, was to "live for others rather than for herself; to live, yes, and often to die for them" (599). Yet the death of Helga's fourth child, a "sickly infant," reveals the "futile torture" of her compliance (*Quicksand* 131). The disappointing issue of Helga's pain has "no vitality," suggesting that Helga has "ruined her [own] life" without providing for the life of the race (133). Helga's sacrifice—like Larsen's sacrifice of the "first truly sexual" black heroine as well as a potential black female artist—offers a bleak prognosis for the New Negro woman.

Helga's subjection to motherhood testifies to the constraints on black female sexuality, which even in the sexually liberated 1920s could not go unpunished, and represents the seeming impossibility of black female artistry. The violent destruction of Helga's subjectivity through the relentless process of reproduction (a seemingly "natural" process) provides a metaphor for the death of an artist limited, as Larsen demonstrates, by social determinants. Ironically, Helga, who has been a consumer for most of the novel—for her "art" depends on displaying her own consumption, particularly of clothing— finally creates something besides her own image. Yet she produces children who, far from expressing her self, consume the mother-artist. If Edith Summers Kelley depicted a mother-as-artist, endowing her heroine with "superior" qualities chiefly to demonstrate the price of women's reproductive ignorance, Larsen presents the artist-as-mother, using a monstrous vision of maternity to represent the apparent incompatibility of creation and procreation. Ironically, W. E. B. Du Bois lavished praise on *Quicksand* because he deemed its plot less "defeatist" than those of Julia Peterkin and its themes less prurient than those of Claude McKay. Making no reference to Helga's biracial or maternal identities—or to the quagmire in which they leave her— Du Bois lauded Helga as "typical of the new, honest, young fighting Negro woman—the one on whom 'race' sits negligibly" and whose life is "darkened, not obliterated by the shadow of the Veil" ("Two Novels" 202).

Neither Larsen nor Kelley could voice a direct challenge to the reproductive order of early twentieth-century America. Yet both succeeded in demythologizing the concept of mother love, which apparently has little relevance to their reluctant mothers. Helga thus finds that her child is but a "sop of consolation for the suffering and horror through which she had passed" during labor (127). Her thoughts echo Judith Pippinger's, affirming that "nature's reward for all the anguish" of childbirth is little better than a "deformed abortion" (Kelley, *Weeds* 348). It is a measure of the authors' profound disillusionment with motherhood that in their groundbreaking depictions of childbirth, the newborn infant is not only divested of all sentimental appeal but bears the brunt of its mother's scorn and anger.

In these two novels of the twenties, motherhood—once the defining activity of womanhood—becomes a life-threatening enemy. Larsen's "appalling blackness of pain" and Kelley's "No Man's Desert of pain" offer maternal metaphors that describe both the physical pain of childbirth and the psychological and artistic price of women's lack of reproductive agency. Ironically, a quarter of a century after Pauline Hopkins imagined the rebirth of the black race—claiming for her unmarried black mother the status accorded to white "true" women, and appealing to white women to join a cross-racial struggle against racial and sexual oppression—Larsen and Kelley suggest that black and white women indeed share a common fate. Yet far from affirming the racially redemptive aspects of motherhood championed by Hopkins, much less confirming Frances E. W. Harper's vision of the twentieth century as the dawn of a transformative "woman's era," images of maternity in the 1920s suggest that in their role as childbearers, women are not the literal and symbolic mothers of liberation but merely instruments of reproduction.

Epilogue: Representing Motherhood at Century's End

IN THE FIRST YEAR of the twentieth century, Pauline Hopkins posed a rhetorical question to the readers of the *Colored American Magazine:* "Of what use is fiction to the colored race at the present crisis in its history?" ("Prospectus" 195–96). Her answer, embodied in *Contending Forces* and in her three other novels, was that racial protest literature could bring about profound social change but only if it could effectively cross what W. E. B. Du Bois would call "the problem of the Twentieth Century . . . the problem of the color line" (*Souls* xxxi). For Hopkins the issue of motherhood proved an effective vehicle for appealing simultaneously to black and white women and, indeed, for exposing the color line itself as a disabling fiction.

As the preceding chapters suggest, however, *Contending Forces* was unique among early twentieth-century fictions of maternity in its ability not only to deconstruct but also to reconstruct motherhood. For Hopkins's immediate literary daughters, dismantling the ideal of the "mother-woman" produced decidedly less hopeful narratives, stories shaped and delimited by the very ideologies that they sought to critique. Certainly, the optimism and agency implicit in Sappho Clark's reclamation of motherhood found no echo in the hopeless resignation of Judith Pippinger or Helga Crane.

The increasing fatalism of maternal fictions reflects, in part, the trajectory of early twentieth-century mothers' movements. A case in point is the Sheppard-Towner Maternity and Infancy Protection Act. The product of a cross-class alliance between "grass-roots mothers, club women, and Children's Bureau officials," Sheppard-Towner provided funding for prenatal and infant health clinics as well as educational materials for pregnant women and mothers (Ladd-Taylor, "My Work" 321). Passing Congress by a wide margin in 1921, the Sheppard-Towner Act not only epitomized the success of Progressive Era organizing on behalf of women and children—in 1918, for example, eleven million women contributed to the Children's Bureau's baby-saving campaign—but also seemed to symbolize women's new political efficacy (328). But the increasing political conservatism of the 1920s made it impossible to extend the act's provisions beyond its initial five-year period. When Sheppard-Towner came up for renewal in 1926, opponents denounced its female administrators as socialists, and conservative senators repealed the law two years later, voting down fourteen subsequent attempts between 1928 and 1932 to reverse the repeal (337–38).

Besides the devaluation of maternity implicit in the repeal of Sheppard-Towner, the loss of the first welfare measure targeted at women and children had disproportionate effects on working-class and nonwhite mothers, widening the divisions that maternalist ideals had temporarily bridged. The attenuation of women's cross-racial and cross-class alliances in the immediate aftermath of suffrage, and the largely unsuccessful efforts of second-wave feminists to forge similar alliances, are evident in contemporary welfare-reform rhetoric, which reinforces the notion of separate "classes" of mothers.[1] As Mimi Abramovitz, Gwendolyn Mink, and many others have demonstrated, the welfare policies and practices that encourage some women to remain at home while forcing others into low-wage work have historically been "predicated on racist assumptions that some women (that is, white women) are fit to be mothers and homemakers and thus 'deserve' subsidies allowing them to remain in the home [while] other women (that is, women of color and immigrant women) are deemed 'unfit' nurturers . . . and thus are viewed as better suited to fulfill the demands for certain kinds of market labor" (Chang 271).

In Michigan the contradictions of such policies were made particularly vivid in 1994 when, just as Gov. John Engler proposed making work or school mandatory for all mothers on welfare, a middle-class Ann Arbor college student lost custody of her young son precisely *because* she was enrolled in college. In the Ann Arbor case the child's father won custody because the father's *mother* was willing to stay home to care for her grandchild, while the child's mother—because she was in school—could not. Equating "good" mothering with the absence of day care, this ruling suggested that the best place for middle-class mothers was in the home. Yet for other mothers (in this case, welfare mothers), Governor Engler's plan implied that full-time, stay-at-home mothering was a sign of pathological dependency.

Given the persistent racism of welfare mythology, the inadequately maternal middle-class mother (the mother who should stay home but won't) is most often coded white, while the so-called welfare queen (the alleged drain on national prosperity) is usually coded black. The normalization of such discrepancies in the 1990s makes the similarities between Edith Summers Kelley's and Nella Larsen's narratives all the more striking, for they reflect a moment in history when the problem of maternity solicited fictional responses that resonated across lines of color and class.

The persistence of racial and maternal hierarchies at the turn into the twenty-first century gives us occasion to ask once again, "Of what use is fiction?" How do recent images of maternity reflect and reshape the cultural landscape of motherhood? Certainly, the 1990s saw pregnancy and childbirth covered—or uncovered—by the media in unprecedented ways, from *Vanity Fair*'s August 1991 cover photo of a very pregnant and nearly nude Demi Moore to the first live broadcast of childbirth on the Internet in June 1998 (reported by abcnews.com under the headline "Congratulations! It's a URL!"). Meanwhile, the increasing viability of surrogate motherhood, cloning, and genetic engineering promises to take us into a brave new world of reproductive technologies beside which the technology of birth control appears less revolutionary than routine.[2]

Back to the Future

Nonetheless, recent depictions of motherhood in literature and film draw us inexorably to the past, reframing the early twentieth-century True Mother—and her opposite, the nonmaternal New Woman—in ways that reflect our current racial preoccupations. The fall 1998 film season saw the release of two movies, Jonathan Demme's *Beloved* and Carl Franklin's *One True Thing*, whose dissimilarities speak volumes about racial constructions of maternity at the end of the century. Based on novels of the same title by Toni Morrison and Anna Quindlen, the movies present more radically dichotomized images of motherhood than the novels themselves, though the novels are, unquestionably, worlds apart.[3] Juxtaposing public policy and popular culture, we might ask how, on the eve of the twenty-first century, these films rehabilitated historically intertwined myths of motherhood and race. Specifically, how does nostalgia for the "good" white mother depend upon and sustain fear of the "bad" black mother and vice versa? If, as E. Ann Kaplan argues in *Motherhood and Representation,* the "maternal sacrifice paradigm" governing nineteenth-century melodrama persisted in twentieth-century films—so that, depending on a viewer's identification, the "ideal, self-sacrificing mother threatens to collapse into the evil phallic one" (77)—how is this dichotomy enacted across films marketed for highly segregated film audiences? I want to suggest that, while the novel *Beloved* effectively confronts

the maternal legacies of slavery, in ways that the movie unfortunately atten-
uates, the novel *One True Thing* depends on a racially exclusive construction
of white maternity, in ways that the movie unfortunately intensifies.

Despite the well-intentioned efforts of everyone involved in the movie *Beloved*, the film failed to reproduce two of the novel's most stunning achievements: its ability to convey the invisible, as well as the visible, wounds of slavery, and its insistence that the brutality of slavery affected both genders equally.
Certainly, the marketing strategy for the film *Beloved* relied upon a distortion
of the novel's themes. Titling their respective reviews "The Haunting," "Haunted by the Past," and "Bewitching Beloved," the *Village Voice,* the *New Yorker,*
and *Time* magazine walked a fine line between acknowledging the novel's central metaphor and sensationalizing the film as one more tale of the supernat-
ural (Hoberman 155, Denby 248, Corliss 75). Full-page ads in the *New York
Times* trumpeted the film's cultural significance by proclaiming *Beloved* "One
of the Best Films of the Decade" and predicting that "'Beloved' will swim in
your bloodstream and echo through your bones" like a "spooky beauty and a
natural wonder." At the same time, the movie was pitched as a bitter-but-
necessary spoonful of medicine—a sort of antidote to the disease of racism—
in ads instructing potential movie goers that "America . . . needs to remember its past."

Of course, the novel *Beloved* refuses to provide an easily digestible history
lesson. Rather, it gradually reveals not so much the fact of Sethe's infanticide
but the horrors of its causes and consequences. Morrison's heroine endures
such unspeakable crimes that her decision to murder her children rather than
subject them to slavery becomes comprehensible, if not heroic. *Beloved* thus
shares with Harriet Jacobs's *Incidents in the Life of a Slave Girl* (1861) a critique of conventional morality as inapplicable to slave women's sexual and
maternal realities. Jacobs explicitly asked her readers not to judge her by white
standards: "O, ye happy women, whose purity has been sheltered from childhood, who have been free to choose the objects of your affection, whose
homes are protected by law, do not judge the poor desolate slave girl too severely! If slavery had been abolished, I, also, could have married the man of
my choice; I could have had a home shielded by the laws; and I should have
been spared the painful task of confessing [my affair with a white man]; but
all my prospects had been blighted by slavery. I wanted to keep myself pure,
but . . . I was struggling alone in the powerful grasp of the demon Slavery;
and the monster proved too strong for me" (54). Similarly, having witnessed
the violence done to Sethe's maternal body (when schoolteacher's nephews
steal her milk) and her spirit (when she hears her "human" and "animal"
characteristics enumerated), Morrison's readers are in a position to under-

stand the dark humor of Sethe's offhand comment, upon contemplating having another child with Paul D., that "unless carefree, motherlove was a killer" (*Beloved* 132).

Like *Contending Forces, Beloved* defines mother love as contextual and contingent, even as it insists on remembering slavery's literal and metaphoric scars. Sethe's back, like Grace Montfort's, bears the indelible marks of slavery; yet Morrison, like Hopkins, suggests that the always informing presence of slavery need not be forever incapacitating. Morrison rewrites Hopkins's presentation of redemptive motherhood in one crucial way, however. While Sappho Clark is symbolically healed through selfless devotion to her long-denied child, Sethe recovers only when she renounces a "too-thick" bond with the ghost of her infant daughter and comes to recognize herself as her own "best thing" (273).

Despite the novel's ultimately empowering ending, and despite white director Jonathan Demme's apparently unself-conscious comment that he was "slavish" in translating the novel to the screen (Corliss 76), the movie *Beloved* failed to garner the almost unanimous praise accorded the novel. While it received generally positive reviews, just three weeks after the movie's opening a *New York Times* headline announced that "Despite Hope, 'Beloved' Generates Little Heat Among Moviegoers." Not surprisingly, the film performed especially poorly at suburban malls; more surprisingly, the film did not attract younger black audiences, drawing its audience most heavily from black women older than thirty (Weinraub B4). In *Black Women as Cultural Readers* Jacqueline Bobo argues that black women have long been critical consumers of mainstream Hollywood depictions of black women as "dominating matriarchal figures," "ill-tempered wenches," and "wretched victims" (33). Accustomed to resisting the "ideological domination" of such filmic stereotypes, black female viewers of *Beloved* had ample reason to welcome Demme's more complex rendering of Sethe.

Yet the movie seriously undermines both the power and the meaning of Morrison's novel by depicting Sethe's and Paul D.'s experiences during slavery in a few fragmentary and disconnected images. Such images—unframed by a larger narrative of the more subtle, yet more damaging, degradations of life at Sweet Home plantation—reduce slavery's effects to the sum of discrete, physically brutal acts, so that Sethe's own murder of her child appears less heroically resistant than mindlessly reflexive. Certainly, the movie's almost total exclusion of Paul D.'s story turns the novel's focus on re-membering the black family into a psychodrama of mother-daughter relationships, a drama that, for a nonresistant viewer, might easily confirm the "pathological" aspects of the "black matriarchy" criticized by Daniel Patrick Moynihan in his infamous 1965 report. For contemporary viewers still inclined to view black women as dangerously powerful, the movie's final image of a weakened and bedridden Sethe would be almost as comforting as the earlier scene in which Beloved is successfully exorcized. Since the movie avoids the past of slavery almost as scrupulously as Morrison insists upon it, white viewers could easily conclude that the "damage" that must be set right is caused by Sethe's too-powerful assertion of mother love, not by the history that conditioned her actions.

Nonetheless, Paul D.'s reminder that Sethe is her "own best thing" affirms an identity for black women outside (in this case, subsequent to) motherhood. Anna Quindlen's novel *One True Thing,* on the other hand, resuscitates the nineteenth-century white ideal of motherhood as a (literally) all-consuming activity; thus the novel's motherly heroine, Kate Gulden (played in the movie by Meryl Streep), is glorified precisely in proportion to her progressive physical decline. If Sethe's literary mother is the indomitable Sappho Clark, Kate might descend from Adele Ratignolle, the "mother-woman" Kate Chopin satirized. Told from the perspective of Kate's daughter, Ellen, Quindlen's 1994 novel depicts the final months of Kate's fatal struggle with cancer, a struggle that prompts her career-driven daughter to discover her softer, more maternal side.[4]

On the surface, the narrative's sympathies are with the thoroughly modern Ellen, who accuses her father, a philandering literature professor, of causing her mother's death through his self-absorbed dependency on his wife's domestic services (49). But despite this hint that the traditional 1950s marriage often proves lethal to the "angel in the house," the novel ultimately celebrates Ellen's own growing capacity for self-abnegation. Ellen initially insists on an "essential difference" between her mother's role as the "ideal faculty wife" and Ellen's own high-powered career in journalism (44, 50). But her father's accusation that she "has no heart" (23) so wounds her that she leaves her job in Manhattan and returns to her provincial hometown to care for her dying mother.

During the course of her reluctant maternal service Ellen learns that she has seriously underestimated her mother's intelligence and courage, manifested most dramatically in her mother's decision to end her own life. Though the question of whether Ellen has assisted her mother's suicide brings a contemporary twist to Hollywood's time-honored dying mother plot, Kate's death serves the same symbolic function as the death of any good woman in a sentimental novel: It enforces an appreciation of the "female" virtues of self-sacrifice and self-denial. Accordingly, when her mother dies, Ellen returns to New York but pursues a kinder, gentler career as a therapist specializing in adolescent girls, a job that weds her intellectual interests to her newfound heart by casting her as a surrogate mother to innumerable young women.

Thus, while *One True Thing* appears to offer a feminist tale of mother-daughter bonding, and its ending suggests a happy resolution to the dilemma of career versus family, it actually supports an age-old conception of women's essentially maternal nature. It thus indirectly assures readers that white women, defined historically as the "fittest" mothers, have not completely jettisoned this identity. Indeed, the novel's most significant intertext is *Anna Karenina*, one of several books that Ellen and Kate, desperate to find an interest in common, read together. After her mother's death Ellen signals her own belated appreciation of selfless maternity by fondly recalling her mother's criticism of the novel: "I will never again be able to think that Anna [Karenina] did the right thing when she closed the door and ran after Vronsky; I will always think of little Seryozha shivering in the hallway, waiting for Maman to return, as I sometimes wait for mine, pausing with the telephone receiver in my hand to make a call and then remembering that the woman I need to speak with has been dead for nearly a decade" (281).

Ellen's nostalgia for the maternal presence that she spent her adult life rejecting is an understandable expression of her grief. Unfortunately, the novel as a whole appears nostalgic not only for the one good mother at its center but for the social fabric of which she was a part. That this social fabric depends on clearly demarcated racial boundaries becomes clear when Ellen returns to her formerly beloved New York City after her mother's funeral, a return that Quindlen represents through a seemingly inexplicable reference to *The Wizard of Oz*. Upon entering the Village, Ellen muses, ambiguously: "There's no place like home. . . . There's no place like home." To which her friend obligingly replies, "We're not in Kansas anymore" (270).

That Greenwich Village is not, and can never be, the quintessential white, rural, and safe space immortalized in *The Wizard of Oz* is suggested by the novel's lone reference to an African American figure, who appears precisely at this moment. Less a character than a nameless, menacing embodiment of urban life, he is described generically as a "young black man with a squeegee, the skin tight on his facial bones" (269), and his only action is to look up from his hotdog cart to hurl profanities at the car full of white passengers from the suburbs. This apparently gratuitous detail seems to be Quindlen's way of demonstrating that Ellen's return to the life of a single career woman is not only disappointing but dangerous.

If we take seriously Toni Morrison's assertion that "the fabrication of an Africanist persona is reflexive; an extraordinary meditation on the self; a powerful exploration of the fears and desires that reside in the writerly conscious" (*Playing* 17), what does it mean that an inexplicably hostile African American man stands, metonymically, for the amaternal landscape of contemporary urban life? How does the white fear of black presence that this scene unconsciously reveals reinforce a longing for the racially pure white mother, uncorrupted by the touch of the city, the "profanity" of blackness?

The novel's racist subtext is not directly reproduced in the movie. Instead, the movie version of *One True Thing* adds color to the novel's all-white suburban setting by supplying an African American extra who plays a member of Kate's philanthropic organization, "The Minnies." Yet Meryl Streep's costuming as Kate Gulden works against such calculated diversity by invoking the sanitized white mother from the *Father Knows Best* era. Although the movie, like the novel, is set in the 1990s, Kate appears repeatedly in 1950s-style aprons; indeed, in a subtle echoing of the novel's *Wizard of Oz* motif, she first appears dressed up as Dorothy for a costume party. As part of its nostalgia for midcentury domestic bliss, the film indirectly associates the comforts of home with the supposed absence of racial discord in the pre–civil rights era. Thus the movie's black "Minnie" not only lacks the hostility of the novel's one African American character but is virtually indistinguishable from her white peers, since she shares with them the perquisites of upper-middle-class domesticity, namely, the leisure to spend endless hours decorating the town square for Christmas.

The movie audience is encouraged to laugh along with Ellen at her mother's anachronistic apron wearing but only to heighten viewers' eventual realization of the heroic strength that undergirds the good *white* mother's domesticity. Thus, if the marketing of *Beloved* reduced its plot to the "spooky" story of a murderous black mother and her trouble-making progeny, *One True Thing* produces narrative pleasure by demonstrating that the 1950s (white) mother really did know best. Indeed, the movie intensifies the novel's privileging of maternal over "selfish" female behavior by suggesting that Ellen will reproduce her mother's selfless nurturing. While the novel devotes considerable space to Ellen's return to New York City after her mother's funeral, the movie closes on an image of Ellen kneeling at her mother's grave, patiently teaching her father how to plant flower bulbs.

One True Thing's nostalgic reinscription of the white middle-class nuclear family stands in stark contrast with the ending of *Beloved*, in which Sethe's daughter Denver establishes herself as an independent, self-supporting member of Cincinnati's black community. Significantly, Denver's journey away from the haunted house on Bluestone Road is facilitated not by her biological mother but by a community of thirty black women who provide physical and spiritual nourishment by leaving food for her destitute family and collectively exorcizing the ghost of Beloved. In this respect Morrison is very much Hopkins's literary daughter, for the multiplicity of characters serving important maternal functions in *Beloved*—including Baby Suggs, Paul D., Amy Denver, Stamp Paid, and Lady Jones—works against an essential or unitary definition of "true" motherhood.

Other Mothers

Beloved and *One True Thing* thus make a dramatic contrast as much through their depictions of daughters as through their respective tributes to black and white mothers. As in Hopkins, Chopin, Wharton, Kelley, and Larsen, a mother's influence and value are best understood through the legacy that she leaves her daughter. Where Hopkins and Wharton suggest that a daughter need not repeat her mother's story, Kelley's heroine produces a daughter to take her place in a senseless round of reproduction, and both Chopin's and Larsen's heroines pass on their own experience of maternal abandonment to their children. Alone among the authors discussed in this book, Hopkins depicts without ambivalence the positive legacies of motherhood, perhaps because her definition of motherhood includes not only the nurturance of a biological mother but also the support of community members who function as what Patricia Hill Collins calls "othermothers." By dramatizing the importance of othermothers in securing Sappho's safe passage from violated daughter to contented mother, *Contending Forces*, like *Beloved*, offers a compelling representation of the "fluid and changing boundaries" between "biological mothers [and] other women who care for children in African and African American communities" (Collins 119).

The Other mother appears in quite a different context in *One True Thing*. If Hopkins deconstructed the nineteenth-century True Mother by questioning the biological basis of both race and maternal instinct, the late twentieth century saw the construction of a new category of othermothers, valorized because they embody the apparently foreign function of mother love. Besides the African American squeegee wielder, the only person of color in Quindlen's novel is the Ecuadoran American home health-care worker, Teresa Guerrera, who steps in to care for Kate when the job becomes overwhelming for Ellen. Because Quindlen makes much of Ellen's response to Teresa's racial difference—Ellen remarks upon meeting Teresa that "she had a slight accent and her teeth were very white against her dark face" (117) and later finds comfort in Teresa's "soft and slightly accented voice" (265)—it is difficult to disassociate Teresa's superior maternal instincts from her ethnoracial identity. When Ellen asks her, "Why do you do this kind of work? You could be working in the hospital nursery, bathing babies," Teresa replies: "Anyone can bathe a baby . . . not everyone can do this" (123). Of course, not everyone *has* to do this particular maternal work; much as a woman of color might be expected to provide care if Ellen had children, Teresa steps in here to care for Ellen's mother's infantlike needs, insisting, for example, on changing the mother's soiled bedsheets, though this is not part of her professional duties (175). Depicting Teresa as somehow "naturally" better than Ellen at performing this function, Quindlen upholds the notion—as convenient to middle-class women's current needs as the notion of inferior mothering was to early twentieth-century nativists—that women of color are endowed with extraordinary caregiving qualities.

Thus, even as it celebrates white maternal sacrifice, *One True Thing* extends to non–African American women the myth of the all-nurturing (yet inadequately maternal) black woman, who has been prized as a nurturer of white children but not recognized as a worthy mother to her own. Analyzing a spate of recent films that use the "cheerful-caregiver-of-color" theme—including *Clara's Heart* (1988), *Passion Fish* (1992), and *Corrina, Corrina* (1994)—Sau-ling C. Wong argues that "in a society undergoing radical demographic and economic changes, the figure of the person of color patiently mothering white folks serves to allay racial anxieties." Wong further suggests that "by conceding a certain amount of spiritual or even physical dependence on people of color—as helpers, healers, guardians, mediators, educators, or advisors—without ceding actual structural privilege, the care-receiver preserves the illusion of equality and reciprocity with the caregiver" (69).

While I agree with Wong's analysis, it is important to recall that even such falsely comforting images exist alongside filmic images of "bad" black mothers, images certain to produce further racial anxieties, for instance, 1994's *Losing Isaiah* (featuring Halle Berry as a belatedly recovered, crack-addicted mother) or 1991's *Boyz N the Hood*. Michele Wallace has characterized the latter film's maternal figures as falling into one of two camps: those who are "white-identified and drink espresso (the Buppie version), or [those] who call their sons 'fat fucks' and allow their children to run in the streets while they offer blow jobs in exchange for drugs (the underclass version)" (124). Wallace finds these specific images all the more damaging given the film's failure to more fully characterize these women: "We never find out what Tre's mother does for a living, whether or not Doughboy's mother works, is on welfare, or has ever been married, or anything whatsoever about the single black mother whose babies run into the street" (123).

Certainly, white mothers are not exempt from negative portrayal in recent movies, but it is interesting to note that "evil" white mother figures, such as those in *Serial Mom* (1994) or *Hush* (1998), are frequently represented in the genres of satire or horror, not "realism." Such generic distancing makes them unlikely to displace the sentimental white mother—as invoked in such dramas as *Steel Magnolias* (1989), *Little Women* (1994), or *Stepmom* (1999)—in the popular imagination.

My point in analyzing two recent representations of motherhood is not to imply that fictional images of motherhood produced in the 1990s are indistinguishable from those produced in the 1890s or that depictions of motherhood are uniquely susceptible to racist subtexts. Rather, I want to suggest that *One True Thing,* no less than *Beloved,* is "about" race, and that motherhood remains one key arena in which national racial anxieties are worked out. The cultural meanings of motherhood have shifted profoundly enough that it is difficult to invoke, without irony, what Hopkins called the "glory" and "joy" of motherhood; yet as at the start of the twentieth century, race remains a predictable subtext in popular constructions of maternity. To the extent that racial ideologies continue to underwrite fictional and filmic images of maternity, helping to define what it means to be an authentic American mother, and to the extent that the "good" mother remains both a cherished national myth and an intensely racialized ideal, motherhood may indeed be America's one true thing.

Notes

Introduction

1. My use of the term *True Motherhood* is meant to echo the nineteenth-century ideal of True Womanhood, defined by Barbara Welter as encompassing "piety, purity, submissiveness, and domesticity" (21). While the True Mother of the nineteenth century embodied all these qualities and more—her defining virtue was a limitless capacity for self-sacrifice—the qualities most desirable in twentieth-century mothers were very much in debate at the turn of the century, when burgeoning sexology, birth control, eugenics, and parent-education movements rejected sentimental ideals of motherhood in favor of scientific principles. Thus, if "representations of a sanctified motherhood formed the primary cornerstone for commercially successful writing in the United States of the nineteenth century" (S. Smith 1), desanctified images of motherhood became one hallmark of writing in the twentieth.

2. A representative text from England is Frances Swiney's *The Awakening of Women; or, Woman's Part in Evolution,* an early feminist defense of eugenics, which went through three editions between 1899 and 1908 and was translated into Dutch and French during the same years. Swiney's preface provides a particularly striking articulation of how a collective, democratic conception of female literacy might advance the early twentieth-century women's movement: "I have written for the crowd, not for the student. I have avoided as much as possible technical and scientific phraseology, and long columns of statistics. The woman who thinks and reads can verify my statements . . . and I plead with her, provided she agrees with my premises, to enter the band of teachers for the enlightenment and advancement of the majority. The average woman, occupied with many things, to whom study would be an added burden, would not open the book, if it were a purely scientific, erudite treatise . . . and it is that woman I would fain reach, influence, and enlist, as an active, sympathetic worker in the higher and purer development of our race" (vi). For discussions of the New Woman question as it intersected with eugenic debates in Britain, see Ledger, Chrisman, and Barash.

3. *Race* was, of course, a highly ambiguous term at the turn of the century. It could serve

as a synonym for *nation* or *population,* refer to a particular racial or ethnic group, or both. As Carole McCann argues, "In the [racial betterment] discourse of the dominant white culture, [general and specific] senses of the word were conflated to refer simultaneously to native-born Americans of Western European descent and to the nation as a whole" (14). Thus, for example, when MacLean stresses the importance of perpetuating "the race," she would seem to refer to the human race as a whole; yet her comment elsewhere in *Wage-Earning Women,* that "one alien race after another, lured to the mills, crowds the earlier arrival and underbids it oftentimes" (11), suggests that she is chiefly concerned with defending the rights of native-born working women.

4. Katrina Irving's *Immigrant Mothers,* for example, focuses on nativist constructions of the immigrant mother rather than on immigrant women's own narratives.

5. For an analysis of *private* discussions of motherhood among working-class and immigrant women, primarily in the context of child-study and mothers' clubs, see Grant, *Raising Baby by the Book.* For a discussion of attempts to Americanize Native American mothers, see K. Tsianina Lomawaima, *They Called It Prairie Light: The Story of Chilocco Indian School.*

6. Of course, these ideas were frequently overlapping; while the True Mother's cardinal virtue was self-sacrifice, the New Mother typically combined an instinctive desire for children with a scientific and/or civic interest in improving the race.

7. Studies from the late 1980s tended to use psychoanalytic frameworks; see, for example, Marianne Hirsch, *The Mother/Daughter Plot: Narrative, Psychoanalysis, Feminism,* and Jane Silverman Van Buren, *The Modernist Madonna: Semiotics of the Maternal Metaphor.* More recent studies situate maternal narratives in relation to a variety of historical discourses, giving more extended attention to race; see Laura Doyle, *Bordering on the Body;* Stephanie Smith, *Conceived by Liberty;* and Eva Cherniavsky, *That Pale Mother Rising.*

8. For pioneering black feminist criticism published before the 1990s, see, for example, Hazel Carby, *Reconstructing Womanhood;* Barbara Christian, *Black Women Novelists;* Gloria Hull, *Color, Sex, and Poetry;* Alice Walker, *In Search of Our Mother's Gardens;* Mary Helen Washington, *Invented Lives;* Deborah McDowell, "'The Changing Same'"; Barbara Smith, "Toward a Black Feminist Criticism"; and Hortense Spillers, "Mama's Baby, Papa's Maybe."

9. For a review of recent scholarship that "interrogates whiteness," see Fishken. Although cross-racial literary scholarship proliferated in the 1990s, Elizabeth Ammons's *Conflicting Stories,* Nina Miller's *Making Love Modern,* and Martha J. Cutter's *Unruly Tongue* are among the few thoroughly integrated studies of American *women's* writing. Several studies of U.S. women's literary traditions published in the 1990s either focus exclusively on white women writers or include a single African American writer in a final chapter; see, for example, Suzanne Clark's *Sentimental Modernism;* Susan Harris's *19th-Century American Women's Novels;* Ann Romines's *The Home Plot;* Helen Fiddyment Levy's *Fiction of the Home Place;* Susan Rosowski's *Birthing a Nation;* and Karen Tracey's *Plots and Proposals.* Perhaps an even greater number focus exclusively on African American or other minority women writers, continuing the important work of examining African American, Latina, Native American, and Asian women's writing as distinct traditions. My point is not that every study of American women's writing should strive arbitrarily for racial balance but simply that work remains to be done in exploring how

traditions of writing by white women and women of color are (or are not) mutually informing.

10. While existing studies of motherhood and race in American culture have not focused on this crucial time period, they provide important foundations for my work. Smith and Cherniavsky have examined the imbrication of race and maternity in the nineteenth century, while Doyle provides a trans-Atlantic and transhistorical perspective on the figure of the race mother, covering a range of romantic and modernist writers from Britain and the United States. Doyle's argument, that "hierarchies of race and gender require one another as co-originating and co-dependent forms of oppression" and that these "co-dependent structures of race and sex converge especially on the mother" (21), is particularly useful to my analysis. However, with the exception of Toni Morrison, Doyle does not consider how black women writers have used the trope of the race mother, nor does she consider how, from a black feminist perspective—and particularly in the context of early twentieth-century racial uplift efforts—the race mother could signify personal or political empowerment as well as reproductive subservience.

11. Indeed, so pervasive was the equation of managed maternity with national well-being that even as (white, native) mothers were defined as guardians of the nation's "good American blood" (Monroe 130), the nation itself was figured in maternal terms: "In recognition of its duties as Step-mother," wrote one eugenicist, "the State will in self defense protect its maternal arms from the influx of undesirables" (Helen Baker 108).

12. Of course, representations of motherhood were not produced exclusively by women writers. From Stephen Crane's portrait of a dysgenic immigrant mother in *Maggie: A Girl of the Streets* (1893) to Upton Sinclair's veiled depiction of childbirth and maternal mortality in *The Jungle* (1905) to the murder-inducing pregnancy in Theodore Dreiser's *An American Tragedy* (1925) and certainly to Ernest Hemingway's notorious depiction of childbirth in "Indian Camp" (1924), one could trace a similar conjunction of race, class, and reproductive anxieties in male-authored naturalist and modernist fiction. Yet such texts make no attempt to portray maternity from a mother's perspective; indeed, the white doctor in "Indian Camp" pronounces that the Native American woman's cries during childbirth "are not important" (16).

13. See, for example, Ardis and Smith-Rosenberg.

14. While Tompkins, Tate, and Romero, among others, have demonstrated that the nineteenth-century sentimental novel was in fact a decidedly political enterprise, the association of the sentimental with popular (and therefore "trivial") feminine concerns persists. For the writers that I discuss, the problem with the nineteenth-century "woman's novel" was not its sentimentality per se but its evasion of the less-than-romantic details of domesticity and maternity. They frequently signal their rejection of this tradition within their own novels, as when Kate Chopin lampoons the "bygone heroine of romance" (*Awakening* 51) or Edith Summers Kelley has her heroine complain that novels always "end when they git married" and "never tell what happens after" (*Weeds* 120).

Chapter 1: Maternal Metaphors

1. Recent historical studies have pointed out the centrality of race to maternalist arguments, which were used equally but somewhat differently by African American and white feminists. Black and white women shared a belief in "the fundamental responsibility of

women, as mothers, or potential mothers, for the welfare of their own children, and, thus, society's children" (Lasch-Quinn 111). But maternalist discourse carried a double burden for black women, who sought to counter both racial and sexual stereotypes by promoting the image of a supermoral black mother on whose shoulders the black race would advance. Like the specter of white race suicide, the imperative of black racial uplift in a period marked by intensified racial violence placed a particular premium on black women's biological and cultural work as mothers. See, for example, Boris; Ladd-Taylor, *Mother-Work*; and Mink, *The Wages of Motherhood*.

2. See Rudwick and Meier for a description of black male efforts at inclusion at the exposition.

3. Ladd-Taylor distinguishes the politically conservative members of the National Congress of Mothers from "progressive maternalists," who were active in the formation of the U.S. Children's Bureau, and from feminists like Crystal Eastman and Charlotte Perkins Gilman (*Mother-Work* 7–9).

4. Key's insistence on women's inviolable right to sexual fulfillment led her, for example, to defend unwed mothers and repudiate the concept of illegitimacy (Cott 45–46).

5. The competitive politics of population transcended national boundaries, particularly in the aftermath of World War I. In December 1918 an unsigned editorial in the *General Federation of Women's Clubs Magazine* placed domestic "problems of maternity" in an international context. Noting that "France at the present rate will require 260 years for repopulation—Germany 40 years," and bemoaning the "steady decrease of native American stock," it endorsed the following prescription: "If we are to establish a peace which will be built on true and lasting foundations we must . . . be willing to look our misdeeds and mistakes in the face while we say, 'Never again.' Never again should the young manhood of the country be found to such a degree unfit. Never again should mothers be forced to admit that in ignorance were their babies born and reared. Never again should those who are working in the Home service of the Red Cross be able to report such home conditions as were revealed during the late epidemic" ("Problems" 19).

6. For a discussion of the similarly conjoined concerns of American nativism and American modernism, see Walter Benn Michaels, *Our America*.

Chapter 2: Reconstructing Motherhood

1. Frances E. W. Harper used this term in "Woman's Political Future," her 1893 address to the World's Congress of Representative Women, reprinted in Loewenberg and Bogin. For discussions of black women's political activism during the woman's era, see Giddings and Guy-Sheftall.

2. See also Tate, *Domestic Allegories of Political Desire;* Foster, *Written by Herself;* and duCille, *The Coupling Convention*.

3. The topic of black matriliny has recently received much critical attention, prompted in part by Alice Walker's tribute to her literary mother, Zora Neale Hurston, in *In Search of Our Mother's Gardens* (1983). Following Walker's lead, most critics have focused on late twentieth-century writers' relationships to their early twentieth-century predecessors, often taking Hurston and Walker as representative of the dynamics of black matrilineage. See, for example, Dianne F. Sadoff, "Black Matrilineage: The Case of Alice Walker and Zora Neale Hurston," and Molly Hite, "Romance, Marginality, and Matrilineage: *The Color*

Purple and *Their Eyes Were Watching God."* Deborah E. McDowell takes a wider view in "'The Changing Same': Generational Connections and Black Women Novelists," where she compares the paradigms of nineteenth- and twentieth-century black women's fiction.

4. Hazel Carby's excellent analysis of *Contending Forces* as an exposé of "the violent act of rape and its specific political use as a device of terrorism" (*Reconstructing* 132) does not address the connection between rape and violated maternity; likewise, in "Unsettled Frontiers: Race, History and Romance in Pauline Hopkins's *Contending Forces,"* Carla Peterson examines the novel's critique of "nationalist and imperialist ideology from a black feminist perspective" (180) but does not consider the centrality of motherhood to early twentieth-century black feminist thought. Claudia Tate, on the other hand, usefully identifies *Contending Forces* with what she calls the "maternal discourse [of] antebellum social protest" (*Domestic* 23), but her argument that the novel inscribes the "mother's Law" (*Domestic* 174) does not consider the text's considerable ambivalence about motherhood.

5. For a discussion of how both novels signify on the "matrifocal values" articulated by Harriet Beecher Stowe's *Uncle Tom's Cabin,* see Ammons, "Stowe's Dream." According to Ammons, while Harper shares Stowe's "reverence for motherhood" (179), Wilson provides a portrait of "vicious mother rule" through the character of Mrs. Bellmont (182). While *Contending Forces* continues *Our Nig*'s critique of idealized maternity, Hopkins focuses not on the potential violence *of* mothers but on the effect of racialized violence *on* mothers and on the possibility of restoring mother-child relationships damaged by this violence. It thus shares with *Iola Leroy* what Elizabeth Young has identified as the "narrative trajectory of maternal quest and reunion" (274). Yet unlike *Iola Leroy* or *Our Nig, Contending Forces* questions the biological basis of racial difference, using the instability of racial categories as a basis for interrogating nineteenth-century notions of motherhood.

6. On the tenets of True Womanhood, see Welter.

7. A number of feminist historians have examined the intersection of racial and sexual ideologies in early twentieth-century maternalist discourses; see especially Eileen Boris, "The Power of Motherhood." I am concerned with how maternalism's basic assumptions that women's work as mothers entitled them to political voice, that in order to "protect, nurture, and train children, mothers must have access to the conditions that will allow them to flourish as persons" (Brush 430)—underwrote fictional as well as political uses of maternity.

8. The magazine's stated mission, "to develop and intensify the bonds of that racial brotherhood, which alone can enable a people to assert their racial rights as men," suggests that race goals were implicitly black male goals. See "Editorial and Publishers' Announcements," 60. On Hopkins's role as editor of the *Colored American Magazine,* and her dismissal when Booker T. Washington assumed control of the magazine, see Johnson and Johnson, 4–9.

9. Here Hopkins draws on a convention of slave narratives, in which the violent abuse of slave mothers in particular testified to the brutality of the slave system. Her depiction of Grace's violation bears a striking resemblance, for instance, to Frances Greene's "The Slave-Wife" (1845), whose hero describes his pregnant wife's punishment as follows: "She was bound to the stake; and while cruel and vulgar men mocked her agony, THERE *our babe was born!"* (qtd. in Sanchez-Eppler 45). Though Hopkins does not

explicitly connect the pool of blood at Grace's feet with the blood of childbirth, the image is suggestive.

10. In *The Black Image in the White Mind,* George Fredrickson argues that late nineteenth-century American interpretations of Darwin facilitated a reformulation of racist tenets originally developed to defend slavery; thus, "by appealing to a simplistic Darwinian or hereditarian formula, white Americans could make their crimes against humanity appear as contributions to the inevitable unfolding of biological destiny" (254–55). See also John Haller, *Outcasts from Evolution.*

11. For a discussion of this and other racist treatises published at the turn of the century, see Judith A. Berzon, *Neither White Nor Black,* 25–35.

12. See, for example, Richard Yarborough's introduction to *Contending Forces,* where he argues that "Hopkins never challenges the basic assumption that races can be ranked qualitatively" (xxxvi) and concludes that the novel demonstrates "how difficult it was for black writers to reject widely accepted concepts of race and culture" (xli). More recent critics have demonstrated, however, that Hopkins was a deliberately "radical experimenter" whose "dense polyvocality" makes her less a parrot of nineteenth-century racial ideologies than a "model of early modernist innovation" (Ammons, Afterword 211, 218). See also the many fine essays on Hopkins in Gruesser, *The Unruly Voice.*

13. These related assertions support Gerda Lerner's observation that "the myth of the black rapist of white women is the twin of the myth of the bad black woman—both designed to apologize for and facilitate the continued exploitation of black men and women" (193). See also Angela Davis, "Rape, Racism, and the Myth of the Black Rapist" in *Women, Race, and Class,* 172–201.

14. For a discussion of the ways in which contemporary feminist theorists have inadvertently reinforced this association, see Margaret Homans, "'Women of Color' Writers and Feminist Theory," 73–94.

15. According to John Brandt's *Anglo-Saxon Supremacy* (1915), "Anglo-Saxon women have wonderful tact in arranging cozy-corners, dens," while immigrants "continue to live . . . in the same miserable hut, generally in one, or two, dark, dirty, dingy rooms" (qtd. in Irving 47).

Chapter 3: The Romance "Plot"

1. While the work of Sigmund Freud and Havelock Ellis gained a considerable American audience in the first two decades of the century, extended treatments of female sexuality in fiction were rare. Even when female desire was crucial to the plot of a novel, as in Theodore Dreiser's *Sister Carrie,* it was depicted primarily in terms of its emasculating effects on the male protagonist. In England, of course, D. H. Lawrence offered more explicit treatments of woman's sexual nature, though his images typically explored what Sandra Gilbert and Susan Gubar have called the "corrosiveness of female desire" (*War* 38).

2. The woman question was one of several social issues that Chopin and Wharton engaged in their fiction. See Martha Fodaski Black, who argues that Chopin "locates the personal in a social milieu that implies the relationship between the two" and that *The Awakening* is thus "as much 'problem' literature as an Ibsen play or Shaw polemic" (98–99). See also Helen Taylor's analysis of gender and race in Chopin's works. On Wharton's

sustained engagement with social and political issues, see Elizabeth Ammons's *Edith Wharton's Argument with America* and Dale Bauer's *Edith Wharton's Brave New Politics*.

3. Patricia S. Yaeger offers the most sustained and persuasive linguistic analysis of *The Awakening*.

4. While neither Chopin nor Wharton was, strictly speaking, a biological determinist, both were strongly influenced by Darwin, particularly his theories of sexual selection. See Bender, *The Descent of Love*.

5. Of Ward's gynaecentric theory, Gilman wrote: "Nothing so important to humanity has been advanced since the theory of evolution, and nothing so important to women has ever been given to the world" (qtd. in Lane 278–79). Ward, first president of the American Sociological Society, made a distinction between "gynesis" (or natural evolution) and "telesis" (or social evolution), a distinction apparent in Gilman's work. Equally important to Gilman was Ward's description of women as the predominant force in evolution. The influence of Gilman's own evolutionary theories was profound. Thorstein Veblen's well-known *Theory of the Leisure Class* (1899), for example, appeared a year after *Women and Economics;* following Gilman, Veblen applies evolutionary theory to economics in order to describe capitalism's construction of women as "conspicuous consumers."

6. Like Pauline Hopkins, Gilman believed that the principles of evolution did not negate, but made more imperative, human work for social reform. Gilman also resembled Hopkins in her tendency to domesticate evolutionary theory. As Gilbert and Gubar have noted, Gilman bolstered her critique of the private home in *Herland* not by rejecting domesticity but by extending the idea of home "so the race is viewed as a family and the world as its home" (*Sexchanges* 75).

7. For a discussion of the ongoing tension between Lamarckian and Mendelian interpretations of heredity, see Hasian, 18–20.

8. See Gail Bederman's chapter called "'Not to *Sex*—But to *Race!*' Charlotte Perkins Gilman, Civilized Anglo-Saxon Womanhood, and the Return of the Primitive Rapist" in *Manliness and Civilization* for a detailed discussion of why Gilman would have seen no contradiction between her feminism and her racism, because "her feminism was inextricably rooted in the white supremacism of 'civilization'" (122).

9. In her autobiography Gilman describes her own infantilization under Mitchell's care. Told to "have your child with you all the time," Gilman recalls: "I made a rag baby, hung it on a doorknob and played with it. I would crawl into remote closets and under beds— to hide from the grinding pressure of that profound distress" (*Living* 96).

10. Chopin's fable begins: "There was once an animal born into this world, and opening his eyes upon Life, he saw above and about him confining walls, and before him were bars of iron through which came air and light from without; this animal was born in a cage" ("Emancipation" 177). While Chopin refers to this animal as a "he," the restrictive rules guiding proper female behavior were much on her mind when she wrote this tale, during her first season as a society belle. In her commonplace journal she copied approvingly Anna Bromwell Jamison's observation that a girl's moral education consisted chiefly of proscriptions ("you must not do this—you must not say that—you must not think so") as well as her conclusion that suppressing female "passions, powers, tempers [and] feelings" was "monstrous" (Toth and Seyersted 54).

11. In "Life's Empty Pack," her provocative essay on female psychosocial development, Sandra Gilbert suggests that "for women the myth that governs personality may be based on such a moment, a confrontation of the dead mother that is as enduring and horrifying to daughters as Freud . . . claimed the nightmare of the dead father was to sons" (365). I am indebted to Gilbert's reading of *Summer* as a family romance of a "dead mother," "orphan daughter," and "adoptive father." But where Gilbert focuses on the incestuous process by which the daughter must give herself over to the symbolic father, I am interested specifically in Wharton's representation of Charity's diminishing voice as a function of a pre-scripted romantic and reproductive "plot."

12. Wharton's description in *A Backward Glance* of her own attempts to discuss sex with her mother suggest a similar absence, or abnegation, of maternal modeling:

> Life, real Life, was . . . running over me in vague tremors when I rode my poney [*sic*] or raced & danced & tumbled with "the boys." . . . [When] I asked my mother "What does it mean?" I was always told . . . "It's not nice to ask about such things." . . .
>
> A few days before my marriage, I was seized with such a dread of the whole dark mystery, that I summoned up courage to appeal to my mother, & begged her, with a heart beating to suffocation, to tell me "what being married was like." Her handsome face at once took on the look of icy disapproval which I most dreaded. "I never heard such a ridiculous question!" she said impatiently; & I felt at once how vulgar she thought me.
>
> But in the extremity of my need I persisted. "I'm afraid Mamma—I want to know what will happen to me!"
>
> The coldness of her expression deepened to disgust.

Wharton observes that such interchanges "did more than anything else to falsify & misdirect my whole life" (qtd. in Erlich 27–28).

13. Gilbert reads this scene as the novel's "originary heart of darkness where [Charity] will find and lose her mother" and suggests that the mother's "death paroxysm . . . parodies the paroxysm of birth" ("Life's Empty Pack" 369). If this is true, Wharton's horrifying description of this mother—whose "broken teeth" and "dreadful glistening leg" make her look "like a dead dog in a ditch" (250)—offers a grim picture of childbirth. In Edith Summers Kelley's *Weeds,* which I discuss in the next chapter, a woman in labor is indeed shown to be dehumanized, and in language remarkably similar to Wharton's, Kelley describes this woman as a "wild, doglike creature" (343).

14. See also Carolyn Heilbrun, who notes that "the heroines of most novels by women have either no mothers, or mothers who are ineffectual and unsatisfactory. Think of George Eliot; think of Jane Austen; think of the Brontës. As a rule, the women in these novels are very lonely." The motherless heroines of early twentieth-century novels can be added to Heilbrun's list of nineteenth-century examples, and like their fictional predecessors, Charity and Edna "have no women friends" (Heilbrun 118).

15. The story that Edna imagines revises Chopin's own fiction, for in many of her earlier stories a woman's sexual life follows exactly the pattern that Mandelet describes. See, for example, "Athénaïse" (1897), in which a heroine first runs off with her lover, then comes to her senses and returns to her husband.

16. Another instance is when Victor Lebrun usurps his black maid's responsibility for

answering the door, and she "grumble[s] a refusal to do part of her duty when she had not been permitted to do it all" (111). Edna refers to this woman as "plainly an anomaly" (111), though it is not clear if this is because she speaks at all or because she insists on doing her job (presumably in contrast to the "naturally" lazy darker races).

17. Much of Chopin's short fiction depicts Creole, Cajun, and black women not only as "naturally" sexual and maternal but also as less bound by proscriptions against female self-expression. In "A Night in Acadie," for example, Chopin writes that Zaïda "carried herself boldly and stepped out freely and easily, like a negress. There was an absence of reserve in her manner; yet there was no lack of womanliness" (487). For a discussion of Chopin's representation of patriarchal discourse in her short fiction, see Martha Cutter, "Losing the Battle but Winning the War: Resistance to Patriarchal Discourse in Kate Chopin's Short Fiction." See also Sandra Gunning, "Rethinking White Female Silences," in *Race, Rape, and Lynching.*

Chapter 4: Hard Labor

1. Representative titles include "Mother Heart," *Overland Monthly* (1921); "My Mother's Impelling Influence," *American Mercury* (1921); "Mother of His Children," *Scribner's* (1921); "Hundred Percent Mother," *Good Housekeeping* (1923); and "Fun of Being a Mother," *Pictorial Review* (1927). As Nancy Cott points out, however, the tensions surrounding motherhood in the 1920s were high, especially because more and more women were "refusing" motherhood: nearly one quarter of the women who came of age in the 1920s would remain childless (165). The cultural anxiety produced by the changing definition of motherhood is reflected in other articles that appeared beside the traditional homages to motherhood: "Wanted: Motives for Motherhood," *Outlook* (1921); "Working Mothers," *New Republic* (1925); as well as "What About the Children? The Question of Mothers and Careers," *Harper's* (1927).

2. For a discussion of the historical connections between birth control, feminism, and eugenics, see Gordon, *Woman's Body,* esp. 126–35. Gordon argues that "the polemical function of eugenic arguments for feminists was often to give teeth to their moralism, to provide a punishment with which to threaten those who would ignore or despise women's demands for equality" (126). Carole McCann places Sanger's alliance with eugenicists in the context of her uneven relationship with the medical profession, whose efforts to restrict contraceptive prescriptions Sanger resisted. According to McCann, eugenicists were "powerful allies against the medical hegemony" who "helped dissociate birth control from sexual controversy" (19). McCann argues that Sanger was compelled to ally herself with eugenicists because of the medical establishment's intransigence as well as the "official silence about birth control on the part of other women's rights organizations" (27); the League of Women Voters, the National Woman's Party, and the Children's Bureau all refused to endorse birth control publicly (19).

3. As Linda Gordon notes, from its first issue the *Birth Control Review* published eugenic and race suicide arguments. Guy Irving Burch, director of the American Eugenics Society, was a regular contributor to the *Review;* he favored birth control because it would "prevent the American people from being replaced by alien or Negro stock, whether it be by immigration or by overly high birth rates among others in this country" (qtd. in Gordon 283).

4. Kelley may intend a subtle reference to the larger context of early twentieth-century race suicide debates by noting that the community schoolhouse is adorned with an "impressive print of Roosevelt" (11).

5. For differing accounts of Sanger's changing allegiances, see Gordon (249–300), Reed (97–105 and 129–39), and Chesler (269–86). While Gordon in particular condemns Sanger's retreat from radical politics, she allows that, given Sanger's experience with the legal system during the trials for *The Woman Rebel* and for her Brownsville clinic, she had good reason to suppose that winning the legal right for doctors to prescribe contraception was the best that could be hoped for. The question of Sanger's motives has occasioned much scholarly debate, as has the issue of her alleged racism. Carole McCann provides a balanced summary of these debates by placing Sanger's shifting rhetoric within "the political terrain and discursive horizons of her time" (4).

6. The birth control movement's more conservative emphasis in the 1920s was part of a general turn away from radical politics that affected inquiry into many aspects of sexuality and reproduction. Christina Simmons notes, for example, that while the sex radicals of the early decades of the century continued to explore female sexuality and birth control in the 1920s, "they discussed these matters . . . with a more exclusive attention to the attitudes and behavior of middle-class youth than had their predecessors" (111).

7. Likewise, in the *Birth Control Review* the eugenic effects of birth control were emphasized over self-determination for women. According to Ethel Klein, only 4.9 percent of all articles in the *Birth Control Review* in 1921–29 made reference to the issue of women's self-determination (64).

8. For a discussion of the nineteenth-century social purity movement in relation to eugenics discourses, see Gordon, 116–35. Among the many medical and sociological studies of female sexuality in the 1920s were those by Robert Latou Dickinson and Lura Beam, William J. Robinson, and Katharine B. Davis.

9. For a discussion of the increasing scientification of child rearing in the early twentieth century, see Ehrenreich and English, 183–210.

10. In their ethnographic study of "Middletown" (Muncie, Indiana), for example, Robert and Helen Lynd found that while nearly all of the town's middle-class wives used birth control, fewer than half of the working-class wives did. Katharine Davis's 1922 study of contraceptive use among one thousand college alumnae and women's club members found that nearly 75 percent of these women used contraceptives, suggesting a strong connection between education (and thus class) and access to birth control (Kennedy 136).

11. See Adams for an analysis of early twentieth-century male depictions of childbirth, including Ernest Hemingway's infamous short story "Indian Camp" and William Carlos Williams's less well-known "A Night in June." For an examination of women writers' increasingly forthright depictions of childbirth in the 1930s, see Rabinowitz.

12. Richard Connell's "Weeds," the story of a "mentally defective pauper" who bears four children while in an asylum, appeared in the March and April 1922 issues of the *Birth Control Review.*

13. Sinclair nominated *Weeds* for a Civil Liberties Union award, presumably because of its depiction of the dehumanizing effects of sharecropping. Sinclair also shared Kelley's concern for the injustice of denying birth control to the poor, though he took the more common approach of soliciting sympathy for the innocent child. In his *Book of Life* he

wrote: "A poor unwanted little waif of a soul, which never sinned, and had nothing to do with the matter, is brought into a hostile world, to suffer neglect and perhaps starvation, in order to punish parents who did not happen to be sufficiently strong-willed to practice continence in marriage" (1:65).

14. As in *Contending Forces, The Awakening,* and *Summer,* the mother cannot be depended upon as a model or guide; like Hopkins's Sappho, Chopin's Edna, and Wharton's Charity, Judith will be a motherless mother. Given the maternal mortality rate in the early decades of the century, the preponderance of "motherless mothers" in literature of this period is not surprising. According to Ethel Klein, despite medical advances, maternal mortality remained high and "thirty percent of the women born around 1900 and married during the 1920s did not survive to late motherhood" (51).

15. Kelley may have taken her inspiration for this scene from D. H. Lawrence's "The Horse Dealer's Daughter" (1922), which also features a near drowning in a horse pond. Yet as she did with *The Awakening,* Kelley borrows from Lawrence in order to revise his story. Where the doctor in "Horse Dealer's Daughter" rescues the heroine from drowning—and thereby seals their sexual and marital union—Kelley's heroine saves herself and, soon after, determines to stop sexual relations with her husband.

Chapter 5: Fatal Contractions

1. In her introduction to *Quicksand* and *Passing,* Deborah McDowell notes Larsen's tendency to write "unconvincing" endings, attributing this shortcoming to the historical difficulty of depicting unconventional black heroines. She observes that Jessie Fauset and Zora Neale Hurston produced equally unsatisfactory endings, in which their heroines "retreat from the brink of independence and self-realization" into more conventional roles (xi). I would suggest, however, that *Quicksand*'s "retreat" is unique in that Helga's loss of freedom is attributed directly to the physical demands of reproduction and indirectly to the problems of the biracial female artist.

2. Most recent critics of *Quicksand* have focused on its representation of black female sexuality (McDowell, Introduction; duCille, *Coupling*), its reworking of the myth of the tragic mulatto (Gray, McLendon), or its intersecting thematics of gender and race (Hostetler). While some of these critics address issues of embodiment, they do not recognize the images of maternity that recur throughout the novel, nor do they address the novel's inclusion of characters who endorse eugenic discourses mandating increased childbearing for the black middle class. In *Psychoanalysis and Black Novels* Claudia Tate offers an intriguing psychoanalytic interpretation, but she focuses on Helga as a daughter rather than as a mother.

3. McDowell argues that "Helga is divided psychically between a desire for sexual fulfillment and a longing for social respectability" and that "Larsen's narrative strategies mirror her heroine's dilemma," for Larsen herself was caught between "narrative expression and repression" of female sexuality (Introduction xvii).

4. As Loralee MacPike has suggested, in nineteenth-century literature the metaphor of childbirth often registers a comment on the legitimacy of female sexuality, and "she who is wanton pays, whether through a difficult birth or through 'postpartum psychosis'" (59–60). MacPike demonstrates the essentially conservative narrative function of childbirth, noting that "any female sexual license threatens a society in which marriage and childbearing must be controlled to insure the continuation of that society in its present form"

(62). Of course, Helga atones for her sexuality not only through painful labor but also, like so many nineteenth-century "fallen women," with her life.

5. For contrasting views of how Nella Larsen's own biracial identity may have influenced her work, see Thadious Davis, *Nella Larsen,* and George Hutchinson, "Nella Larsen."

6. In one of his more impassioned statements on this subject Du Bois vows: "I shall forgive the white South much in its final judgment day . . . but one thing I shall never forgive, neither in this world nor the world to come: its wanton and continued and persistent insulting of the black womanhood which it sought and seeks to prostitute to its lust" ("Damnation" 517).

7. While Carter appears to echo Roosevelt, it is important to recall their differences. While Roosevelt and white eugenicists focused attention on racial betterment, stressing the evolutionary importance of middle-class white women's reproductive compliance, African Americans were concerned with the survival of the black race. Much as slavery's definition of black women as chattel demanded a resistant politics of reproduction, the incidence of lynching at the turn of the twentieth century compounded black fears of "race suicide" because of declining birthrates.

8. For a discussion of the antilynching crusade of the 1920s, including an attempt to pass a federal antilynching bill, see Giddings (176–81 and 206–10), and Hall. Giddings credits black women's efforts, particularly the work of the Anti-Lynching Crusaders, with decreasing the number of lynchings "from 301 between 1919 and 1923 to 100 between 1924 and 1928" (177). Certainly, antilynching plays would have helped to stir public sentiment against lynching.

9. Performed only three times—in school auditoriums and small theaters in Washington, D.C., New York City, and Cambridge—*Rachel* reached a limited number of white playgoers. Because Grimké's appeal was, in her words, "not primarily to the colored people, but to the whites" ("'Rachel,' the Play" 413) she published the play with her own money in 1919. According to Gloria Hull, *Rachel* received much more attention in its printed form, garnering nearly fifty reviews and notices. Many of these appeared in white newspapers, suggesting that *Rachel* did finally reach its intended audience although with mixed success.

10. Nellie McKay argues that many critics "objected to the propaganda aspects of the plot because they held firmly to the belief that black drama, as well as other forms of Afro-American creative writing, should focus strictly on artistic concerns and not become involved in political issues" (134). Yet as I have suggested, it was the explicit goal of the play (sponsored, after all, by the NAACP) to effect social change. Clearly, it was the play's representation of Rachel's willful rejection of motherhood, and not its overall "propaganda" against lynching, that offended some viewers.

11. McFalls and Masnick's study of African American attitudes toward birth control corrects the racist assumptions of earlier studies, which held that African Americans virtually did not use birth control and that the declining black birthrate in the early decades of the century was primarily the result of venereal disease rather than a deliberate attempt to limit family size. Refuting these claims, McFalls and Masnick note that "those blacks with the socioeconomic and educational characteristics most conducive to good health had the lowest fertility and the highest childlessness," suggesting the use of birth control primarily among middle-class blacks (90).

12. Though *Rachel* makes no reference to birth control per se, Rachel's motivations for avoiding motherhood were apparently shared by many middle-class African Americans. In a 1921 article for the journal *Social Hygiene,* Dr. Charles V. Roman observed, "The scarcity of children among educated colored people is one of the most striking phases of the social-hygiene problem as it affects the race. . . . In private practice I have frequently heard intelligent and upright colored women say they would rather die than to bring children into the world to suffer what they had suffered" (45).

13. Several other black female playwrights recognized drama's potential to educate the public about the travesty of lynching. Propaganda plays against lynching include Myrtle Smith Livingston's *For Unborn Children* (1926), about the lynching of a black man who dares to become involved with a white woman; Mary Burrill's *Aftermath* (1919), in which a black soldier returns from serving in World War I to find that his father has been lynched; and Regina Andrews's *Climbing Jacob's Ladder* (1931), which depicts a lynching that takes place during a Sunday morning church service. Georgia Douglas Johnson, who was a member of the Anti-Lynch Crusade Organization, wrote at least three antilynching plays, including *Safe, A Sunday Morning in the South,* and *Blue-Eyed Black Boy* (Perkins 10). *Safe,* which was never published, makes the connection between maternity and lynching most explicit. Johnson's notes for this work specify that a young mother "snuff out the life of her baby at the same time" that a black boy is "strung up" by a lynch mob (Hull 163).

14. Even though "The Closing Door" was published three years after *Rachel* was first performed, a draft of the more radical story formed the inspiration for the play (Hull 128); Grimké most likely toned down the sentiments of "The Closing Door" when she envisioned how the story would play on the stage. That she should rework this material is not surprising because, as Gloria Hull notes, nearly all of Grimké's dramatic and fictional work dealt in some way with the issue of lynching (131).

15. For an analysis of contemporaneous birth control propaganda plays, including Lawrence Langner's *Wedded: A Social Comedy* (1914); Rose Pastor Stokes and Alice Blache's *Shall the Parents Decide?* (1916); and Susan Glaspell's *Chains of Dew* (1922), see Gainor.

16. Jessie Rodrique has documented that not only were African Americans using birth control as it was made available in clinics but were "active and effective participants in the establishment of local clinics and in the birth control debate" (138).

17. See David Kennedy for a discussion of Sanger's reliance on this emotional (possibly apocryphal) story and its rhetorical usefulness for the birth control movement (15–19).

18. Burrill's portrayal of Mrs. Jaspar's double burden reflects an enduring theme in Afrocentric ideologies of motherhood. According to Patricia Hill Collins, "In contrast to the cult of true womanhood in which work is defined as being in opposition to and incompatible with motherhood, work for Black women has been an important and valued dimension of Afrocentric definitions of Black motherhood" (124).

19. See Hutchinson, "Nella Larsen," for a perceptive analysis of how biracial identity is "subtly resisted, quietly repressed, or openly mocked" (328). See also his *Harlem Renaissance in Black and White* for an exhaustive study of the interracial intellectual commerce that came to fruition in the artistic productions of the Harlem Renaissance. As I argue in "The New 'New Negro,'" the suspicion of biracial authors and characters as inauthentically black persists in recent Harlem Renaissance scholarship; the taint of inauthenticity seems to adhere most readily to women writers and their female characters, as when

Houston Baker erroneously interprets black women writers' use of mulatto characters as "an implicit approval of white patriarchy" (Baker 25).

20. Helga's difficulty in constructing an identity is typical of the black female bildungs-roman. Sondra O'Neale has identified recurring characteristics of this genre, from Harper's *Iola Leroy* (1892) to Toni Cade Bambara's *The Salt Eaters* (1980). Especially relevant to *Quicksand* (which O'Neale does not discuss) is the tendency of mulatto heroines to be "repelled by sex" and to avoid pregnancy because of the "racial curse involved in their own procreation" (35). That Helga's fear of marriage and motherhood stems from her own familial history is clear when she tells Axel Olsen, "If we were married, you might come to be ashamed of me, to hate me, to hate all dark people. My mother did that" (88). Helga's story thus reproduces what O'Neale calls a motif of "skin-conscious mothers who beget more skin-conscious daughters" (28).

21. Larsen consistently encourages her readers to see Helga as she sees herself, that is, as a piece of art. In the opening chapter, for example, she literally frames Helga with her boudoir, noting that "an observer would have thought her well fitted to that framing of light and shade" (2).

Epilogue

1. On the decline of social provisions for women and children in the United States, the contrast between 1960s and 1990s welfare debates, and the unfailing racism of welfare mythology, see Kornbluh; Kittay; Glenn, "From Servitude to Service Work"; and Mink, "The Lady and the Tramp (II)."

2. For an analysis of second-wave feminist fiction that confronts such technologies, see Adams, *Reproducing the Womb.* Certainly, these technologies have no better chance of equalizing reproductive agency among different groups of women than did earlier technologies; on the disparate uses to which the Norplant contraceptive has been put, for example, see Margot E. Young, "Reproductive Technologies and the Law: Norplant and the Bad Mother."

3. While these two films are not necessarily representative, their origins in critically acclaimed novels by Morrison, recipient of the 1993 Nobel Prize for literature, and Quindlen, a popular and respected columnist-turned-novelist, give them a certain cultural cachet, regardless of their box-office earnings.

4. It is, in other words, an extension of such late 1980s and early 1990s films as *Baby Boom* and *Fatal Attraction,* which dramatize the rewards of uncovering, and the dangers of repressing, the career woman's "natural" maternal instincts. On maternal myth making in other recent Hollywood films, see Diane Raymond, "Not as Tough as it Looks."

Works Cited

Abramovitz, Mimi. *Regulating the Lives of Women: Social Welfare Policy from Colonial Times to the Present.* Rev. ed. Boston: South End, 1996.

Adams, Alice E. *Reproducing the Womb: Images of Childbirth in Science, Feminist Theory, and Literature.* Ithaca, N.Y.: Cornell University Press, 1994.

Alexander, William. "The Higher Education of Women." In *History of the Colored Race in America.* 592–620. New Orleans: Palmetto, 1887.

Allen, Grant. *The Woman Who Did.* Boston: Roberts Bros., 1895.

Ammons, Elizabeth. Afterword to *The Unruly Voice: Rediscovering Pauline Elizabeth Hopkins.* Ed. John Cullen Gruesser. 211–19. Urbana: University of Illinois Press, 1996.

———. *Conflicting Stories: American Women Writers at the Turn into the Twentieth Century.* New York: Oxford University Press, 1992.

———. *Edith Wharton's Argument with America.* Athens: University of Georgia Press, 1980.

———. "Stowe's Dream of the Mother-Savior: *Uncle Tom's Cabin* and American Women Writers Before the 1920s." In *New Essays on Uncle Tom's Cabin.* Ed. Eric J. Sundquist. 155–95. New York: Cambridge University Press, 1986.

Ardis, Ann. *New Women, New Novels: Feminism and Early Modernism.* New Brunswick, N.J.: Rutgers University Press, 1990.

Baker, Helen LaReine. *Race Improvement or Eugenics: A Little Book on a Great Subject.* New York: Dodd, Mead, 1912.

Baker, Houston. *Workings of the Spirit: The Poetics of Afro-American Women's Writing.* Chicago: University of Chicago Press, 1991.

Bakhtin, Mikhail. *The Dialogic Imagination.* Austin: University of Texas Press, 1981.

Bambara, Toni Cade. *The Salt Eaters.* New York: Random House, 1980.

Barash, Carol L. "Virile Womanhood: Olive Schreiner's Narratives of a Master Race." In *Speaking of Gender.* Ed. Elaine Showalter. 269–81. New York: Routledge, 1989.

Bauer, Dale M. *Edith Wharton's Brave New Politics.* Madison: University of Wisconsin Press, 1994.

Beckham, Albert Sidney. "Applied Eugenics." *Crisis* 28 (August 1924): 177–78.

Bederman, Gail. *Manliness and Civilization: A Cultural History of Gender and Race in the United States, 1880–1917.* Chicago: University of Chicago Press, 1995.

Bender, Bert. *The Descent of Love: Darwin and the Theory of Sexual Selection in American Fiction, 1871–1926.* Philadelphia: University of Pennsylvania Press, 1996.

Benstock, Shari. *No Gifts from Chance: A Biography of Edith Wharton.* New York: Scribner's, 1994.

Berg, Allison. "The New 'New Negro': Recasting the Harlem Renaissance." *College Literature* 25, no. 3 (Fall 1998): 172–80.

Berlant, Lauren. *The Anatomy of National Fantasy: Hawthorne, Utopia, and Everyday Life.* Chicago: University of Chicago Press, 1991.

Berzon, Judith. *Neither White Nor Black: The Mulatto Character in American Fiction.* New York: New York University Press, 1978.

Birnbaum, Michele. "Alien Hands: Kate Chopin and the Colonization of Race." *American Literature* 66 (1994): 301–23.

Birney, Alice. "Address of Welcome." In *Work and Words of the National Congress of Mothers (First Annual Session).* 6–10. New York: Appleton, 1897.

Black, Martha Fodaski. "The Quintessence of Chopinism." In *Kate Chopin Reconsidered.* Ed. Lynda Boren and Sara de Saussure Davis. 95–113. Baton Rouge: Louisiana University Press, 1992.

Blanchard, Phyllis. "Sex in the Adolescent Girl." In *Sex in Civilization.* Ed. V. F. Calverton and S. D. Schmalhausen. 538–61. New York: Macaulay, 1929.

Bobo, Jacqueline. *Black Women as Cultural Readers.* New York: Columbia University Press, 1995.

Bogle, Bonnie. "Negro Womanhood's Greatest Needs." *Messenger,* April 1927: 109.

Boris, Eileen. "The Power of Motherhood: Black and White Activist Women Redefine the 'Political.'" In *Mothers of the New World.* Ed. Seth Koven and Sonya Michel. 213–45. New York: Routledge, 1993.

Brinton, Daniel G. *Races and Peoples: Lectures on the Science of Ethnography.* New York: Hodges, 1890.

Brooks, Gwendolyn. *A Street in Bronzeville.* New York: Harper, 1945.

Brown, Elsa Barkley. "'What Has Happened Here': The Politics of Difference in Women's History and Feminist Politics." In *"We Specialize in the Wholly Impossible": A Reader in Black Women's History.* Ed. Darlene Clark Hine, Wilma King, and Linda Reed. 39–54. Brooklyn, N.Y.: Carlson, 1995.

Brown, Hallie Q. "Discussion of Speech by Sarah J. Early." In *World's Congress of Representative Women.* Ed. May Wright Sewall. 724–29. Chicago: Rand, McNally, 1894.

———. "Negro Womanhood's Greatest Needs." *Messenger,* May 1927: 198–99.

Bruce, Philip Alexander. *The Plantation Negro as a Freeman.* New York: Putnam, 1889.

Brush, Lisa. "Love, Toil, and Trouble: Motherhood and Feminist Politics." *Signs* 21 (Winter 1996): 429–54.

Burrill, Mary. *They That Sit in Darkness.* 1919. In *Black Female Playwrights: An Anthology of Plays before 1950.* Ed. Kathy A. Perkins. 67–74. Bloomington: Indiana University Press, 1989.

Carby, Hazel V. Introduction to *The Magazine Novels of Pauline Hopkins.* Schomburg Library of Nineteenth-Century Black Women Writers, ed. Henry Louis Gates, Jr. xxix–l. New York: Oxford University Press, 1988.

———. *Reconstructing Womanhood: The Emergence of the Afro-American Woman Novelist.* New York: Oxford University Press, 1987.

Carroll, Charles. *The Negro a Beast.* 1900. Miami: Mnemosyne, 1969.

Carter, Elmer. "Eugenics for the Negro." *Birth Control Review* 16 (June 1932): 169–70.

Chang, Grace. "Undocumented Latinas: The New 'Employable Mothers.'" In *Mothering: Ideology, Experience, Agency.* Ed. Evelyn Nakano Glenn, Grace Chang, and Linda Rennin Force. 259–85. New York: Routledge, 1994.

Cherniavsky, Eva. *That Pale Mother Rising: Sentimental Discourses and the Imitation of Motherhood in 19th-Century America.* Bloomington: Indiana University Press, 1995.

Chesler, Ellen. *Woman of Valor: Margaret Sanger and the Birth Control Movement in America.* New York: Doubleday, 1992.

Chopin, Kate. "Athénaïse." In *The Awakening and Other Stories.* Ed. Sandra M. Gilbert. 229–61. New York: Penguin, 1984.

———. *The Awakening.* 1899. In *The Awakening and Other Stories.* Ed. Sandra M. Gilbert. 43–176. New York: Penguin, 1984.

———. "Emancipation: A Life Fable." In *The Awakening and Other Stories.* Ed. Sandra M. Gilbert. 177–78. New York: Penguin, 1984.

———. "La Belle Zoraïde." In *The Awakening and Other Stories.* Ed. Sandra M. Gilbert. 195–200. New York: Penguin, 1984.

———. "A Night in Acadie." In *The Complete Works of Kate Chopin.* Ed. Per Seyersted. 484–99. Baton Rouge: Louisiana State University Press, 1969.

Chrisman, Laura. "Empire, 'Race,' and Feminism at the Fin de Siècle: The Work of George Egerton and Olive Schreiner." In *Cultural Politics at the Fin de Siècle.* Ed. Sally Ledger and Scott McCracken. 45–65. Cambridge: Cambridge University Press, 1995.

Christian, Barbara. *Black Women Novelists: The Development of a Tradition.* Westport, Conn.: Greenwood, 1980.

Clark, Suzanne. *Sentimental Modernism: Women Writers and the Revolution of the Word.* Bloomington: Indiana University Press, 1991.

Clifford, Carrie W. "Votes for Children." *Crisis* 10 (August 1915): 185.

Collins, Patricia Hill. *Black Feminist Thought: Knowledge, Consciousness, and the Politics of Empowerment.* New York: Routledge, 1990.

Connell, Richard. "Weeds." *Birth Control Review* 6 (March 1922): 38–39; 6 (April 1922): 61–62.

Coolidge, Mary. *Why Women Are So.* New York: Henry Holt, 1912.

Cooper, Anna Julia. "Discussion of the Same Subject." In *World's Congress of Representative Women.* Ed. May Wright Sewall. 711–15. Chicago: Rand, McNally, 1894.

———. *A Voice from the South.* 1892. Schomburg Library of Nineteenth-Century Black Women Writers, ed. Henry Louis Gates, Jr. New York: Oxford University Press, 1988.

Corliss, Richard. "Bewitching Beloved." *Time,* October 5, 1998: 75–77.

Cott, Nancy F. *The Grounding of Modern Feminism.* New Haven, Conn.: Yale University Press, 1987.

Cotten, Sallie. "A National Training School for Women." In *Work and Words of the National Congress of Mothers (First Annual Session).* 208–19. New York: Appleton, 1897.

Crane, Stephen. *Maggie: A Girl of the Streets.* 1893. Reprint, New York: W. W. Norton, 1979.

Culley, Margaret, ed. *The Awakening,* by Kate Chopin. New York: W. W. Norton, 1976.

Cutter, Martha. "Losing the Battle but Winning the War: Resistance to Patriarchal Discourse in Kate Chopin's Short Fiction." *Legacy* 11 (1994): 17–36.

Davenport, Benjamin Rush. *Blood Will Tell: The Strange Story of a Son of Ham.* Cleveland: Caxton, 1902.

Davis, Angela. *Women, Race, and Class.* New York: Random House, 1981.

Davis, Katharine B. *Factors in the Sex Life of Twenty-Two Hundred Women.* New York: Harper, 1929.

———. "A Study of the Sex Life of the Normal Married Woman." *Journal of Social Hygiene* 8 (April 1922): 173–88.

Davis, Thadious. *Nella Larsen, Novelist of the Harlem Renaissance: A Woman's Life Unveiled.* Baton Rouge: Louisiana State University Press, 1994.

De Koven, Marianne. *Rich and Strange: Gender, History, Modernism.* Princeton, N.J.: Princeton University Press, 1991.

Denby, David. "Haunted By the Past." *New Yorker,* October 26, 1988: 248–53.

Dickinson, Mary Lowe. "Response to Address of Welcome." In *Work and Words of the National Congress of Mothers (First Annual Session).* 11–21. New York: Appleton, 1897.

Dickinson, Robert L., and Lura Beam. *A Thousand Marriages: A Medical Study of Sex Adjustment.* Baltimore: Williams and Wilkins, 1940.

Dittmar, Linda. "When Privilege Is No Protection: The Woman Artist in *Quicksand* and *The House of Mirth.*" In *Writing the Woman Artist: Essays on Poetics, Politics and Portraiture.* Ed. Suzanne W. Jones. 133–54. Philadelphia: University of Pennsylvania Press, 1991.

Dixon, Thomas. *The Clansmen: An Historical Romance of the Ku Klux Klan.* New York: Grosset and Dunlap, 1905.

———. *The Leopard's Spots: A Romance of the White Man's Burden, 1865–1900.* New York: Doubleday, 1902.

Dorr, Rheta Childe. *What Eight Million Women Want.* Boston: Small, Maynard, 1910.

Doyle, Laura. *Bordering on the Body: The Racial Matrix of Modern Fiction and Culture.* New York: Oxford University Press, 1994.

Dreiser, Theodore. *An American Tragedy.* New York: Boni and Liveright, 1925.

———. *Sister Carrie.* New York: B. W. Dodge, 1907.

Du Bois, W. E. B. "Black Folk and Birth Control." *Birth Control Review* 16 (June 1932): 166–69.

———. "The Damnation of Women." 1921. In *The Seventh Son: The Thought and Writings of W. E. B. Du Bois.* Ed. Julius Lester. Vol. 1: 511–26. New York: Random House, 1971.

———. *The Souls of Black Folk.* 1903. Reprint, New York: Bantam, 1989.

———. "Returning Soldiers." *Crisis* 17 (May 1919): 13–14.

———. "Two Novels." *Crisis* 35 (June 1928): 202.

duCille, Ann. *The Coupling Convention: Sex, Text, and Tradition in Black Women's Fiction.* New York: Oxford University Press, 1993.

———. "The Occult of True Black Womanhood: Critical Demeanor and Black Feminist Studies." *Signs* 19 (Spring 1994): 591–629.

Dunbar-Nelson, Alice. "Woman's Most Serious Problem." *Messenger,* March 1927: 73+.

Durham, Robert Lee. *The Call of the South.* Boston: L. C. Page, 1908.

"Editorial and Publishers' Announcements." *Colored American Magazine,* May 1900: 60–64.

Ehrenreich, Barbara, and Deirdre English. *For Her Own Good: 150 Years of the Experts' Advice to Women.* Garden City, N.Y.: Doubleday, 1979.

Elliott, R. S. "The Story of Our Magazine." *Colored American Magazine,* May 1901: 43–48.

Emerson, William. "Are You a 100% Mother?" *Woman's Home Companion,* January 1922: 25, 56.

Erlich, Gloria C. *The Sexual Education of Edith Wharton.* Berkeley: University of California Press, 1992.

Fauset, Jessie. "Oriflamme." 1920. In *Black Sister: Poetry by Black American Women, 1746–1980.* Ed. Erlene Stetson. 64. Bloomington: Indiana University Press, 1981.

Felski, Rita. *Beyond Feminist Aesthetics: Feminist Literature and Social Change.* Cambridge, Mass.: Harvard University Press, 1989.

———. *The Gender of Modernity.* Cambridge, Mass.: Harvard University Press, 1995.

Fishken, Shelley Fisher. "Interrogating 'Whiteness,' Complicating 'Blackness': Remapping American Literary Culture." *American Quarterly* 47 (1995): 428–66.

Foster, Frances Smith. *Written by Herself: Literary Production by African American Women, 1746–1892.* Bloomington: Indiana University Press, 1993.

Foster, J. Ellen. "The Civil and Political Status of Women." In *World's Congress of Representative Women.* Ed. May Wright Sewall. 439–45. Chicago: Rand, McNally, 1894.

Fredrickson, George. *The Black Image in the White Mind: The Debate on Afro-American Character and Destiny, 1817–1914.* New York: Harper and Row, 1971.

Gaines, Kevin. *Uplifting the Race: Black Leadership, Politics, and Culture in the Twentieth Century.* Chapel Hill: University of North Carolina Press, 1996.

Gainor, J. Ellen. "Chains of Dew and the Drama of Birth Control." In *Susan Glaspell: Essays on Her Theater and Fiction.* Ed. Linda Ben-Zvi. 165–93. Ann Arbor: University of Michigan Press, 1995.

Gardener, Helen. "Heredity in Its Relation to a Double Standard of Morals." In *World's Congress of Representative Women.* Ed. May Wright Sewall. 374–86. Chicago: Rand, McNally, 1894.

———. "The Moral Responsibility of Women in Heredity." In *Work and Words of the National Congress of Mothers (First Annual Session).* 130–47. New York: Appleton, 1897.

———. "Woman as an Annex." In *World's Congress of Representative Women.* Ed. May Wright Sewall. 488–99. Chicago: Rand, McNally, 1894.

Gates, Henry Louis, Jr. Foreword to *Contending Forces: A Romance Illustrative of Negro Life North and South,* by Pauline Hopkins. Schomburg Library of Nineteenth-Century Black Women Writers, ed. Henry Louis Gates, Jr. vii–xxii. New York: Oxford University Press, 1998.

———. *The Signifying Monkey: A Theory of African-American Literary Criticism.* New York: Oxford University Press, 1988.

Gere, Anne Ruggles. *Intimate Practices: Literacy and Cultural Work in U.S. Women's Clubs, 1880–1920.* Urbana: University of Illinois Press, 1997.

Giddings, Paula. *When and Where I Enter: The Impact of Black Women on Race and Sex in America.* New York: Bantam, 1984.

Gilbert, Sandra M. Introduction to *The Awakening,* by Kate Chopin. 7–33. New York: Penguin, 1984.

————. "Life's Empty Pack: Notes toward a Literary Daughteronomy." *Critical Inquiry* 11 (1985): 355–84.

————. "The Second Coming of Aphrodite: Kate Chopin's Fantasy of Desire." *Kenyon Review* (Summer 1983): 42–66.

Gilbert, Sandra M., and Susan Gubar. *The Madwoman in the Attic: The Woman Writer and the Nineteenth-Century Literary Imagination.* New Haven, Conn.: Yale University Press, 1979.

————. *Sexchanges.* Vol. 2 of *No Man's Land: The Place of the Woman Writer in the Twentieth Century.* New Haven, Conn.: Yale University Press, 1991.

————. *The War of the Words.* Vol. 1 of *No Man's Land: The Place of the Woman Writer in the Twentieth Century.* New Haven, Conn.: Yale University Press, 1988.

Gilman, Charlotte Perkins. "Educated Bodies." *Woman's Journal,* June 1904: 178–90.

————. *Herland.* 1915. Reprint, New York: Pantheon, 1979.

————. *His Religion and Hers: A Study of the Faith of Our Fathers and the Work of Our Mothers.* New York: Century, 1923.

————. *The Home: Its Work and Influence.* New York: McClure, Phillips, 1903.

————. *The Living of Charlotte Perkins Gilman: An Autobiography.* 1935. Reprint, New York: Arno, 1972.

————. *The Man-Made World; or, Our Androcentric Culture.* New York: Charlton, 1911.

————. "Our Brains and What Ails Them." 1912. In *Charlotte Perkins Gilman: A Nonfiction Reader.* Ed. Larry Ceplair. 219–34. New York: Columbia University Press, 1991.

————. "Should Women Use Violence?" 1912. In *Charlotte Perkins Gilman: A Nonfiction Reader.* Ed. Larry Ceplair. 212–19. New York: Columbia University Press, 1991.

————. "Why I Wrote 'The Yellow Wallpaper.'" 1913. In *The Captive Imagination: A Casebook on "The Yellow Wallpaper."* Ed. Catherine Golden. 51–53. New York: Feminist Press, 1992.

————. *Women and Economics.* Boston: Small, Maynard, 1898.

————. "The Yellow Wallpaper." 1892. In *The Charlotte Perkins Gilman Reader.* Ed. Ann J. Lane. 3–19. New York: Pantheon, 1980.

Glenn, Evelyn Nakano. "From Servitude to Service Work: Historical Continuities in the Racial Division of Paid Reproductive Labor." *Signs* 18 (Autumn 1992): 1–43.

————. "Social Constructions of Mothering: A Thematic Overview." In *Mothering: Ideology, Experience, Agency.* Ed. Evelyn Nakano Glenn, Grace Chang, and Linda Rennin Force. 1–29. New York: Routledge, 1994.

Goldman, Emma. *Marriage and Love.* New York: Mother Earth, 1911.

Goodman, Charlotte. Afterword. In *Weeds,* by Edith Summers Kelley. 353–66. New York: Feminist Press, 1982.

Gordon, Linda. *Woman's Body, Woman's Right: Birth Control in America.* 2d ed. New York: Penguin, 1990.

Graham, Shirley. *It's Morning.* 1940. In *Black Female Playwrights: An Anthology of Plays before 1950.* Ed. Kathy Perkins. 211–24. Bloomington: Indiana University Press, 1989.

Grant, Julia. *Raising Baby by the Book: The Education of American Mothers.* New Haven, Conn.: Yale University Press, 1998.

Gray, Jeffrey. "Essence and the Mulatto Traveler: Europe as Embodiment in Nella Larsen's *Quicksand.*" *Novel* 27 (1994): 257–70.

Grimké, Angelina Weld. "The Closing Door." *Birth Control Review* 3 (September 1919): 10–14; 3 (November 1919): 8–12.

———. *Rachel.* In *Black Theater, U.S.A.: Forty-five Plays by Black Americans.* Ed. James V. Hatch. 139–72. New York: Free Press, 1974.

———. "'Rachel' the Play of the Month: The Reason and Synopsis by the Author." 1920. In *Selected Works of Angelina Weld Grimké.* Ed. Carolivia Herron. Schomburg Library of Nineteenth-Century Black Women Writers, ed. Henry Louis Gates, Jr. 413–16. New York: Oxford University Press, 1991.

Gruesser, John Cullen, ed. *The Unruly Voice: Rediscovering Pauline Elizabeth Hopkins.* Urbana: University of Illinois Press, 1996.

Gubar, Susan. "'The Blank Page' and the Issues of Female Creativity." In *The New Feminist Criticism: Essays on Women, Literature, and Theory.* Ed. Elaine Showalter. 292–313. New York: Pantheon, 1985.

Gunning, Sandra. *Race, Rape, and Lynching: The Red Record of American Literature, 1890–1912.* New York: Oxford University Press, 1996.

Guy-Sheftall, Beverly. *Daughters of Sorrow: Attitudes toward Black Women, 1880–1920.* Brooklyn, N.Y.: Carlson, 1990.

Hackley, E. Azalia. *The Colored Girl Beautiful.* Kansas City: Burton, 1916.

Hall, Jacquelyn Dowd. *Revolt against Chivalry: Jessie Daniel Ames and the Women's Campaign against Lynching.* New York: Columbia University Press, 1993.

Haller, Mark. *Eugenics: Hereditarian Attitudes in American Thought.* New Brunswick, N.J.: Rutgers University Press, 1963.

Haller, John. *Outcasts from Evolution: Scientific Attitudes of Racial Inferiority, 1859–1900.* Urbana: University of Illinois Press, 1971.

Harcourt, Alfred, to Edith Summers Kelley. April 6, 1923. Kelley Papers. Morris Library. Southern Illinois University at Carbondale.

Harper, Frances E. W. "The Afro-American Mother." In *Work and Words of the National Congress of Mothers (First Annual Session).* 67–71. New York: Appleton, 1897.

———. "Enlightened Motherhood." 1892. In *A Brighter Coming Day: A Frances E. W. Harper Reader.* Ed. Frances Smith Foster. 285–92. New York: Feminist Press, 1990.

———. *Iola Leroy, or Shadows Uplifted.* 1892. Schomburg Library of Nineteenth-Century Black Women Writers, ed. Henry Louis Gates, Jr. New York: Oxford University Press, 1988.

———. "Woman's Political Future." In *World's Congress of Representative Women.* Ed. May Wright Sewall. 433–38. Chicago: Rand, McNally, 1894.

Harper, Ida A. "Women in Municipal Government." In *World's Congress of Representative Women.* Ed. May Wright Sewall. 451–57. Chicago: Rand, McNally, 1894.

Harris, Susan. *19th-Century American Women's Novels: Interpretive Strategies.* Cambridge: Cambridge University Press, 1990.

Hasian, Marouf Arif, Jr. *The Rhetoric of Eugenics in Anglo-American Thought.* Athens: University of Georgia Press, 1996.

Hatch, James V., ed. *Black Theater, U.S.A.: Forty-five Plays by Black Americans, 1847–1974.* New York: Free Press, 1974.

Heilbrun, Carolyn. *Writing a Woman's Life.* New York: W. W. Norton, 1988.

Hemingway, Ernest. "Indian Camp." In *In Our Time.* 15–19. New York: Scribner's, 1925.

Herrick, Robert. "A Feline World." *Bookman* 69 (1929): 1–6.

———. "Hermaphrodites." *Bookman* 69 (1929): 485–89.

———. "A Study in Black." *New Republic* 57 (December 26, 1928): 172–73.

Higginbotham, Evelyn Brooks. "African-American Women's History and the Metalanguage of Race." *Signs* 17 (Winter 1992): 251–74.

Hirsch, Marianne. *The Mother/Daughter Plot: Narrative, Psychoanalysis, Feminism.* Bloomington: Indiana University Press, 1989.

Hite, Molly. "Romance, Marginality, and Matrilineage: *The Color Purple* and *Their Eyes Were Watching God.*" In *Reading Black, Reading Feminist.* Ed. Henry Louis Gates, Jr. 431–53. New York: Penguin, 1990.

Hoberman, James. "The Haunting." *Village Voice,* October 20, 1998: 155.

Holland, W. W. "Photography for Our Young People." *Colored American Magazine,* May 1902: 5–7.

Homans, Margaret. "'Women of Color' Writers and Feminist Theory." *New Literary History* 25 (1994): 73–94.

Hopkins, Pauline. "Club Life among Colored Women." *Colored American Magazine,* August 1902: 273–77.

———. *Contending Forces: A Romance Illustrative of Negro Life North and South.* 1900. Schomburg Library of Nineteenth-Century Black Women Writers, ed. Henry Louis Gates, Jr. New York: Oxford University Press, 1988.

———. "Echoes from the Annual Convention of Northeastern Federation of Colored Women's Clubs." *Colored American Magazine,* October 1903: 709–13.

———. "Famous Women of the Negro Race: Artists." *Colored American Magazine,* September 1902: 362–67.

———. "How a New York Newspaper Man Entertained a Number of Colored Ladies and Gentlemen at Dinner in the Revere House, Boston, and How the Colored American League Was Started." *Colored American Magazine,* March 1904: 151–60.

———. "Literary Workers." *Colored American Magazine,* April 1902: 366–71.

———. "Prospectus . . . of the New Romance of Colored Life, 'Contending Forces.'" *Colored American Magazine,* September 1900: 195–96.

———. "Some Literary Workers." *Colored American Magazine,* March 1902: 277–80.

Hostetler, Ann E. "The Aesthetics of Race and Gender in Nella Larsen's *Quicksand.*" *PMLA* 105 (1990): 35–46.

Howard, June. *Form and History in the Naturalist Novel.* Chapel Hill: University of North Carolina Press, 1985.

Howe, Julia Ward. "The Moral Initiative as Related to Woman." In *World's Congress of Representative Women.* Ed. May Wright Sewall. 314–21. Chicago: Rand, McNally, 1894.

Hughes, Langston. *The Negro Mother and Other Dramatic Recitations.* Salem, N.H.: Ayer, 1931.

Hull, Gloria. *Color, Sex, and Poetry: Three Women Writers of the Harlem Renaissance.* Bloomington: Indiana University Press, 1987.

Hurston, Zora Neale. *Their Eyes Were Watching God.* 1937. Reprint, Urbana: University of Illinois Press, 1978.

Hutchinson, George. *The Harlem Renaissance in Black and White.* Cambridge, Mass.: Harvard University Press, 1995.

———. "Nella Larsen and the Veil of Race." *American Literary History* 9 (1997): 329–49.

Irving, Katrina. *Immigrant Mothers: Narratives of Race and Maternity, 1890–1925.* Urbana: University of Illinois Press, 2000.

Iseman, M. S. *Race Suicide.* New York: Cosmopolitan Press, 1912.

Jacobs, Harriet. *Incidents in the Life of a Slave Girl.* 1861. Reprint, Cambridge, Mass.: Harvard University Press, 1987.

Johnson, Abby A., and Ronald M. Johnson. *Propaganda and Aesthetics: The Literary Politics of Afro-American Magazines in the Twentieth Century.* Amherst: University of Massachusetts Press, 1979.

Johnson, Georgia Douglas. *Bronze: A Book of Verse.* Boston: B. J. Brimmer, 1922.

Kaplan, E. Ann. *Motherhood and Representation: The Mother in Popular Culture and Melodrama.* New York: Routledge, 1992.

Kaplan, Carla. "The Erotics of Talk: 'That Oldest of Human Longing' in *Their Eyes Were Watching God.*" *American Literature* 67 (1995): 115–42.

Kelley, Edith Summers. "Can an Artist Exist in America?" Kelley Papers. Morris Library. Southern Illinois University at Carbondale.

———. "Helicon Hall: An Experiment in Living." 1934. Kelley Papers. Morris Library. Southern Illinois University at Carbondale.

——— to Upton Sinclair. July 24, 1934. Kelley Papers. Morris Library. Southern Illinois University at Carbondale.

———. Kelley Papers. Morris Library. Southern Illinois University at Carbondale.

———. *Weeds.* 1923. Reprint, New York: Feminist Press, 1982.

Kellogg, Vernon. *Darwinism Today.* New York: Henry Holt, 1907.

Kennedy, David. *Birth Control in America: The Career of Margaret Sanger.* New Haven, Conn.: Yale University Press, 1970.

Key, Ellen. *The Century of the Child.* Trans. Frances Mary. New York: Putnam's, 1909.

———. *The Woman Movement.* Trans. Mamah Bouton Borthwick. New York: Putnam's, 1912.

Kittay, Eva Feder. "Dependency, Equality, and Welfare." *Feminist Studies* 24, no. 1 (Spring 1998): 32–43.

Klein, Ethel. *Gender Politics: From Consciousness to Mass Politics.* Cambridge, Mass.: Harvard University Press, 1984.

Koch, Felix J. "Little Mothers of Tomorrow." *Crisis* 14 (October 1917): 289–92.

Kornbluh, Felicia. "The Goals of the National Welfare Rights Movement: Why We Need Them Thirty Years Later." *Feminist Studies* 24, no. 1 (Spring 1998): 65–78.

Koven, Seth, and Sonya Michel, eds. *Mothers of a New World: Maternalist Politics and the Origins of Welfare States.* New York: Routledge, 1993.

Ladd-Taylor, Molly. *Mother-Work: Women, Child Welfare, and the State, 1890–1930.* Urbana: University of Illinois Press, 1994.

———. "'My Work Came Out of Agony and Grief': Mothers and the Making of the Sheppard-Towner Act." In *Mothers of a New World.* Ed. Seth Koven and Sonya Michel. 321–42. New York: Routledge, 1993.

Ladd-Taylor, Molly, and Lauri Umansky, eds. *"Bad" Mothers: The Politics of Blame in Twentieth-Century America.* New York: New York University Press, 1998.

Lane, Ann J. *To Herland and Beyond: The Life and Work of Charlotte Perkins Gilman.* New York: Pantheon, 1990.

Larsen, Nella. *Quicksand* and *Passing.* Ed. Deborah E. McDowell. New Brunswick, N.J.: Rutgers University Press, 1989.

Lasch-Quinn, Elisabeth. *Black Neighbors: Race and the Limits of Reform in the American Settlement House Movement, 1890–1945.* Chapel Hill: University of North Carolina Press, 1993.

Lawrence, D. H. "The Horse Dealer's Daughter." 1922. In *The Norton Anthology of English Literature.* 4th ed. Ed. M. H. Abrams. Vol. 2: 2168–83. New York: W. W. Norton, 1979.

Ledger, Sally. "The New Woman and the Crisis of Victorianism." In *Cultural Politics at the Fin de Siècle.* Ed. Sally Ledger and Scott McCracken. 22–44. Cambridge: Cambridge University Press, 1995.

Lerner, Gerda. *Black Women in White America: A Documentary History.* New York: Vintage, 1979.

LeSueur, Meridel. *The Girl.* Rev. ed. Albuquerque, N.M.: West End Press, 1978.

Levy, Helen Fiddyment. *Fiction of the Home Place: Jewett, Cather, Glasgow, Porter, Welty, and Naylor.* Jackson: University Press of Mississippi, 1992.

Littell, Robert. "The Negro Players." *New Republic,* May 30, 1923: 21.

Lock, Robert Heath. *Recent Progress in the Study of Variation, Heredity and Evolution.* London: John Murray, 1906.

Locke, Alain, ed. *The New Negro.* 1925. Reprint, New York: Simon and Schuster, 1992.

Loewenberg, Bert James, and Ruth Bogin, eds. *Black Women in Nineteenth-Century American Life: Their Words, Their Thoughts, Their Feelings.* University Park: Penn State University Press, 1976.

Lomawaima, K. Tsianina. *They Called It Prairie Light: The Story of Chilocco Indian School.* Lincoln: University of Nebraska Press, 1993.

Lootens, Barbara. "A Struggle for Survival: Edith Summers Kelley's *Weeds.*" *Women's Studies* 13 (1986): 103–13.

Lynd, Robert S., and Helen Merrell Lynd. *Middletown: A Study in Modern American Culture.* New York: Harcourt, Brace, and World, 1929.

MacLean, Annie Marion. *Wage-Earning Women.* New York: Macmillan, 1910.

MacPike, Loralee. "The Fallen Woman's Sexuality: Childbirth and Censure." In *Sexuality and Victorian Literature.* Ed. Don Richard Cox. 54–71. Knoxville: University of Tennessee Press, 1984.

McCann, Carole R. *Birth Control Politics in the United States, 1916–1945.* Ithaca, N.Y.: Cornell University Press, 1995.

McClintock, Anne. " 'No Longer in a Future Heaven': Nationalism, Gender, and Race." In *Becoming National: A Reader.* Ed. Geoff Eley and Ronald Grigor Suny. 260–84. New York: Oxford University Press, 1996.

McDowell, Deborah E. " 'The Changing Same': Generational Connections and Black Women Novelists." *New Literary History* 18 (1987): 281–302.

———. Introduction to *Quicksand* and *Passing,* by Nella Larsen. Ed. Deborah E. McDowell. ix–xxxviii. New Brunswick, N.J.: Rutgers University Press, 1989.

McDougald, Elise Johnson. "The Double Task: The Struggle of Negro Women for Sex and Race Emancipation." *Survey Graphic* 6 (March 1925): 691.

McFalls, Joseph A., Jr., and George S. Masnick. "Birth Control and the Fertility of the U.S. Black Population, 1880–1980." *Journal of Family History* 6 (1981): 89–106.

McKay, Nellie. "'What Were They Saying?': Black Women Playwrights of the Harlem Renaissance." In *The Harlem Renaissance Re-examined*. Ed. Victor A. Kramer. 129–47. New York: AMS Press, 1987.

McLendon, Jacquelyn Y. *The Politics of Color in the Fiction of Jessie Fauset and Nella Larsen*. Charlottesville: University Press of Virginia, 1995.

Mailloux, Steven. *Rhetorical Power*. Ithaca, N.Y.: Cornell University Press, 1989.

Martin, Anne. "Everywoman's Chance to Benefit Humanity: An Everlasting Benefit You Can Win in a Week." *Good Housekeeping*, February 1920: 20–21, 144–48.

Mercer, Hamilton. "Messages of Love." *Overland Monthly*, May 1920: 437.

Michaels, Walter Benn. *Our America: Nativism, Modernism, and Pluralism*. Durham, N.C.: Duke University Press, 1995.

Miller, Kelly. "The Risk of Woman Suffrage." *Crisis* 10 (November 1915): 37–38.

Miller, Nina. *Making Love Modern: The Intimate Public Worlds of New York's Literary Women*. New York: Oxford University Press, 1999.

Mink, Gwendolyn. "The Lady and the Tramp: Gender, Race, and the Origins of the American Welfare State." In *Women, the State, and Welfare*. Ed. Linda Gordon. 92–122. Madison: University of Wisconsin Press, 1990.

———. "The Lady and the Tramp (II): Feminist Welfare Politics, Poor Single Mothers, and the Challenge of Welfare Justice." *Feminist Studies* 24, no. 1 (Spring 1998): 55–64.

———. *The Wages of Motherhood: Inequality in the Welfare State, 1917–1942*. Ithaca, N.Y.: Cornell University Press, 1995.

Monroe, Anne Shannon. "Adventuring in Motherhood." *Good Housekeeping*, May 1920: 28–29, 128–38.

Morrison, Toni. *Beloved*. New York: Alfred A. Knopf, 1987.

———. *Playing in the Dark: Whiteness and the Literary Imagination*. Cambridge, Mass.: Harvard University Press, 1992.

———. "Unspeakable Things Unspoken: The Afro-American Presence in American Literature." *Michigan Quarterly* 28, no. 1 (Winter 1989): 1–34.

Mossell, Mrs. N. F. (Gertrude). *The Work of the Afro-American Woman*. 1894. Schomburg Library of Nineteenth-Century Black Women Writers, ed. Henry Louis Gates, Jr. New York: Oxford University Press, 1988.

Moynihan, Daniel Patrick. *The Negro Family: The Case for National Action*. Washington, D.C.: U.S. Government Printing Office, 1965.

Murray, Anna. "Negro Children of America." In *Report of the National Congress of Mothers*. 174–77. New York: Appleton, 1905.

"The New Negro Woman." *Messenger*, July 1923: 757.

North, Michael. *The Dialect of Modernism: Race, Language, and Twentieth-Century Literature*. New York: Oxford University Press, 1994.

Omolade, Barbara. "Black Women and Feminism." In *The Future of Difference*. Ed. Hester Eisenstein and Alice Jardine. 247–57. Boston: G. K. Hall, 1980.

O'Neale, Sondra. "Race, Sex and Self: Aspects of Bildung in Select Novels by Black American Women Novelists." *MELUS* 9 (Winter 1988): 25–37.

Owen, Chandler. "Black Mammies." *Messenger*, April 1923: 670.

Perkins, Kathy, ed. *Black Female Playwrights: An Anthology of Plays before 1950*. Bloomington: Indiana University Press, 1989.

Peterson, Carla. "Unsettled Frontiers: Race, History and Romance in Pauline Hopkins's *Contending Forces*." In *Famous Last Words*. Ed. Alison Booth. 177–96. Charlottesville: University Press of Virginia, 1993.

Prasch, Thomas. "From Murphy Brown to L.A. Law: Dan Quayle in California." *Ryder Magazine*, July 1992: 24–30.

"Problems of Maternity." *General Federation of Women's Clubs Magazine*, December 1918: 19.

Quindlen, Anna. *One True Thing*. New York: Random House, 1994.

Rabinowitz, Paula. *Labor and Desire: Women's Revolutionary Fiction in Depression America*. Chapel Hill: University of North Carolina Press, 1991.

Raymond, Diane. "Not as Tough as It Looks: Images of Mothering in Popular Culture." In *Sexual Politics and Popular Culture*. Ed. Diane Raymond. 131–46. Bowling Green, Ohio: Popular Press, 1990.

Reed, James. *From Private Vice to Public Virtue: The Birth Control Movement and American Society since 1830*. New York: Basic, 1978.

Rich, Adrienne. *Of Woman Born: Motherhood as Experience and Institution*. New York: W. W. Norton, 1976.

Roberts, Dorothy. *Killing the Black Body: Race, Reproduction, and the Meaning of Liberty*. New York: Pantheon, 1997.

Robinson, William J. *America's Sex, Marriage, and Divorce Problems: Based on 30 Years Practice and Study*. New York: Eugenics Publishing, 1928.

——. *Eugenics, Marriage, and Birth Control: Practical Eugenics*. 2d ed. New York: Critic and Guide, 1922.

Rodrique, Jessie M. "The Black Community and the Birth Control Movement." In *Passion and Power: Sexuality in History*. Ed. Kathy Peiss and Christina Simmons. 138–54. Philadelphia: Temple University Press, 1989.

Rogers, J. A. "The Critic." *Messenger*, April 1925: 165–66.

Roman, Charles V. "The American Negro and Social Hygiene." *Social Hygiene* 7 (1921): 41–47.

Romero, Lora. *Home Fronts: Domesticity and Its Critics in the Antebellum United States*. Durham, N.C.: Duke University Press, 1997.

Romines, Ann. *The Home Plot: Women, Writing, and Domestic Ritual*. Amherst: University of Massachusetts Press, 1992.

Roosevelt, Theodore. "Address to the First International Congress in America on the Welfare of the Child." *National Congress of Mothers Magazine*, April 1908: 174–76.

——. "Sixth Annual Message." 1906. *A Compilation of the Messages and Papers of the Presidents*. Vol. 9: 7403–50. New York: Bureau of National Literature, 1909.

Rosowski, Susan J. *Birthing a Nation: Gender, Creativity, and the West in American Literature*. Lincoln: University of Nebraska Press, 1999.

——. "The Novel of Awakening." In *The Voyage In: Fictions of Female Development*. Ed. Elizabeth Abel, Marianne Hirsch, and Elizabeth Langland. 49–68. Hanover, N.H.: New England University Press, 1983.

Rudwick, Elliott M., and August Meier. "Black Man in the 'White City': Negroes and the Columbian Exposition, 1893." *Phylon* 26, no. 4 (Winter 1965): 354–61.

Russett, Cynthia Eagle. *Sexual Science: The Victorian Construction of Womanhood.* Cambridge, Mass.: Harvard University Press, 1989.

Rydell, Robert W. *All the World's a Fair: Visions of Empire at American International Expositions, 1876–1916.* Chicago: University of Chicago Press, 1987.

Sadoff, Dianne F. "Black Matrilineage: The Case of Alice Walker and Zora Neale Hurston." *Signs* 11 (Autumn 1985): 4–26.

Sanchez, George J. *Becoming Mexican American: Ethnicity, Culture, and Identity in Chicano Los Angeles, 1900–1945.* New York: Oxford University Press, 1993.

Sanchez-Eppler, Karen. "Bodily Bonds: The Intersecting Rhetorics of Feminism and Abolition." *Representations* 24 (Fall 1988): 28–59.

Sanger, Margaret. "Birth Control and Racial Betterment." *Birth Control Review* 3 (February 1919): 11–12.

———. "The Civilizing Force of Birth Control." In *Sex in Civilization.* Ed. V. F. Calverton and S. D. Schmalhausen. 525–37. New York: Macaulay, 1929.

———. *Motherhood in Bondage.* New York: Brentano's, 1928.

———. *Woman and the New Race.* 1920. Reprint, New York: Maxwell, 1969.

Sewall, May Wright. Introduction to *World's Congress of Representative Women.* Ed. May Wright Sewall. 1–8. Chicago: Rand, McNally, 1894.

———. "Introductory Address." In *World's Congress of Representative Women.* Ed. May Wright Sewall. 13–18. Chicago: Rand, McNally, 1894.

———. "Prefatory Comments: The Solidarity of Human Interests." In *World's Congress of Representative Women.* Ed. May Wright Sewall. 632–33. Chicago: Rand, McNally, 1894.

Sherman, Stuart P. "Fresh Harvest." *Literary Review,* December 15, 1923: 363.

Showalter, Elaine. "The Death of the Lady (Novelist): Wharton's *House of Mirth.*" *Representations* 9 (Winter 1985): 133–149.

———. *Sexual Anarchy: Gender and Culture at the Fin de Siècle.* New York: Penguin, 1990.

Simmons, Christina. "Marriage in the Modern Manner: Radicalism and Reform in America, 1914–41." Ph.D. diss. Brown University, 1982.

Sinclair, Upton. *The Book of Life.* 2 vols. Girard, Kans.: Haldeman-Julius, 1921.

———. *The Jungle.* New York: Doubleday, 1905.

Smith, Barbara. "Toward a Black Feminist Criticism." In *The New Feminist Criticism: Essays on Women, Literature, and Theory.* Ed. Elaine Showalter. 168–85. New York: Pantheon, 1985.

Smith, Stephanie. *Conceived by Liberty: Maternal Figures and Nineteenth-Century American Literature.* Ithaca, N.Y.: Cornell University Press, 1994.

Smith-Rosenberg, Carroll. "The New Woman as Androgyne: Social Disorder and Gender Crisis, 1870–1930." In *Disorderly Conduct: Visions of Gender in Victorian America.* 245–96. New York: Alfred A. Knopf, 1985.

Spender, Dale. *Man-Made Language.* London: Routledge, 1980.

Spillers, Hortense. "Mama's Baby, Papa's Maybe: An American Grammar Book." *Diacritics* 17 (Summer 1987): 65–81.

Stallings, Laurence. "None But the Brave." *New York World,* December 7, 1923: 13.

Stoddard, Lothrop. *The Rising Tide of Color against White World-Supremacy.* New York: Scribner's, 1920.

Swiney, Frances. *The Awakening of Women; or, Woman's Part in Evolution*. London: Reeves, 1899.

Tate, Claudia. *Domestic Allegories of Political Desire: The Black Heroine's Text at the Turn of the Century*. New York: Oxford University Press, 1992.

———. *Psychoanalysis and Black Novels: Desire and the Protocols of Race*. New York: Oxford University Press, 1998.

Tayleur, Eleanor. "The Negro Woman." *Outlook* 76 (1904): 266–72.

Taylor, Helen. *Gender, Race, and Region in the Writings of Grace King, Ruth McEnery Stuart, and Kate Chopin*. Baton Rouge: Louisiana State University Press, 1989.

Terrell, Mary Church. "What Role Is the Educated Negro Woman to Play in the Uplifting of Her Race?" 1902. In *Quest for Equality: The Life and Writings of Mary Eliza Church*. Ed. Beverly Washington Jones. 151–56. Brooklyn, N.Y.: Carlson, 1990.

Tompkins, Jane. *Sensational Designs: The Cultural Work of American Fiction, 1790–1860*. New York: Oxford University Press, 1985.

Toth, Emily. *Kate Chopin: A Life of the Author of "The Awakening."* New York: William Morrow, 1990.

Toth, Emily, and Per Seyersted. *Kate Chopin's Private Papers*. Bloomington: Indiana University Press, 1998.

Tracey, Karen. *Plots and Proposals: American Women's Fiction, 1850–90*. Urbana: University of Illinois Press, 2000.

Van Buren, Jane Silverman. *The Modernist Madonna: Semiotics of the Maternal Metaphor*. Bloomington: Indiana University Press, 1989.

Veblen, Thorstein. 1899. *The Theory of the Leisure Class: An Economic Study of Institutions*. New York: Macmillan, 1912.

Walker, Alice. *In Search of Our Mother's Gardens*. New York: Harcourt, 1983.

Wallace, Michele. "*Boyz N the Hood* and *Jungle Fever*." In *Black Popular Culture*. Ed. Gina Dent. 123–31. Seattle: Bay Press, 1992.

Ward, Lester. "Our Better Halves." *Forum* 6 (November 1888): 274–75.

Washington, Mary Helen. *Invented Lives: Narratives of Black Women, 1860–1960*. New York: Doubleday, 1987.

Weinraub, Bernard. "Despite Hope, 'Beloved' Generates Little Heat Among Moviegoers." *New York Times*, November 9, 1988: B4.

Weeks, Mary Harmon, ed. *Parents and Their Problems: Child Welfare in Home, School, Church, and State*. Washington, D.C.: National Congress of Mothers and Parent Teacher Associations, 1914.

Wells, Ida B., and Frederick Douglass. *The Reason Why the Colored American Is Not in the World's Columbian Exposition*. 1893. In *Selected Works of Ida B. Wells-Barnett*. Schomburg Library of Nineteenth-Century Black Women Writers, ed. Henry Louis Gates, Jr. 46–137. New York: Oxford University Press, 1991.

Welter, Barbara. *Dimity Convictions: The American Woman in the Nineteenth Century*. Athens: Ohio University Press, 1976.

Wharton, Edith. "Beatrice Palmato." In *Edith Wharton: A Life*, by R. W. B. Lewis. 544–58. New York: Harper, 1975.

———. *The House of Mirth*. 1905. Reprint, New York: Bantam, 1984.

———. *Summer*. 1917. Reprint, New York: Harper and Row, 1979.

———. "The Valley of Childish Things and Other Emblems." In *Collected Short Stories of Edith Wharton.* Ed. R. W. B. Lewis. Vol. 1: 58–63. New York: Scribner's, 1968.

Wiggam, Albert Edward. *The Fruit of the Family Tree.* New York: Blue Ribbon, 1922.

Williams, Fannie Barrier. "The Club Movement among Colored Women of America." 1900. In *A New Negro for a New Century: An Accurate and Up-to-Date Record of the Upward Struggles of the Negro Race.* Ed. Booker T. Washington, N. B. Wood, and Fannie Barrier Williams. 379–428. New York: Arno, 1969.

———. "The Intellectual Progress of the Colored Women of the United States since the Emancipation Proclamation." In *World's Congress of Representative Women.* Ed. May Wright Sewall. 696–711. Chicago: Rand, McNally, 1894.

———. "Some Perils of Women's Clubs." *New York Age,* December 28, 1905: 6.

Williams, Rhonda M., and Carla L. Peterson. "The Color of Memory: Interpreting Twentieth-Century U.S. Social Policy from a Nineteenth-Century Perspective." *Feminist Studies* 24, no. 1 (Spring 1998): 7–25.

Williams, William Carlos. "A Night in June." In *The Farmers' Daughters: The Collected Stories of William Carlos Williams.* 136–43. Norfolk, Conn.: New Directions, 1961.

Wilson, Harriet E. *Our Nig; or, Sketches from the Life of a Free Black.* 1859. Reprint, New York: Vintage, 1983.

Wines, Michael. "Appeal of 'Murphy Brown' Now Clear at White House." *New York Times,* May 20, 1992: A1+.

Wolff, Cynthia Griffin. Introduction to *Summer,* by Edith Wharton. v–xxvii. New York: Harper and Row, 1979.

Wong, Sau-ling C. "Diverted Mothering: Representations of Caregivers of Color in the Age of Multiculturalism." In *Mothering: Experience, Ideology, Agency.* Ed. Evelyn Nakano Glenn, Grace Chang, and Linda Rennin Force. 67–91. New York: Routledge, 1993.

The Work and Words of the National Congress of Mothers. New York: Appleton, 1897.

Wyman, Tillie Buffum Chace. Review of *Rachel. Journal of Negro History.* 1921. In *Selected Works of Angelina Weld Grimké.* Ed. Carolivia Herron. 447–49. New York: Oxford University Press, 1991.

Yaeger, Patricia S. "'A Language Which Nobody Understood': Emancipatory Strategies in *The Awakening.*" *Novel* 20 (1987): 197–219.

Yarborough, Richard. Introduction to *Contending Forces,* by Pauline Hopkins. xxvii–xlvii. New York: Oxford University Press, 1988.

Young, Elizabeth. "Warring Fictions: *Iola Leroy* and the Color of Gender." *American Literature* 64 (1992): 273–97.

Young, Margot E. "Reproductive Technologies and the Law: Norplant and the Bad Mother." *Marriage and Family Review* 21 (1995): 259–81.

Index

Postpartum depression, 59–60. *See also* Madness

Power. *See* Agency, female

Pregnancy, 5; Chopin's depiction of, 62, 65; contemporary depictions of, 135; Hopkins's depiction of, 108; inevitability of, 10, 61, 71, 72, 87, 88, 92, 128; Kelley's depiction of, 92–97; Larsen's depiction of, 103–5, 125–26, 128; male writers' depictions of, 147n.12; Wharton's depiction of, 67, 71, 77. *See also* Birth control; Childbirth; Motherhood

"Primitive Motherhood" (Cushing), 26

Private sphere. *See* Public vs. private spheres

Progressive Era: emphasis of, on race and evolution, 4, 5; as focus of study, 6; population politics in, 16, 148n.5; women's contributions to, 4, 6, 17, 18–31, 133–34. *See also specific works*

Psychoanalysis and Black Novels (Tate), 155n.2

Public vs. private spheres: gender basis of, 8; motherhood as link between, 4, 7–8, 15–31, 79–80, 109, 149n.7

Quayle, Dan, 1, 2–3

Quicksand (Larsen), 10, 11, 102, 104, 106, 118–31, 155n.1. *See also* Larsen, Nella

Quindlen, Anna, 11, 135–36, 138–43

Race: alliances across, 133–35; defined, 145n.3; determinism based on, 33, 35, 40–41; as factor in sexual violence against black women, 33, 34, 41–42, 45–51, 108, 112, 115, 136, 149nn.4–5; Hopkins's view of, as not intrinsic, 34–35, 46–47; intractibility of binary categories of, 11, 102, 105–6, 118–31, 155n.1, 157n.19; literary analysis across, 6–7, 9, 12; and patriarchy, 18; permeability of boundaries of, in the U.S., 11–12, 47; value of reproduction to, 1–5, 78–87, 107–8; at World's Columbian Exposition, 19–20, 26. *See also* Dialect; Eugenics; Motherhood; "Race mother"; Racial uplift; Reproduction; Violence, racial; White supremacy; *specific races*

—hierarchies based on, 4–6, 9, 40, 73–74, 135, 147n.10; as reinforced by Chopin and Wharton, 54–55, 72–77; as reinforced by contemporary depictions of motherhood, 135–43; as reinforced by rhetoric of universal womanhood, 18–31

Race death. *See* Race suicide

"Race mother": construction of, 9, 15–31, 33; Hopkins on redemptive power of, 9, 43–44, 47–51, 131, 133, 137, 141; Larsen on, 120; scholarship on, 147n.10; and True Motherhood, 9, 33, 45, 47, 48, 52, 62, 131, 141. *See also* Motherhood: as racial duty

Races and Peoples (Brinton), 4

Race suicide: *Birth Control Review* on, 153n.3; black, 13, 107, 113–14, 156n.7; white, 1–2, 5, 8, 30, 75. *See also* Birth control; Birthrate; Lynching; Motherhood: black women's refusal of

Race Suicide (Iseman), 80

Rachel (Grimké), 13, 112–16, 118, 121, 126

Racial progress. *See* Racial uplift

Racial uplift: African American women's contributions to, 1, 2, 5, 9–10, 15, 16, 18, 23–24, 27, 33, 36–40, 42–43, 45–51, 147n.1, 155n.2. *See also* "Race mother"

Rape. *See* Sexual violence

Raphael, 112

Reading. *See* Women's club movement, black; Women's club movement, white

Realism. *See* Naturalism

The Reason Why the Colored American Is Not in the World's Columbian Exposition (Wells and Douglass), 19–20

Recent Progress in the Study of Variation, Heredity, and Evolution (Lock), 75

Reproduction: as defeating women's artistic ambitions, 10–11, 59–60, 88, 89, 91–93, 98, 103–8, 118, 121–26, 128–31, 155n.1; Gilman's emphasis on, 55–61; materialist critique of, 78–101; racial value of, 1–14, 16, 20–31, 54–61, 74, 77–87, 105–11, 118, 126, 130; voluntary, calls for, 31, 79, 107; vs. women's emancipation, 1, 3, 5, 16, 23, 61, 71, 77, 82–84, 87. *See also* Birth control; Body, mother's; Childbirth; Motherhood; Pregnancy; Race; Sexuality, women's

Republican Motherhood, 8

"Returning Soldiers" (Du Bois), 109

Rich, Adrienne, 6

Rich and Strange (De Koven), 12

The Rising Tide of Color against White World-Supremacy (Stoddard), 1, 81

"The Risk of Woman Suffrage" (Miller), 107

Roberts, Dorothy, 2–3

Robinson, William J., 82, 154n.8

Rodrique, Jessie, 157n.15

Rogers, J. A., 107

ALLISON BERG is an assistant professor of American culture and writing at James Madison College, Michigan State University. She previously taught at St. Mary's College of Maryland, where she codirected the women's studies program. Her publications include numerous articles on American literature, popular culture, and pedagogy.

The University of Illinois Press
is a founding member of the
Association of American University Presses.

———————————————————

Composed in 10.5/13 Minion
by Celia Shapland
for the University of Illinois Press
Manufactured by Thomson-Shore, Inc.

University of Illinois Press
1325 South Oak Street
Champaign, IL 61820-6903
www.press.uillinois.edu